Labour, the state, social movements and the challenge of neo-liberal globalisation

Manchester University Press

Critical Labour Movement Studies

Series editors
John Callaghan
Steven Fielding
Steve Ludlam

Labour, the state, social movements and the challenge of neo-liberal globalisation

edited by
Andrew Gamble, Steve Ludlam,
Andrew Taylor and Stephen Wood

Manchester University Press
Manchester and New York
distributed exclusively in the USA by Palgrave

Published by Manchester University Press
Oxford Road, Manchester M13 9NR, UK
and Room 400, 175 Fifth Avenue, New York, NY 10010, USA
www.manchesteruniversitypress.co.uk

Distributed exclusively in the USA by
Palgrave, 175 Fifth Avenue, New York,
NY 10010, USA

Distributed exclusively in Canada by
UBC Press, University of British Columbia, 2029 West Mall,
Vancouver, BC, Canada V6T 1Z2

British Library Cataloguing-in-Publication Data
A catalogue record for this book is available from the British Library

Library of Congress Cataloging-in-Publication Data applied for

ISBN   978 0 7190 7586 5 *hardback*

First published 2007

16 15 14 13 12 11 10 09 08 07   10 9 8 7 6 5 4 3 2 1

Typeset
by Florence Production Ltd, Stoodleigh, Devon
Printed in Great Britain
by The Cromwell Press Ltd, Trowbridge

Contents

Part III Patterns of resistance across the globe

Series editors' foreword

The start of the twenty-first century is superficially an inauspicious time to study labour movements. Political parties once associated with the working class have seemingly embraced capitalism. The trade unions with which these parties were once linked have suffered near-fatal reverses. The industrial proletariat looks both divided and in rapid decline. The development of multi-level governance, prompted by 'globalisation' has furthermore apparently destroyed the institutional context for advancing the labour 'interest'. Many consequently now look on terms such as the 'working class', 'socialism' and 'the labour movement' as politically and historically redundant.

The purpose of this series is to give a platform to those students of labour movements who challenge, or develop, established ways of thinking and so demonstrate the continued vitality of the subject and the work of those interested in it. For despite appearances, many social democratic parties remain important competitors for national office and proffer distinctive programmes. Unions still impede the free flow of 'market forces'. If workers are a more diverse body and have exchanged blue collars for white, insecurity remains an everyday problem. The new institutional and global context is moreover as much of an opportunity as a threat. Yet, it cannot be doubted that, compared with the immediate post-1945 period, at the beginning of the new millennium, what many still refer to as the 'labour movement' is much less influential. Whether this should be considered a time of retreat or reconfiguration is unclear – and a question the series aims to clarify.

The series will not only give a voice to studies of particular national bodies but will also promote comparative works that contrast experiences across time and geography. This entails taking due account of the political, economic and cultural settings in which labour movements have operated. In particular this involves taking the past seriously as a way of understanding the present as well as utilising sympathetic approaches drawn from sociology, economics and elsewhere.

John Callaghan
Steven Fielding
Steve Ludlam

List of figures and tables

Figures

Tables

Contributors

Andreas Bieler is senior lecturer in Politics and International Relations at the University of Nottingham, UK. His main research interest is in the area of trade unions and European integration. He has published *The Struggle for a Social Europe: trade unions and EMU in times of global restructuring* (Manchester University Press, 2006).

David Coates holds the Worrell Chair in Anglo-American Studies at Wake Forest University in North Carolina, USA. His recent publications include *Varieties of capitalism, varieties of approaches* and *Prolonged labour – the slow birth of New Labour* (both Palgrave, 2005).

Bill Dunn lectures in the School of Politics and International Studies at the University of Leeds, UK. His research interests are in political economy, labour, social and spatial aspects of economic restructuring, and Marxism. His publications include 'Capital Movements and the Embeddedness of Labour', in *Global Society*.

Michael Gillan is a lecturer in Industrial Relations and Labour Studies at the University of Western Australia. His research interests include contemporary political and economic development in South Asia, the 'internationalisation' of higher education, and labour relations in the restructuring of the global domestic appliance industry.

Anibel Ferus-Comelo is an independent Educator and Researcher based in India. Chapter 11 is based on her doctoral research in economic geography at the University of London. Her research interests are industrial relations, gender and development.

Nazım Güveloğlu is based in the Department of Political Science and Public Administration at the Middle East Technical University, Ankara, Turkey. He has published '"Birey ve Toplum" İkiliğine Karşı Tarihsel Materyalizmin Nesnesi Olarak Toplumsal İlişkiler' in *Praksis*.

Rod Lambert is an industrial sociologist who specialises in Australian and Southeast Asian labour studies. He lectures at the University of Western Australia, and has published numerous articles on labour movements, industrial relations and globalisation. He has taught in several continents, is coordinator of the Research Committee on Labor Movements RC44 of the International Sociological Association. He is the Western Australian Trade and Labour Council's regional coordinator, and a founder of the Southern Initiative on Globalisation and Trade Union Rights.

Adam David Morton is Senior Lecturer in the School of Politics and International Relations at the University of Nottingham, UK. His main research interest is in the political economy of development. His book, *Images of Gramsci: hegemony and passive revolution in the global political economy* was published in 2006 in the *Reading Gramsci Series*.

Beata Mtyingizana is Lecturer in the Department of Sociology at Rhodes University, South Africa. Her research interests are labour movements, employment relations, development studies and social theory. She has published 'A Survey of Industrial Relations Practices in Mozambique' in *Labour relations in Mozambique: law, praxis and economic implications with international comparisons*, edited by Peter E. Coughlin (Maputo, Econ Policy Research Group, 2005).

Mario Novelli is a full-time Researcher in the Centre for Studies of Globalisation, Education and Societies at the University of Bristol, UK. His research explores the impact of neo-liberalism on international development, and particularly issues of labour rights, social movements and education in low income countries. He is also Chair of the Colombia Solidarity Campaign, UK.

Austina J. Reed is a doctoral candidate in political science at McMaster University in Hamilton, Canada, and a graduate research fellow with the Institute on Globalization and the Human Condition and the Interuniversity Research Center on Globalization and Work. Her main research interests are the political economy of labour migration and the politics of citizenship, as well as globalization and international labour standards.

Vivien A. Schmidt is Jean Monnet Professor of European Integration and Professor of International Relations at Boston University, USA. Her research interests span European political economy and democracy. Her book *The futures of European capitalism*, was published in 2002 by Oxford University Press which will publish her *Democracy in Europe, the EU and national polities* (forthcoming).

Darcy du Toit is professor of law at the University of the Western Cape in Cape Town, South Africa, specialising in labour law. The sixth edition of his *Labour law through the cases* appeared in 2005, published by LexisNexis Butterworths. He is co-author with Chris Todd and Craig Bosch of *Business transfers and employment rights in South Africa*, published in 2004 by LexisNexis Butterworths.

Charlotte A. B. Yates is full professor of Political Science and Director of Labour Studies at McMaster University in Hamilton, Canada. Her main research interests are the political economy of labour markets and union renewal. In 2003, she co-edited with Peter Fairbrother *Trade Unions in Renewal: A Comparative Study* (Continue Books; Re-issued under Routledge). Her article 'Challenging misconceptions about organizing women into unions' was published in *Gender, Work and Organization* in November 2006, and her report on changing labour markets in the auto parts sector is forthcoming.

Abbreviations

ABVP	Akhil Bharatiya Vidyarthi Parishad
ACTU	Australian Council of Trade Unions
AFL	American Federation of Labor
AFL-CIO	American Federation of Labor-Congress of Industrial Organisations
AITUC	All India Trade Union Congress
AIWA	Asian Immigrant Women Advocates
AKP	Justice and Development Party
ANC	African National Congress
BCEA	Basic Conditions of Employment Act
BJP	Bharatiya Janata Party
BMS	Bharatiya Mazdoor Sangh
CADTM	Le Comité pour l'Annulation de la Dette du Tiers Monde
CAW	Canadian Auto Workers
CCMA	Commission for Conciliation, Mediation and Arbitration
CCOO	Confederación Sindical de Comisiones Obreras
CCT	Comissao Consultiva Do Trabalho
CEACR	Committee of Experts on the Application of Conventions and Recommendations CEACR
CFDT	Confédération Française Démocratique du Travail
CFMEU	Construction, Forestry, Mining and Energy Workers Union
CGIL	Confederazione Generale Italiana del Lavoro
CGT	Confédération Générale du Travail
CGT	Confédération Générale du Travail
CGTP	Confederação Geral dos Trabalhadores Portugueses
CIO	Congress of Industrial Organisations
CITU	Centre for Indian Trade Unions
CME	Coordinated market economies
CMs	contract manufacturers
COBAS	Comitati di Base
CONSILMO	Confederação Nacional do Sindicatos Independetes e Livres de Moçambique
COSATU	Congress of South African Trade Unions
CPGB	Communist Party of Great Britain

CPM	Common Minimum Programme
CSR	Corporate Social Responsibility
CTA	Confederação das Associações Económicas de Moçambique
CUT	Central Unica dos Trabalhadores (United Workers Central)
CWU	Communication Workers Union
DYP	True Path Party
EC	Executive Committee
EIFs	European Industry Federations
EMU	Economic and Monetary Union
EMU	European Monetary Union
EPSU	European Federation of Public Service Unions
ERA	Equal Rights Advocates
ESF	European Social Forum
ETF	European Transport Workers' Federation
ETUC	European Trade Union Confederation
EU	European Union
EZLN	Zapatistas in Mexico
FCS	Forum de Concertação Sindical
FES	Friedrich Ebert Stiftung
FGDS	Fédération de la Gauche Démocratie et Socialiste
FIOM	Federazione Impiegati Operai Metallurgici
FSU	Fédération Syndicale Unitaire
G-10	L'Union Syndicale G10 Solidaires
GATS	General Agreement on Trade in Services
GDs	Grupos Dinamizadores
GEAR	Growth, Employment and Redistribution
GM	General Motors
GSEE	Geniki Synomospondia Ergaton Ellados
GUF	global union federation
HIC	Habitat International Coalition
HMS	Hind Mazdoor Sabha
HP	Hewlett-Packard
IACHR	Inter-American Commission of Human Rights
IAHRC	Inter-American Human Rights Court
ICEM	International Chemical, Energy and Mining
ICFTU	International Confederation of Free Trade Unions
ICRT	International Campaign for Responsible Technology
ICT	information and communications technology
IDA	Industrial Disputes Act
IFAs	international framework agreements
ILO	International Labour Organisation
IMF	International Monetary Fund
INTUC	Indian National Trade Union Congress
ISO	International Organisation for Standardisation
ITS	international trade secretariats
IUF	International Union of Food, Agricultural, Hotel, Restaurant, Catering, Tobacco and Allied Workers' Associations
KCTU	Korean Confederation of Trade Unions KCTU
LME	Liberal market economies

LRA	Labour Relations Act
MNC	multinational corporation
MST	Landless Workers Movement
MÜSIAD	Independent Industrialists' and Businessmen's Association
NAALC	North American Agreement on Labour Cooperation
NAFTA	North American Free Trade Agreement
NCC	National Chamber of Commerce
NCL	National Commission on Labour
NDA	National Democratic Alliance
NEDLAC	National Economic, Development and Labour Council
NGO	non-governmental organisation
NLI	new labour internationalism
NSM	new social movements
OECD	Organisation for Economic Cooperation and Development
OEMs	original equipment manufacturers
OTM	Organisation of Mozambican workers
PCBs	printed-circuit boards
PCF	Parti Communiste Français
PERC	Political Economy Research Centre
PGA	People's Global Action
PKK	Kurdistan Workers' Party
PRE	Programma de Reabilitação Económica
PSI	Public Services International
RDP	Reconstruction and Develoment Programme
RGUN	Rio Global Union Network
RMT	Union of Rail, Maritime and Transport Workers
RP	Welfare Party
RSS	Rashtriya Swayamsevak Sangh
SACP	South African Communist Party
SADC	Southern African Development Community
SATUCC	Southern African Trade Union Coordinating Council SATUCC
SBLC	South Bay Labour Council
SCCOSH	Santa Clara Centre for Occupational Safety and Health
SIGTUR	The Southern Initiative on Globalisation and Trade Union Rights
SIREN	Services, Immigrant Rights, and Education Network
SMU	social movement unionism
SPD	Sozialdemokratische Partei Deutschlands
SUD	Solidaires, Unitaires et Démocratiques
SVTC	Silicon Valley Toxics Coalition
SWP	Socialist Workers Party
TESMA	Tamil Nadu Essential Services Maintenance Act
TINA	There is no alternative
TISK	Turkish Employers' Confederation
TNCs	transnational corporations
TOBB	Union of Turkish Chambers and Stock Exchanges
TUC	Trades Union Congress
TÜSIAD	Turkish Industrialists' and Businessmen's Association
UAW	United AutoWorkers
UNCHR	United Nations Commission for Human Rights

UPA	United Progressive Alliance
VHP	Vishwa Hindu Parishad
VRS	voluntary retirement schemes
WFTU	World Federation of Trade Unions
WSF	World Social Forum
WTO	World Trade Organisation

1

Introduction: labour, the state, social movements and the challenge of neo-liberal globalisation

Andrew Gamble, Steve Ludlam, Andrew Taylor and Stephen Wood

Since the 1980s organised labour has taken a beating. Using even the crudest measures – numbers of members, density of membership, political influence – trade unions have been in decline. So substantial has this decline been commentators have not been reluctant to write labour's obituary. This volume of essays is intended to be a contribution to challenging this image.

Whilst it would be foolish to deny the facts of decline, two points are worth noting. First, however great its decline, organised labour remains a substantial social, economic and political presence. That it is sometimes unable to translate this presence into real influence in society, workplace or polity does not alter this. Second, the picture of decline can be too much influenced by a focus on the old industrial economies of the North, including Australasia. The industrialisation of China and India, the outsourcing of manufacturing and, increasingly, service industries from North America and Western Europe means that the global working class is growing at a faster rate than at any time in history. Whether or not this growing global proletariat will transform itself into organised labour remains an open question but history shows that, sooner or later, workers will seek to organise to defend themselves.

The title of this book identifies what we believe are the three most important factors influencing labour in the global economy and the possible transformation of disparate labour forces into labour movements. Labour must be seen in the context of the state. State theory has continued to stress the state's role with reference to labour, and labour looks to state action as part of its defensive and protective strategies. Generally, the state's relationship with labour takes two forms: the repressive and the integrative. This is not an 'either/or' relationship, the two responses can and do coexist, and equally state policy can emphasise repression or integration. Which predominates at a particular time depends on what used to be called 'the balance of class forces'. State policy, as several of the chapters in this volume show, is essentially a balance between repression and integration. States, being essentially instruments of the economically dominant, need labour and their role is to encourage its productivity but whether they need labour to be organised is a very different issue. A theme explored in this collection is the sheer variety of relationships between the state and labour. If, however, we can identify any common aspect in the state-labour relationship it is that states – by a variety of strategies – aspire to hinder labour organising, but if that fails they will try to prevent labour developing a consciousness of its separate interests.

Until recently there was a tendency to regard labour as *the* social movement. This is no longer sustainable. As organised labour has retreated and as politics and the issues it deals with have become more complex and fragmented, so has the group universe. Organised labour cannot now realistically claim to embrace in an all encompassing way labour's interests. Put simply, labour exists in a far more complex world than it once did. To some extent this reflects the multiple identities of individuals as, for example, worker, parent, consumer and citizen. These multiple identities require multiple articulation and mobilisation, which may sometimes be contradictory. The traditional aspiration of unions to fold these multiple identities and interests into the single categories of 'work' and 'worker' capable of expression by a single organisation was always unrealistic. The fit of identity and organisation was inevitably imperfect and organised labour often ignored other identities – for example, gender and ethnicity – to the detriment and disaffection of the individuals concerned. Labour remains society's central identity but now organised labour is only one of many organisations seeking to advance individual and collective interests. The logical conclusion, and one explored by several chapters, is that labour must co-operate extensively and intensively with related organisations on the principle that the sum will be greater than its parts. The creation and management of social movement unionism is not easy, and it is prey to internal conflict but then so were traditional labour movements. If labour is to exercise the influence its social and economic importance warrants, then it must do so as part of coalitions. Some will be permanent, some temporary, some domestic and some international.

Opponents and supporters often present neo-liberal globalisation as labour's mortal enemy. There is much truth in this. A US textile worker or British car worker seeing their job disappear abroad is hardly likely to rejoice at globalisation; the peasant, however, who finds employment in a textile or car factory is brought into a historical process which, history suggests, will eventually produce a higher standard of life and bring about a social revolution. There is undoubtedly a tension at the heart of globalisation (the neo-liberal is redundant, there is only one variety) between its economic and political impacts. This process is not new. It has been at work in its present form since the 1840s, and history shows globalisation to be both destructive and constructive. Old social and economic orders – industrial and non-industrial alike – collapse before it and new ones emerge; it is in this dual process there lie the seeds of the next phase of development. The old organised labours of the industrial and now post-industrial world are forced to adapt on the pain of extinction whilst the new and emerging labours find themselves presented with opportunities. A point made frequently in this collection is that current globalisation differs from previous manifestations because it is not merely an 'economic' phenomenon. Globalisation can be seen as part of democratisation, 'good governance' (free, competitive elections, the right to organise, the rule of law, and so on) comes as standard and this offers labour opportunities to organise and act in a range of spheres ranging from the local to the global. It is certainly the case that in too many parts of the world that state (or company) sponsored death squads take a terrible toll of those seeking to put substance into good governance. If it is true that, as the old civil rights adage has it: 'If they're shooting at you then you must doing something right', then the djinn of political freedom is out of the globalisation bottle. Whether and to what extent labour will be able to benefit from globalisation's positive side is not a question this collection can hope to answer but even if the situation is one of 'three steps forwards, two steps back', then labour has advanced.

The conference on which this collection of essays is based was concerned about the protection of labour in the hostile environment of neo-liberal capitalist globalisation. The collection is divided into three sections. The first presents key theoretical arguments; the second considers the impact of neo-liberalism in a variety of states; the third offers case studies of labour movement responses to the challenge of neo-liberal capitalist globalisation. The first asserts the centrality of the concept of labour in social theory (Coates); and analyses comparatively the labour strategies of the developed states (Schmidt). The second section investigates the potential of institutions of global governance to protect labour (Reed and Yates), and presents a series of case studies addressing the impact of labour legislation and labour movements and the rise of neo-liberalism (Du Toit, Mtyingizana, Güveloğlu, Gillan) covering South Africa, Mozambique, Turkey and India. In the third section case studies examine the role of trade unions struggling to protect labour in the face of political and market pressures. In particular they focus on the tendency of trade unions in these circumstances to work strategically as part of wider social movements seeking to protect entire communities from economic dislocation and exploitation. The general problems of such strategies are discussed (Dunn) and their prospects illustrated in the southern hemisphere (Lambert), of workers in the global electronics industry in India and California (Ferus-Comelo), of unions combating privatisation in the most difficult circumstances imaginable in Columbia (Novelli), and of the recent engagement of European trade unions with the anti-globalisation movements in the European Social Forums (Bieler and Morton).

This collection is based on papers selected from those given at the conference 'Labour Movements in the Twenty-First Century: Employment, States, Capital, Trade Unions and Social Movements' held in Sheffield in July 2004. The Political Economy Research Centre (PERC) hosted the conference, and it was co-organised by the UK Political Studies Association's Labour Movement's Specialist Group, the British Journal of Industrial Relations and Sheffield University's Institute of Work Psychology. The editors would like to acknowledge the enormous help and support provided by Sylvia McColm, the PERC administrator whose organisational skills did so much to make the conference a success. We would also like to thank the Sheffield postgraduate students who provided support to the organisers and delegates and finally we would like to thank those who travelled from all parts of the globe to give papers and participate in the discussions.

Part I
Theory

2
The category of labour: its continued relevance in social theory

David Coates

It is a remarkable, and in many ways disturbing, feature of the modern academic condition in the majority of English-speaking universities in the Western world that, at the very moment that more people are engaged in paid work than at any time in human history, it is necessary to argue again for the centrality of the category of 'labour' to any full understanding of the world in which that work is taking place. Yet that argument has to be made, and has to be made strongly, because of late 'labour' as a category has been drained of its content in the dominant discourses of the academic world, and labour as a set of social interests has been pushed to the margins of the public policy agenda that academic discourse helps to shape. It is a draining and a marginalisation that we need both to understand and to counter.

Generational defeat

How then to understand it? The argument to be developed here is that the marginalisation of labour concerns in academia, and the subordination of labour interests in the world of public policy, are best understood as by-products of a generational defeat of the intellectual forces of the Left. Of course, to talk in the language of victory and defeat is to talk in the language of the dramatic, and so is normally to be avoided: but not on this occasion – for dramatic times require a language of equal force, and we do live in dramatic times. The times are certainly dramatic, and potentially disastrous, in a public world dominated in 2006 by American military power and the alliance of US President George W. Bush and British Prime Minister Tony Blair; and if we are to shape that public world in better ways, we also need to make the times dramatic in the academic circles and opinion-making processes in which we participate. We need to understand that public world, and we need to struggle there to re-establish a radical labour presence within it.

The public world is set in ways that make that re-establishment not only necessary but also difficult. Globally the Cold War has gone, and with it any credible alternative to the worldwide spread of capitalism. *Economically* and in consequence, the forces of private ownership are everywhere on the advance, new industrial powers are challenging existing international divisions of labour, and key players in leading capital markets have a freedom to cross national boundaries that is of an unprecedented scale. *Socially*, the number of people obliged to sell their labour power in order to survive has doubled in a generation, and is now doubling again. Indeed and contrary to how it is normally portrayed, the enhanced ability of capital to relocate itself globally is not primarily the product of the new information technology that moves it from place to place. It is primarily the product of the fact that, in the increasing number of places to which capital moves, there are more and more workers on which it can latch and grow. The balance of class forces globally has in that sense shifted dramatically in favor of the owners of capital; and because it has, *politically* the class compacts created by post-war social democracy in the majority of the core capitalisms are everywhere under attack. Yet paradoxically, and indeed as a reflection of that same shift in the global balance of forces, social democracy itself flourishes in many of the semi-peripheral spaces of this globalised world, as the poor and dispossessed who occupy those spaces look to the Centre-Left for a political leadership that is no longer available to them from more revolutionary socialist forces. The tragedy of the global poor is that, *ideologically*, the social democracy to which they are turning is itself already weakened, both in content and in confidence, by the stridency of the neo-liberal ideas and policy prescriptions that prevail in the global corridors of power: a stridency that is ultimately anchored in the untrammeled hegemony of the American Centre-Right both at home and abroad.

In consequence, the main global challenges to that hegemony – certainly the main challenges in those regions made key by the disintegration of the Soviet bloc – are overwhelmingly religious and fundamentalist in kind. They are challenges which, at one and the same time, are both progressive in geopolitical terms and profoundly reactionary in social ones. Indeed, it is an outstanding feature of the twenty-first century – perhaps in political terms *the* feature that sets it apart most clearly from the twentieth century – that the main challenge to the global power of capital is no longer coming primarily from the institutions and leadership of the Left. For labour movements are everywhere weakened and in retreat; so that we find ourselves now in an epoch in which the common sense that prevails in the main centres of opinion – certainly in the main centres of opinion in the North if not yet always in the South – that common sense treats issues of class and socialism as outmoded legacies of the twentieth century. Whatever else these times are, they are not good ones for progressive forces of a secular and Enlightenment kind.

As in the world, so in the academy: but it was not always so. In the 1960s and 1970s the dominant frameworks of intellectual thought to be found there were clearly of the Left. Marxism as an intellectual discipline was everywhere ascendant; and with it, labour studies in all their forms were at the core of the academic agenda across the entirety of the social sciences, at least in the United Kingdom. The nature of work, the history of labour, the sources of inequality, the limits of markets, the requirements for social emancipation: all these were the stock-in-trade of radical social science. But not now: now academic units that were once proud to declare themselves 'departments of industrial relations' have long since relabeled themselves as 'departments of personnel management and corporate governance', or some such; and economics departments that once taught Marx, Schumpeter and Keynes as core elements of their syllabus now sell again, as the only truth, the axioms of neoclassical economics. Even in the relatively radical arena of comparative political economy, the dominant paradigm is 'new institutionalist' rather than Marxist; and in consequence in both the debates on globalisation and on the varieties of capitalism, the role and importance of 'labour' is heavily marginalized even in what passes for radical scholarship. Indeed many centre-left intellectuals working in the sub-discipline of comparative political economy spent much of the 1990s selling particular *capitalist* models as worthy of emulation: and while some chose European welfare capitalism (and defended it primarily on social grounds, advocating strong labour movements as harbingers of high-quality economic growth), just as many were drawn to East Asian capitalist models that were characterized by weak unions, intensified work routines and long working days. For even 'new institutionalists' were capable on occasion of missing the dark underside of 'successful' capitalisms, so keen were they to do battle – not with the intellectual forces of the Left – but with neo-liberal economists selling free market capitalism as a universal panacea.

In so doing, that particular generation of the academic Left (among which I count myself) failed adequately to protect a critical intellectual space; and that failure was all the more regrettable because it had just been handed down as something hard-won and of immense value by the generation before us – by intellectual giants like Edward Thompson and Ralph Miliband in the United Kingdom, and by C. Wright Mills and Paul Sweezy in the United States – academics of stature and courage who had fought for a radical agenda and approach in a context of Cold War anti-communism, and who had established that agenda and approach by the sheer quality of their scholarship and the force of their personal presence. But in the main we did surrender the space, and perhaps not surprisingly so. For we inherited it so easily, and many of us failed to grasp with sufficient speed and insight the scale of the shift in social and intellectual forces released upon us all by the ending of capitalism's post-war boom after 1973. Just as European social democracy was caught on the back foot by the crisis of the Keynesianism on which it had long relied to square the contradictory interests of capital and labour, so many academics on the intellectual Left were caught on the back foot too, by the sheer confidence and stridency of the neo-liberal revival that the failure of Keynesianism then made possible. But now, as that neo-liberal alternative itself hits the buffers of its own inadequacies – and does so with increasing visibility before a generation of workers and students with no direct experience of the horrors of Stalinism – the opportunity is emerging again to shift the balance of intellectual forces back towards paradigms of thought and analysis that assert the centrality and importance of labour questions and labour interests. It is an opportunity that, this time, we must *not* waste.

Class blindness

Intellectual spaces are best defended by recognizing the nature of their construction. Intellectual spaces are created by paradigmatic struggle. They are created, that is, by the clash and interplay of dominant theoretical frameworks. Progressive politics requires progressive thought. Empiricism is inevitably and always an intellectual practice of the Right; for it is the Right, not the Left, which has a vested interest in the perpetuation of the view that what exists cannot be changed, and in the associated view that those who conceptualise change are either dreamers or fools. It is the Right, not the Left, who stand to gain most by our failure to explore and to critique the underpinnings of the present. So if the intellectual agenda of the Left *is* to prevail again, those of us who practice it have to understand that under-theorised research is not simply undesirable. It is actually something we literally cannot afford to practice; and that, on the contrary, a solid grounding in radical theoretical systems is vital if progressive purposes are to be reinforced by solid scholarship of an empirical kind.

Of course, we still live in an intellectual world within which fine pieces of radical scholarship occasionally emerge, pieces that deepen our understanding of the present condition of labour. It would be quite wrong to create an impression of some lost golden age, some gilded summer of youth now tarnished by the passage of the seasons. The argument is rather that, since the 1980s, labour studies have been pushed to the margin of one intellectual discipline after another, to our collective cost; and that theoretical systems prioritising labour questions have been pushed away into the darker recesses of the collective academic cupboard. The study of labour process, labour history, labour institutions, not to mention studies of specifically working class communities and of working class industrial experience, all now at best take second place to studies of the needs, history and institutions of capital (which in 2006 tends to carry the euphemistic label of 'business'), and to the life styles and power relationships of higher social classes. Subordinate classes have become harder to 'see' in most modern academic scholarship; and that invisibility is not a product of their social demise. (On the continued presence of working classes, see Panitch and Leys 2000.) It is a product of the rise to dominance, within the academy, of intellectual frameworks that do not choose to 'see' them. The working classes of advanced and developing capitalisms alike have vanished from view, not because they are not there, but because their existence is subsumed into categories of analysis that deny their class character and their systemic centrality.

How then have working class and labour issues been marginalised and hidden from sight in this way? To grasp that, it is worth visualizing the 'doing' of social science research in any one generation as the equivalent of standing on a stage, a stage that is illuminated from the top and back of the theatre by great inverted ice-cream cones of light that bring part of the stage into view while leaving the rest in darkness. As has been argued more fully elsewhere, these searchlights are our theoretical paradigms (Coates 2005). They beam onto the stage of contemporary reality, and bring the light of understanding to the theatre of social action, in exactly the way that Thomas Kuhn argued that first Copernicus and Newton, and later Einstein, did to a stage of natural phenomena that had hitherto been understood in the West largely through the paradigm of Catholic theology and Aristotelian thought (Kuhn 1970). As Thomas Kuhn taught us:

- A well-developed paradigm – in both the social and the natural sciences – is anchored in a distinctive ontology and epistemology. It has a clear view of the

human condition and of the kinds of knowledge of that condition that are open
to the humans participating within it.

- A well-developed paradigm builds on that ontological base, sets of core categories
  for use in analysis. It provides a dynamic conceptual universe, generative of more
  localised explanations that its practitioners create by deploying those concepts
  to locate, isolate, measure and ultimately theorise empirical data.
- A well-developed paradigm also consolidates around itself agreed methodologies,
  a set of main texts, even a number of received truths; and
- a well-developed paradigm also leaves some aspects of social reality unexamined,
  because its concerns are focused elsewhere.

Paradigms in the natural sciences tend to relate to each other in a temporal
sequence. One replaces the other in time, as the new one satisfactorily answers that
key set of issues by which practitioners of the old paradigm had been visibly and
perennially defeated. Aristotelian thought could not explain the movement of the
heavens. Copernicus could. But in the analysis of social phenomena, the relationship
between paradigms in not diachronic in this fashion. It is synchronic. In the social
sciences, paradigms perpetually struggle with each other for dominance, and that
struggle is a permanent feature of the intellectual landscape. It is true that even in the
social sciences, paradigms rise and fall in dominance over time; but they do so while
having to live, even when dominant, in competition with the others; such that, if a
major paradigm is ignored, it is not normally because of its inadequacy as an
explanatory vehicle. It is ignored usually because the social forces whose interests
would be best served by its dominance/consideration have themselves been pushed
out of the central loops of academic and political power. Since the 1980s, it has been
Marxism as a paradigm that has been pushed out in this fashion. Its light has
been dimmed in academia, virtually to the point of extinction, alongside and parallel
to the erosion of the industrial and political power of organised labour. While by
contrast, paradigms that trace their origins back to the writings of Adam Smith, and
to those of Max Weber – paradigms that are not so linked to labour as a social force
– continue to flourish. That cannot be an accidental outcome, or a random
relationship; and it is not.

So when I talk of 'class blindness' in much modern scholarship, I have in
mind scholarship emerging from the two broad paradigmatic formations that hold
centre-stage in the social sciences of the English speaking world in 2006. I have in
mind the intellectual hegemony of modern forms of neoclassical economics, and of
the methodological individualism on which it is based; and I have in mind
too the ostensibly more radical 'new institutionalist' scholarship which, outside
departments of economics, tries to hold the line against the 'rational choice'
mathematical modeling and hypothesis-testing empiricism that is so pervasive:
certainly pervasive across vast swathes of North American graduate programmes in
the social sciences, and no doubt increasingly pervasive in graduate programmes
in the UK as well.

Neo-liberal economics does allow for the study of labour issues, of course, but it
does so predominantly in the form of labour economics: labour, that is, understood
as a factor of production subject to its own laws of supply and demand, and available

for study, like commodities in any other market, only as isolated units offered for sale, and priced optimally when monopoly forces do not intrude into the untrammelled working of the market. With this dominant form of thought as the structuring element in research and policy design, the very institutions called into existence over time by labour forces under challenge – institutions that were created precisely to overcome market weaknesses occasioned by the imbalance of social power between employer and employed – those very institutions have been singled out in neo-liberal scholarship as *the* key barriers to the full realisation of labour's 'true' interests. That is the case both with trade unions as collective bargainers and with governments as providers of social welfare. Little wonder then, that to the degree that the dominant voice emerging from academia is that of conventionally-trained labour economists, then with very few exceptions the policy process in advanced capitalist economies in 2006 is no longer informed by arguments about the importance of collective over individual rights, or about the necessity of creating level playing fields between social actors before the free play of market forces can even begin to generate socially-optimum outcomes. For neo-liberal economics literally lacks the mental furniture through which to conceive of the world and its condition in those more progressive terms.

Of course, that more collectively-focused voice is there still, particularly in continental Europe. It is there in the language of social partnership; and it is there in the associated scholarly defence of strong trade union and welfare rights as 'beneficial constraints' on capital, obliging European employers to seek the high value-added route to profitability by blocking them off from the sweat-shop alternative (Streeck 1997). But that collectivist voice is very muted. It is very much on the defensive. Even in the field of comparative political economy, the main thrust of scholarship has been increasingly driven, not by what we might think of as this 'left face' of the new institutionalism, but by its 'right face'. It has been driven by the scholarship on varieties of capitalism by people like Peter Hall and David Soskice, scholarship which takes the 'firm' as its unit of analysis, and talks the language of 'institutional complementaries' and 'comparative institutional advantage' (Hall and Soskice 2001). This is a body of work which has largely seen itself as performing a vital defensive job against the onslaught of the intellectual and political Right, not least by defending 'coordinated market economies' against 'liberal market economies' as forms of successful capitalism. It is also a body of work, however, that has helped to lock the politics of the Centre-Left into what Greg Albo and others have properly called 'progressive competitiveness' (Albo 1994; Coates 2000; Panitch 1994): the pursuit by left-wing forces of economic advantage for particular national economies by redesigning institutions to strengthen local industrial classes against industrial classes elsewhere that are also being strengthened.

The problem is that the 'right face' of the new institutionalist scholarship in the field of comparative political economy has not always been even-handed in its specification of institutions to be changed by state actors keen to trigger that strengthening. On the contrary, conservative-institutionalists working in the Hall-Soskice framework have been broadly persuaded that, once established, particular varieties of capitalism are so heavily path-dependent that they are extraordinarily difficult to reset at all. In general indeed, in the literature organized around the LME-CME (liberal market economies-coordinated market economies) distinction, the institutions and practices that are frozen into forms that lie beyond political redesign tend invariably to be the institutions of capital. Those must not be touched, lest investment move elsewhere. By contrast, those institutions singled out for redesign, if any can be found at all – and there is much debate within the relevant scholarly literature on this, and much caution on even the possibilities of cherry-picking desirable institutions and practices from one model to another – the institutions and practices singled out for redesign turn out to be the institutions and practices of labour. Education policy has replaced industrial policy with increasing ease in the centre-left programmes sustained by this new institutionalism (Stedward 2003). Reskilling – 'investment in human capital' as the new growth theorists have it – has become the one universal panacea; and being universal, in truth it has turned out to be no panacea at all. For economies cannot get off the treadmill that is international capitalism 'simply by running faster. All they can achieve by that mechanism is temporarily to pass others, until they too respond by running faster, with the long-term consequence of having the whole field increase their speed just to stand still. The victor in such a race', of course, 'is not the runner but the treadmill' (Coates 2000: 254) of capital accumulation on a global scale.

At the very least, by splitting advanced capitalisms into CMEs and LMEs as the only viable contemporary capitalist models, the 'right-face' of the 'new institutionalism' runs the risk of providing a retrospective justification for Thatcherism, and of condemning the labour movements of all but the continental European social democracies to a future of intensified work processes and diminished welfare rights. Since this is not a future that is in any way qualitatively different from that canvassed by neo-liberalism, and since it is a future that ought to be entirely unacceptable to the contemporary Left, it is clear that we need alternative forms of thought through which to think our way out of the mental straightjackets imposed upon us. We need to go beyond neo-liberal or conservative-institutional characterizations of our condition, and we need to do so with increasing speed and determination.

Dialoguing with Marxism

How then best to do that, to make that mental escape? My own view is that we do it best by turning left: by literally, turning left. We do it, that is, by turning our back, by closing our minds, to the powerful intellectual pull exerted upon us by the all-pervasive presence of the neo-liberal paradigm. We do it by breaking entirely with methodological individualism, and with the research strategies and thesis-designs built around the construction and testing of formal abstract models. We do it by anchoring ourselves instead, at the very least, in the *left* face of the new institutionalist scholarship, and then allowing ourselves to feel, through an extensive dialogue, the pull of a revitalised Marxism. My general answer, that is, on how best to escape the constraints of existing modes of thought – how best to re-conceptualise, re-theorise and re-centre 'labour' as our object of study – is to reintroduce Marxism, particularly a pluralistic Marxism of a Gramscian variety,[1] as a major intellectual force across the social sciences, and then to explore the complex articulation of classes and institutions in modern capitalism by bringing together the best of the new institutionalist scholarship with the best of its Marxist equivalent.

That exploration and bringing together is, of course, well underway. There is already a strong body of material – material that, in the language of this chapter, is anchored just as much in the new institutionalist scholarship as it is in Marxism – that recognizes the qualitatively unique character of labour markets in modern capitalism, and the associated *in*appropriateness of analyzing them, as much neo-liberal scholarship does, as just one market amongst many. Against the hegemony of conventional labour market economics, we already possess a strong literature built around the view of markets as socially embedded phenomena (Granovetter 1985; Hollingsworth 1997). We already know that labour markets are highly complex social systems, that have to be understood and studied with a sensitivity to the wider social universes into which they are inserted (Rubery 1994). We already know that, at the very least, this means that the definitions, goals, motivation and stocks of knowledge that individual workers bring to the production process inevitably shape productive outcomes (Buttler *et al.* 1995). We already know that the workings of labour markets are shaped by social forces that lie beyond the immediate control of any one individual labour market actor. That is why labour markets are quintessentially *not* the appropriate territory for forms of analysis based on the interaction of socially abstracted rational individuals (Hutton 1994). That is also why the general neo-liberal enthusiasm for factor 'flexibility' cannot be reduced, in the unique world of labour markets, to a simple capacity to hire and fire; since the resulting insecurity of employment is bound to corrode the capacity of labour – as a self-motivating factor of production – to perform at full capacity (Coates 1999; Rothstein 1990). Labour markets do not perform best when least regulated. They are not like other markets. Which is why we already know that, if neo-liberal intellectuals genuinely want labour to be efficient, they will have to advocate the treatment of workers as people, and not simply as commodities; and yet this is something that neither the theoretical systems nor the policy prescriptions of the intellectual and political Right encourage them on any regular basis to do (Dore 1990).

In other words, we already possess an extensive body of research on the unique role of labour in advanced capitalist economies from scholars whose intellectual origins are institutionalist rather than Marxist (Crouch 2001; Thelen 1998, 2001), and from scholars whose Marxism is regulationist and therefore of a highly institutional kind (Boyer 2001). Moreover, we also possess a rich literature on European welfare capitalism from scholars who wear their Marxism lightly, but wear it nonetheless (Howell 2003; Huber and Stephens 2001; Pontusson 1995, 1997). But what we do not so far possess, from scholars of any kind, is a systematic re-examination of the varieties of capitalism (their success and their adequacy) that is anchored in their impact on labour rather than capital. We lack a 'labour-focused' examination of varieties of capitalism to parallel (and indeed to transcend) the 'firm-focused' analyses of Peter Hall and David Soskice. We lack too any systematic analysis of how different varieties of capitalism are embedded in different forms of non-wage labour: we lack an examination of welfare capitalism that centres its analysis on the articulation of capitalist and domestic modes of production and reproduction. Most of all, and in spite of the fine research emerging on different national capitalist economies and their competitive potential, we lack a solid theorisation of how labour and capital interact at this stage of capitalist development; and so we lack a clear capacity to distinguish that which is endemic to capitalism as a way of organizing economic life from that which is contingent on its particular anchorage in different political, social and cultural contexts. (This is a lack now being addressed in Coates 2005.) Yet it is that capacity to differentiate the endemic from the contingent that is the prime gain of making the proper theoretical move. It is the capacity to locate the underlying drivers, the forces beneath the surface, that only adequate theoretical research can provide. There is no empirical route to those drivers. Finding them requires a theoretical capacity. It is that capacity that we now most need, and that can best be triggered by dialoguing again with Marxism.

Starting with labour

A revitalized Marxism can bring a number of crucial and missing dimensions to our understanding of the position of labour in contemporary capitalism: at least the following four.

First, a serious re-engagement with Marxism as an intellectual paradigm can, at the very least, serve to remind us that starting points are absolutely vital in all forms of analysis; and that to grasp the true nature of contemporary capitalism, it is important to start not with capital but with labour – and indeed with labour in all its forms. A re-engagement with Marxism would remind us that in dealing with capitalism we are dealing simply with the latest manner in which economic activity has been organised historically; and that in consequence it is profoundly misleading (and indeed deeply ahistorical) to restrict our first conceptual move as analysts to the mapping of modern economies as sets of linked markets, as is the habit of most professional economists in the early twenty-first century. The first conceptual move that we should make as students of labour movements has to be deeper than the one they characteristically make. In the manner of Volume 1 of Marx's *Capital*, we have to get beneath the sphere of exchange that preoccupies them, to reach the sphere of production that ought to preoccupy us. Marxism, that is, encourages us to leave the bustle of commodity exchange and the market place behind, to probe first the processes of production from which commodities emerge as available for sale. It helps us to recognise the centrality of production (and its necessarily associated labour processes) to the reproduction of the human condition. For market relationships, though apparently ubiquitous if seen through the eyes of conventional economics, are in truth simply the latest dominant institutional form within which production processes are predominantly organised.

We need always to remember that exchange relationships and commodity production are not endemic to the human condition. Capital is not a perennial presence in the human story. Labour is. As any systematic reading of the early works of Marx makes abundantly clear, what is endemic and perennial to the human condition is the production and reproduction of real life (Marx 1843). Our analysis of economic activity should therefore begin with, and our conceptual schemas should build out from, what is basic to that activity: namely the application of human labour power to the natural world, the humanising of nature itself. What Marxism reminds us is not simply that 'labour' is too important a category to ignore. It reminds us that 'labour' is *the* core category of human life, and needs to be recognised as such.

Second, Marxism also reminds us that, even within capitalism, it is at best superficial, and at worst misleading, to think of economic activity in the language of the neoclassical production function. If economic growth is best seen as the product of the interaction of 'factors of production' – of land, labour, capital and enterprise – then dislocations in that growth process are necessarily only *technical* in kind: the consequence either of inadequacies in the quality and quantity of the factors of production involved, or the product of their limited or distorted interaction. Therein, of course, lies the route to arguments for the full commodi-fication of social life and to the glories of free trade. Marxism by contrast, reminds us that the real barriers to economic growth are *social* rather than technical in origin. They lie in the contradictory nature of the social relationships structuring production in a capitalist economy. They lie in the necessary tension between capital and labour in societies in which class inequalities and the strength of property relationships separate the bulk of the producers from the full ownership of the commodities that their labour produces.

Marxism serves to remind us, that is, that labour markets in a capitalist economy are more than simply social sites, with social dynamics, as even the best of the 'new institutionalist' scholarship still tends to suggest. They are also of necessity sites of exploitation and struggle. We need continually to remember, as we analyse modern economies, that at the heart of the capital-labour relationship stands an unavoidable wage-effort bargain. The struggle over that bargain is invariably experienced by the sellers of labour power as a perennial pressure to surrender more effort for less pay, and to subordinate themselves to an authority structure whose purposes and interests are not their own. Marxism, that is, serves to remind us that under capitalism labour power is treated as a commodity: a commodity moreover whose work rules, work content, work organisation and work pace are geared not to the needs of the suppliers of that commodity, but to some other goal and to the interests of some other social formation. Marxism reminds us not simply that labour is central to the production process of modern economies, but also that the labour so central to production in the modern world experiences its centrality only in an *alienated* form. When we are analysing modern societies, we cannot treat them as organic wholes best studied from above. We have to grasp them as societies riven with class tensions, and in truth and in consequence as societies best studied from below.

Third, Marxism comes, as do all paradigms, with its own conceptual language and ways of visualising the world. We need that alternative visualisation. Against the controlling category of neo-liberal economics – the category of 'the market' – Marxism offers its own: the 'mode of production'. Against the imagery of 'the production function' that is so central to conventional economics, Marxism offers the imagery of linked 'circuits of capital'. It offers circuits of 'merchant capital', circuits of 'industrial capital' and circuits of 'financial capital'. And against the notion that profits accrue through the deployment of 'enterprise', Marxism asserts that, in different ways in each of its circuits of capital, profits accrue only through the extraction of surplus value from the labour of others. According to Marxism, it is labour, not enterprise, that is central to economic growth under capitalism, because it is labour power that alone is capable of generating the surplus on which that growth depends.

In conventional Marxist economics, merchant capital is accumulated by processes of unequal exchange – by buying cheap and selling dear between and within particular modes of production. Industrial capital, by contrast, pays wages that are formally equal to the value of the labour power it purchases. Such capital accumulates only by extracting surplus value from the labour power rewarded in this fashion. Capital can grow only by intensifying the rate of surplus extraction: *absolutely* by lengthening the working day and by increasing the pace and intensity of work, or *relatively* by altering the balance of machinery and labour in the production process itself. In Marxist terms, capital can grow, that is, only by the extraction of either 'absolute' or 'relative' surplus value; and in consequence even advanced capitalist systems are inextricably caught in the contradictions released by the application of machinery to production. It is an application that both increases the mass of profits (by raising the scale of surplus extraction) while simultaneously reducing it (by raising the organic composition of capital). These contradictions are then experienced by both employers and those they employ as generative of perpetual change, instability and flux. Capitalism is, after all, an economic system of immense dynamism. But they are also experienced as generative of profound and normally deepening inequalities: in power, in rewards and in security. For capitalism is more than dynamic. It is also anarchic, and in its anarchy it is necessarily generative of resistance and response. Marxism serves continually to remind us, that is, that capitalism does more than produce commodities. It also produces proletarians; and any analysis of modern systems that fails to recognise this, and to centre that recognition, will have an inflated (and profoundly flawed) view of the various systems' capacity for stability over time.

Finally, by insisting that we think of capitalism as a mode of production with its own internal dynamics and contradictions, Marxism invites us to understand particular national economies as social structures of accumulation of a necessarily precarious kind. It invites us to understand those social structures of accumulation as unstable social formations driven, at one and the same time, by competitive tensions between different sectors and forms of capital, and by competition between capital and labour. Marxism invites us, that is, to see and to prioritise horizontal and vertical social tensions as we trace the performance of whole economies, or of some/all of their constituent institutions, over time. It invites us to understand a capitalist mode of production as a cluster of institutions, processes and social classes that are permanently locked into unstable forms of articulation with modes of production that are *not* capitalist in kind – with pre-capitalist forms of economic organisation globally, and with domestic modes of production internally – articulations which then enable core capitalist economies temporarily to offset some of their endemic contradictions by pushing them out to modes of production that are conceptually, and sometimes genuinely physically, on their edge.

In consequence, Marxism offers us an entirely different take on the nature of the contemporary global economic order. It does not talk to us of 'hyper-globalisation' or its antithesis. It does not require us to be either enthusiastic or skeptical globalisers. It talks instead of the perennially footloose nature of global capital from the very outset of the capitalist period. It talks of the changing weight of mercantile, industrial and financial circuits of capital over time; and it talks of the present stage of capitalist development as one characterized by the generalised and global creation of circuits of industrial capital. It tells us that we are experiencing a second prolonged period of primitive capital accumulation: in the extensive proletarianisation of, on this occasion, predominantly Asian and South American peasantries. It tells us that this is occurring alongside the deepening of processes of relative surplus value extraction from existing labour forces in both core and developing capitalisms. It tells us, that is, that we are seeing the emergence of new and old proletariats together. It takes us to the key global development of our age: the emergence of global labour. That is what we now face: and because we do, far from the class politics of proletarian struggle being somehow behind us and long gone, in truth they have hardly yet begun. Marxism reminds us, that is, that if the present belongs to capital, the future may yet belong to labour: and that given that possibility, theoretical frameworks that marginalise labour interests and labour concerns can have very little purchase on the dominant trajectories of our age.

Conclusions

What is being proposed here is nothing small. It is the complete revamping of the intellectual equipment deployed for the understanding of contemporary capitalism, a revamping that will necessarily involve a re-examination of dominant frameworks of thought across the entirety of the social sciences. For the re-conceptualisation of labour, and its centring in our intellectual concerns, is not something that can be done by focusing on labour alone. Concepts do not come singly. They come in packages; and they do so because the world they conceptualise is full of relationships, and not just of isolated actors. Whatever else people do when they sell their labour power, they do not labour alone. They labour in a context replete with other social actors and forces. So to capture the totality of the world of labour, we need a completely new vocabulary.

Or rather, in truth, we need an old one restored and then understood in all its complexity. This is not to make a virtue of the ancient, but rather to recognise just how much of the intellectual furniture that has come down to us from the past still has immense purchase on the nature of the contemporary world. In fact, there is a real sense in which the vast majority of the dominant languages available to us in the social sciences are old ones. It is certainly always bizarre to hear Marxism dismissed as anachronistic by intellectuals whose own anchorage, whether they know it or not, lies further back still: in the eighteenth century Scottish Enlightenment or beyond. But that anchorage is not a weakness in them. Their intellectual roots have stood the test of time, and that is a very considerable test. So we would do well not to make a fetish of the new when trying to analyse the novel. We would do well rather to remember that conceptual schemas are best judged less by their novelty than by their capacity to explain. We would do well to remember, that is, that at the feast table of intellectual life the proof of the pudding is always in the eating; which is why, given the culinary poverty of the standard modern intellectual diet, it is time again to bring to that feast a wider and more radical menu than is commonplace there.

Note

1   My own predilection for a Gramscian version of Marxism reflects a long-established unease with the reductionism and essentialism characteristic still of much Marxist writing: a tendency to reduce everything to the logics of an economic base, so allowing no room for the relative autonomy of levels; and an associated essentialism, a tendency to pull all forms of labour towards a proletarian core. In truth, given the state of existing scholarship, a bit of essentialism and reductionism is a useful counterweight to the propensity of much new institutionist scholarship to restrict itself to the mapping of variations and to the analysis of surface forms: but two weaknesses do not make one strength. Gramscian Marxism seems the least prone to the Marxian side of these weaknesses.

References

Albo, G. (1994) 'Competitive austerity and the impasses of capitalist employment policy', in R. Miliband and Panitch, L. (eds), *The Socialist Register 1994*.

Boyer, R. (2001) 'The diversity and future of capitalisms: a regulationist analysis', in Hodgson, G., Itoh, M. and Yokokawa, N. (eds), *Capitalism in evolution: global contentions – East and West*, Cheltenham.

Buttler, F., Franz, W., Schetter, R. and Soskice, D. (eds) (1995) *Institutional frameworks and labour market performance: comparative views on the US and German economies*, London.

Coates, D. (1999) 'Labour power and international competitiveness: a critique of dominant orthodoxies', in Panitch, L. and Leys, C. (eds), *Global Capitalism versus Democracy: The Socialist Register 1999*.

—— (2000) *Models of capitalism: growth and stagnation in the modern era*, Cambridge.

—— (2005) 'Paradigms of explanation', in Coates, D. (ed.), *Varieties of capitalism, varieties of approaches*, Basingstoke.

Crouch, C. (2001) 'Welfare regimes and industrial relations systems: the questionable role of path dependency theory', in Ebbinghaus, B. and Manow, P. (eds), *Comparing welfare capitalism*, London.

Dore, R. (1990) 'Two kinds of rigidity: corporate communities and collectivism', in Brunetta, R. and Dell'Arringa, C. (eds), *Labour relations and economic performance*, Basingstoke.

Granovetter, M. (1985), 'Economic action and social structure: the problem of embeddedness', *American Journal of Sociology*, 91:3.

Hall, P. and Soskice, D. (2001) 'An introduction to varieties of capitalism', in Hall, P. and Soskice, D. (eds), *Varieties of capitalism*, Oxford.

Hollingsworth, J. R. (1997), 'Continuities and changes in social systems of production: the cases of Japan, Germany and the United States', in Hollingsworth, J. R. and Boyer, R. (eds), *Contemporary capitalism: the embeddedness of institutions*, Cambridge.

Howell, C. (2003) 'Varieties of capitalism: And then there was one?', *Comparative Politics*, 36:1.

Huber, E. and Stephens, J. (2001) *Development and crisis of the welfare state*, Chicago.

Hutton, W. (1994) *The state we're in*, London.

Kuhn, T. (1970) *The structure of scientific revolutions*, Chicago.

Marx, K. (1843) *The German ideology: part 1*, London.

Panitch, L. (1994) 'Globalization and the state', in Miliband, R. and Panitch, L. (eds), *The Socialist Register 1994*.

—— and Leys, C. (with Albo, G. and Coates, D.) (eds) (2000) *Working classes, global realities: The Socialist Register 2000*.

Pontusson, J. (1995) 'From comparative public policy to political economy: putting political institutions in their place and taking interests seriously', *Comparative Political Studies*, 28:1.

—— (1997) 'Between neo-liberalism and the German model: Swedish capitalism in transition', in Crouch, C. and Streeck, W. (eds), *The political economy of modern capitalism*, London.

Rothstein, B. (1990) 'Marxism, institutional analysis and working class power: the Swedish case', *Politics and Society*, 18:3.

Rubery, J. (1994) 'The British production system: a societal specific system?', *Economy and Society*, 23:3.

Stedward, G. (2003) 'Education as industrial policy: New Labour's marriage of the social and the economic', *Policy and Politics*, 31:2.

Streek, W. (1997) 'Beneficial constraints on the economic limits of rational voluntarism', in Hollingsworth, J. R. and Boyer, R. (eds), *Contemporary capitalism: the embeddedness of institutions*, Cambridge.

Thelen, K. (1998) 'Historical institutionalism in comparative politics', in Polsby, N. (ed.), *Annual Review of Political Science*, 2.

—— (2001) 'Varieties of labour politics in the developed democracies', in Hall, P. and Soskice, D. (eds), *Varieties of capitalism*, Oxford.

3

Labour in the twenty-first century: state strategies

Vivien A. Schmidt

State strategies toward labour in the arenas of both work and welfare have undergone tremendous change in the last thirty years or so. State policies have pushed for the deregulation of labour markets and for the rationalisation of the welfare state. State practices have promoted the decentralisation of wage bargaining and a re-balancing of the traditional post-war compromise to the benefit of business. And state discourses have sought to persuade labour of the necessity and appropriateness of such changes, often by reference to globalisation and Europeanisation (in the EU).

However, there has been no convergence to the same set of state strategies with regard to welfare and work. The highly significant post-war differences in state strategies have certainly narrowed, but they have not disappeared. States are still differentiable along a continuum from 'intervening' to 'hands off', except that the continuum has extended its margins on the hands off end and reduced them on the intervening end. State strategies that were interventionist in the post-war period are now enhancing (France and Italy); those that were 'enabling', remain so (Germany, the Netherlands, Sweden and Denmark); and those that were liberal are even more so (Britain and the United States). While all states have moved along the continuum from *faire* toward *laissez faire*, by doing less on their own and leaving more room for market actors, this has not meant a slide all the way to *laissez faire*. Rather, states have largely turned to *faire faire*, through state direction of what market actors should do. Many also engage in *faire avec*, by collaborating with market actors.

Institutional legacies or path dependencies with regard to state strategies toward labour are only part of the story. Some countries have moved much farther along the continuum than others even when they share similar legacies in terms of post-war systems of welfare and work. These differences are related to states' differing capacities for reform, which is explained in terms of a number of mediating factors. These include countries' differential levels of economic vulnerability; actors' preferences, whether to maintain or to change long-standing policies and practices in the face of economic pressures; states' political institutional capacity to negotiate or impose reform. Public discourse is, as we shall see, particularly important in enhancing political institutional capacity by persuading societal actors not only of the necessity of reform in the face of crisis but also of its appropriateness. Even countries that share similar configurations in terms of state strategies and systems of work and welfare differ greatly in reform capacity, based on these mediating factors. Among liberal states, the UK has demonstrated greater reform capacity than the US; among enabling states, the Netherlands reformed more than Germany, and Denmark more than Sweden; and among enhancing states, France reformed its market economy earlier, Italy, its welfare state.

It is important to note that the European Union (EU) is yet another factor in the explanation of changes in the strategies of its member states. The EU has impacted on national employment and social policies through, for example, EU directives on occupational safety and health and on part-time and temporary employment. Limitations of space, preclude extended analysis (Schmidt 2002a, 2002b, 2002c, 2004).

After a brief introductory section on the continuing divergence in state strategies, I consider in turn liberal, enabling and enhancing state strategies with regard to work and welfare systems. In each of the three types, after providing a general overview of the evolving configuration of work and welfare system, I examine matched pairs of cases to show the importance of the above-mentioned mediating factors for change.

The continuing divergence: liberal, enabling and enhancing state strategies

Although similarities in state policies, practices and discourse seem to suggest tremendous convergence toward 'a one size fits all' neo-liberal model of work and welfare, tremendous diversity remains. The most important factor to explain this is the institutional context. This can be loosely categorised according to three kinds of state strategies related to three main post-war varieties of capitalism and three families of welfare states, all of which have continued to evolve along lines of development from the post-war institutions.

Conceptualising divergent state strategies

State strategies toward labour can be best understood at their most general level when situated along a continuum from 'intervening' to 'hands off' (see Figure 3.1). At the hands off end are the liberal states characteristic of Anglo-Saxon countries like the United States, Britain, Ireland, New Zealand and Australia, which since the mid-1970s only moved farther in a hands off direction, becoming more liberal, often through radical reforms. In the middle are the enabling states, characteristic of a wide range of Continental European and Scandinavian countries, which have on average moved only marginally in a liberal direction, although some countries have moved much farther than others. At the intervening end are the enhancing states characteristic of France and Italy. These countries, often described as *dirigiste* during the post-war years, have undergone transformation through the retreat of the state, but the state still tends to intervene more than either liberal or enabling states.

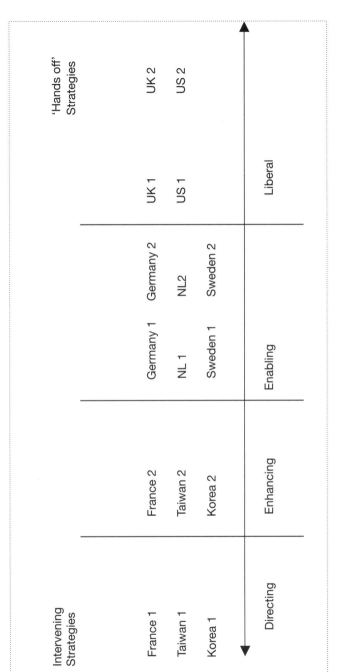

Figure 3.1 Continuum in state strategies toward welfare and work from intervening to hands off (1 = post-war period, 2 = neo-liberal years)

This way of conceiving of the changes in state strategies, while useful in conveying a sense of the market oriented direction of reform, is nevertheless misleading, since it could give the impression that all states are moving toward a *laissez faire* approach to economic governance. In fact, no state has ever been that close to the hands off end of the continuum, including liberal states. Rather than *laissez faire*, as implied by the hands off description, states have moved away from *faire* to *faire faire*. This means markets actors perform functions hitherto performed by the state, but with clear rules as to what that should entail. Deregulation does not mean eliminating all regulation, but creating a different kind of regulation, one in which the state has a more arms'-length relation with market actors through independent regulatory agencies or through laws that establish the rules market actors must follow. Thus, for example, the deregulation of labour markets has involved creating new rules governing work conditions and employee contracts while the reform of the welfare state has often meant that the setting of the rules for pension responsibilities has been shifted to employers.

Equally important, however, reforms of state strategies can mean creating more opportunities for *faire avec* or state action in co-operation with market actors. States that have always played an enabling role have generally continued to prefer this approach, even though they have also often added some *faire faire*. States that moved from a directive role to an enhancing one have generally sought to withdraw from active control over work and welfare-related matters. This entails either setting the rules for market action through *faire faire*, much as in liberal states, or by doing more with market actors through *faire avec*, as in enabling states. In this latter case, they have sought to create the conditions in which the social partners – employers' associations and unions – would interact alone or with the state as coequal in the negotiation of employment contracts and work conditions as well as in oversight of pension funds. Even liberal states have on occasion turned to this kind of *faire avec*, although often without lasting success.

Rather than staying with the conceptualisation of the differences among state strategies as a continuum from intervening to hands off, it would be better to add a conceptualization of such differences in terms of overlapping circles clustered around two axes. Thus, *faire* and *laissez faire* form the y-axis, *faire avec* and *faire faire* the x-axis (Figure 3.2). While these three varieties of state strategies follow quite different internal logics, they nevertheless adopt policies that fit across all four quadrants, although differences in policy emphasis ensure that they inhabit the quadrants to differing degrees.

The differences in internal logics are related to the fact that states' strategies follow from the different varieties of capitalism and families of welfare states in which states are embedded. In the next section, sketches of how state strategies are connected to the different varieties of capitalism and welfare states will be provided. Before turning to this, however, it is important to recognise that the institutional legacies of states and systems of work and welfare are only one of a number of factors that help explain the dynamics of change in state strategies over time. Although path dependence matters, it cannot account for the fact that countries have followed different trajectories even within the same groupings.

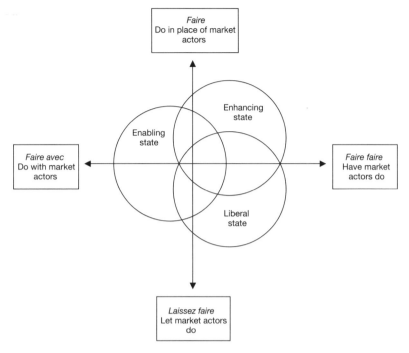

Figure 3.2 State strategies on a four fold scale from *faire* (do in place of market actors)
to *faire avec* (do with market actors) to *faire faire* (have market actors do) to
laissez faire (let market actors do)

Beyond institutional legacies: political institutional capacity and discourse

To explain the dynamics of change, it is useful to point to four other mediating factors in addition to the institutional legacies that follow from long-standing state strategies (see Table 3.1). The first is economic vulnerability. Only where countries are experiencing economic problems are they likely to even consider changing their policies. However, if it is 'broke', the next question is, how do you fix it? The answer depends upon a state's policy preferences, based on interests and values, that involve a debate as to whether to continue with long-standing strategies, on the assumption that the crisis is a momentary one remediable by the old strategies, or to shift to new ones. Most importantly, though, even if it is 'broke' and you know how to fix it, can you fix it? For this, states have to have the political institutional capacity either to impose or negotiate reform. Even if a state has such capacity and prefers certain policies, does it have the discourse required to persuade the relevant actors, those most affected by the reforms as well as the electorate, not only of the policies' necessity but also of their appropriateness, such that the reforms become institutionalised? While institutional legacies, economic vulnerability, and policy preferences are reasonably straightforward, and therefore need little further

Table 3.1 Mediating factors in state strategies in work and welfare

Institutional legacies	Long-standing policies and institutions: liberal, enabling, enhancing
Economic vulnerability	Presence or absence of economic crisis
Policy preferences	Hold to old policy preferences based on interests and values, following pattern of institutional legacies, or open up to new
Political institutional capacity	States' ability to impose or negotiate change depending upon political interactions and institutional arrangements Single actor constellations – UK, France (and Netherlands, Sweden on welfare in 1990s): impose change (given unitary states, statist policymaking, majoritarian representation) subject to sanctions of elections (UK, France) and/or protest (France) Multi-actor constellations – US, Germany, Italy, Denmark, Netherlands, Sweden: negotiate change (bicameral federal/regionalised states, corporatist policymaking, proportional representation) subject to sanctions of lack of agreement (Germany, US, Denmark) or protest (Italy)
Discourse	Ability to change preferences by altering perceptions of economic vulnerabilities, policy legacies and thereby enhance political institutional capacity to impose or negotiate change Ideas: speak to necessity of strategies and appropriateness in term values Coordinative discourse among policy actors to generate ideas and reach agreement: multi-actor systems . . . many voices – speak in harmony or cacophony Communicative discourse between politicians, general public to inform, legitimate ideas: single actor systems. . . . UK single voice, France sometimes two

elaboration, political institutional capacity and discourse are more complicated variables, and thus require further elucidation.

Political institutional capacity
A state's political institutional capacity involves not only the interrelationships of power and interest among major policy actors and the public at any given time but also the institutional arrangements that set the context for the political interactions. In single actor constellations, where governmental power is concentrated in a single authority, the result of unitary institutional structures, statist policymaking processes and majoritarian representation systems, as in the UK and France, the state is generally able to impose reform. This is subject, however, to the sanctions of elections (e.g. UK and France) and protest in the streets (especially France). In multi-actor constellations where governmental power is instead more dispersed through multiple authorities, the result of federal or regionalised institutional

structures, corporatist policymaking processes, and/or proportional representation systems, as in Germany, Belgium, Italy, Denmark, the Netherlands, Sweden, and the US, the state cannot impose. It must therefore negotiate widely, or risk not gaining agreement on reform.

In both kinds of institutional settings, some countries have been more successful than others at bringing about the reform of work and welfare. The single actor UK had greater political institutional capacity than the multi-actor US. Single actor systems do not always come out ahead, especially if one judges reform success not just by government ability to impose but public willingness to accept, which is generally more likely if there has been wide-scale negotiation ahead of time among the most affected policy actors. This helps explain reform success in Italy in the 1990s as well as the Netherlands, Denmark and Sweden at various junctures. Negotiation does not always spell reform success, as evident in the cases of Germany in the 1990s and Italy in the 1980s.

Discourse

Most political scientists would stop at these four factors: legacies, vulnerability, preferences and capacity. This, however, leaves a number of questions unanswered. Why, for example, did some countries regain the capacity to reform after a decade or more of crisis (as in the Netherlands and Italy) whereas others lost it despite years of success (as in Germany)? What enabled some countries to gain public acceptance for reform and others not? Why were some countries able to reform despite little political institutional capacity (such as Italy) while others were not despite high levels of seeming capacity (such as France)?

To answer these questions, I add a fifth factor: discourse. This is because state strategies are also contingent on the presence or absence of a persuasive discourse that serves to generate and legitimate reform. In terms of substantive content, such discourse normally needs to address not just the necessity of change but also its appropriateness through appeal to values.

Discourse, however, is not just about ideas. It is an interactive process, consisting of both a coordinative discourse among policy actors that serves to generate such ideas and a 'communicative' discourse to the public to inform and deliberate about those ideas. Different institutional contexts tend to frame the discourse, however, determining whether the coordinative or communicative discourse has greater emphasis. Single actor states with a concentration of power and authority in the executive tend to privilege the 'communicative' discourse directed toward the general public, so as to legitimate the ideas generated by a restricted policy elite and avoid electoral sanctions or protest. Multi-actor states with greater dispersion of power and authority (the US, Germany, the Netherlands and Denmark) tend to emphasise the coordinative discourse directed toward the multiplicity of actors involved in policy construction in order to gain agreement, although in bigger states, such as the US, the communicative is also very important. Whether coordinative or communicative, the discourse serves to enhance political institutional capacity to reform by persuading key policy actors and/or the public to shift their preferences even if this means going against long-standing policy legacies (Schmidt 2000, 2001, 2002a, chapters 5 and 6, 2002c, 2003; Schmidt and Radaelli 2004).

The continuing differences in state strategies

To understand how these mediating factors affect changing state strategies toward labour in systems of work and welfare, in what follows I consider in turn liberal, 'enabling', and enhancing state strategies with special emphasis on political institutional capacity and discourse. (see Table 3.2).

Liberal state strategies

Countries with liberal state strategies are generally characterized by liberal market economies with market-driven inter-firm relations and market-reliant labour management relations (Hall and Soskice 2001). They tend to be accompanied by liberal welfare states in which welfare is assumed a matter of individual responsibility, distinguishable according to need, provided by the state for the poor, with a comparatively low level of benefits and services (Esping-Anderson 1990). In these countries, the traditionally hands off state has become even more liberal through radical reforms of both work and welfare, even though this has never excluded ad hoc interventionism, especially in the post-war period and even at the beginning of the twenty-first century.

Liberal states' reformist strategies beginning in the 1980s sought to reduce the state's interventionist role by turning to more indirect ways of promoting or ensuring state ends, and by getting private actors to create public goods and carry out public goals, *faire faire* in place of *faire*. Reforms in the work arena were primarily focused on market preservation, as state strategies sought to develop framework legislation to locate decision-making power in companies and to limit the power of organized labour (King and Wood 1999; Wood 2001). For most liberal states, including the US, the UK and New Zealand, this entailed strategies that involved crushing union power in order to promote the decentralisation of the labour markets and passing laws that gave firms maximum flexibility to hire and fire. However, for Ireland it also meant adding a moderate form of corporatism in negotiating wages and work conditions, suggesting that even liberal states can allow for some *faire avec*.

Reforms in the welfare arena were equally ambitious. Liberal state strategies with regard to the employed reinforced individual responsibility for welfare provision as basic pensions became even more basic and pensions were partially privatised above the basic minimum. For the unemployed, while in the 1980s the focus was primarily on reducing unemployment compensation and cutting social assistance, by the mid to late 1990s the focus had shifted to getting people off the welfare rolls through workfare while improving equality of opportunity.

Together, these reforms have produced a situation in which the work arena is characterised by high workforce participation rates, high labour mobility, low job security, big wage inequalities, but also low unemployment. In the welfare arena, the main challenge is poverty, especially because social transfers do not bring the

Table 3.2 Differences in strategies toward work and welfare in liberal, enabling and enhancing states

State strategies	Variety of capitalism	Strategies for work	Family of welfare state	Strategies for welfare
Liberal US UK	**Liberal market economy**	*faire to faire faire* market preservation; locate decision-making in firm, limit power of organised labour (except Ireland, *faire avec*)	Liberal individual responsibility low benefits, services Problem: **poverty**	**Cut low level** > individual responsibility < benefits > private services < workfare
Enabling Denmark Sweden Netherlands Germany	**Coordinated market economy**	*Faire avec and some faire faire* pro competitiveness without jeopardizing non-market coordinating institutions, especially cooperative management labour relations	*Social Democratic* Collective responsibility Very high benefits & services Problem: **Sustainability** Conservative Family responsibility High benefits, low services Problem: **Unemployment** (except Netherlands)	**Retain high level** retain universality, equality modest cuts, user fees public sector jobs/active labour market policy **Maintain level** > individual responsibility modest cuts, no new services need > services, > labour market participation, especially female
Enhancing France Italy	**State-enhanced market economy**	*Faire to faire faire* (France) and some faire avec (Italy) market creation/preservation; locate decision-making in firms, intervene to bail out business, moralise labour market	Conservative Family responsibility (Italy) and state (France) High benefits, low services (Italy) high services (France) Problem: **Unemployment**	**Maintain level** > individual responsibility modest cuts deregulation/privatisation of '*services publics*' need much > labour market participation, especially female (Italy)

poverty level down sufficiently (Scharpf and Schmidt 2000). Despite these general similarities, countries have had different trajectories and different levels of success in their reform efforts, largely due to differences in political institutional capacity and discourse.

The reform success of a single actor state like the liberal UK can be explained in large measure by its political institutional capacity to impose reforms beginning in 1979. The Thatcher government's capacity depended upon a combination of the traditional institutional concentration of power in the executive (the Westminster Model) and a majoritarian electoral system that, given a divided opposition and an unelectable Labour party, allowed the government near dictatorial powers. The government's radical reforms of the organisation of work were accompanied by significant albeit much more modest reforms of the welfare state, especially with regard to health and education. This was mainly because it feared electoral sanctions in areas where the public (and in particular its own electorate) was clearly strongly opposed to any cuts (Pierson 1994; Rhodes 2000; Schmidt 2002a).

Although the Conservative government's single actor political institutional capacity in the 1980s helps explain the swift imposition of radical neo-liberal reform, its lasting success cannot be understood without reference to the transformative power of its communicative discourse.[1] The discourse served to persuade the public not only that reform was necessary, given the economic crisis of the country and that 'there is no alternative' (TINA). Proof of discursive success can be shown not only in the opinion polls that by the mid to late 1980s evidence a shift toward greater acceptance of individual responsibility, materialism and inequalities of income, despite continued support for the universalistic services of health and education (Hetzner 1999; Schmidt 2001). It can also be seen in the fact that the opposition Labour party did not return to power until it had embraced these policies with a 'third way' discourse. This discourse explained that New Labour sought to 'promote opportunity instead of dependence' through positive actions (i.e. workfare) rather than negative actions focused on limiting benefits and services, and by providing 'not a hammock but a trampoline', not 'a hand out but a hand up' (Schmidt 2000a, 2002: Chapter 6).

The more modest success of the multi-actor, liberal US in reforming work and welfare by comparison with single actor UK can be explained by the US's lower political institutional capacity. This is the result of federal institutional structures in which the Congress and the states could counter presidential reform efforts by their own programmes. Business groups and lobbies had tremendous power to block reform and labour little power to promote it in a political system that has ensured that there would rarely be any agreement on reform. Two weak political parties fragmented internally on the left-right dimension as well as regionally by geographical interests that cut across partisan divides made agreement even more unlikely (Dobbin 2002; Howard 1997; Steinmo 1994). In consequence, the US government has had little capacity to introduce strong government run programmes, and has instead largely left to societal actors the public goods tasks generally administered by states in other countries. This is not *laissez faire* but *faire faire*, however, since the state specified the guidelines which societal actors would need to follow, whether corporate actors in carrying out their programmes or the courts in resolving disputes about those guidelines (Dobbin 2002).

The US as a result has consistently been less able to impose radical change than the UK (King and Wood 1999). Although Thatcher and Reagan were equally effective in crushing labour in the early 1980s, the air traffic controllers in the US and the coal miners in Britain, only in the UK was this followed by the government imposition of anti-union laws that effectively broke the back of labour. Hilary Clinton's health care reform proposals in the early 1990s, a rare case in which the US government sought to impose reform akin to a single actor, were a disaster. Hilary Clinton failed to negotiate reform with Congress or industry lobbies, a failure compounded by the complexity of the reform. In contrast, Bill Clinton's success with welfare reform can be attributed to the negotiation process and that it decentralized welfare to the benefit of the states. The shift from a system of *faire* through entitlement programmes to *faire faire* that was actually *laissez faire* to the benefit of the states, which gained block grants that enabled them to allocate the fixed sums as they saw fit (Martin 2000).

In contrast with the UK, the presence of a strong communicative discourse did not have a significant impact, and the absence of a successful coordinative discourse was a problem. The US is arguably the only multi-actor system where the communicative discourse is as important as the coordinative, especially with regard to reframing the coordinative discourse in order to promote agreement in a country where the political institutions militate against agreement. Nevertheless, neither Reagan, the 'great communicator', nor Clinton, were able to overcome the institutional constraints that ensure against rapid reform in the US. Reagan's communicative discourse did arguably better than Clinton's in leaving a lasting influence on the American system, the result of the conservative bias of its institutions and the historically liberal values of the culture that makes it much easier for the state to retreat than to intervene (Dobbin 2002).

Enabling state strategies
Countries with enabling state strategies are generally characterized by coordinated market economies in which inter-firm relations are collaborative and labour-management relations are co-operative (Hall and Soskice 2001). They may be tied to one of two welfare state constellations. Continental European countries have, for the most part, conservative welfare states where welfare is a matter of family responsibility, differentiable according to gender and social status, based on work history, and provided by intermediary groups and the state, with a reasonably high level of benefits but not of services. Scandinavian countries have social-democratic welfare states in which welfare is a matter of collective responsibility, equally accessible to all citizens, to be provided by the state for all at the highest level of benefits and services (Esping-Anderson 1990).

Since the 1980s, the enabling state has not changed its overall strategy even as it has sought to liberalise its market economy and welfare system. In the work arena, the state continues to see its role as promoting greater economic competitiveness without jeopardising non-market-coordinating institutions, especially the co-operative relations between employers' associations and unions (Wood 2001). As a result, enabling states' reform strategies entailed liberalising, deregulating and privatising in consultation and coordination with business and labour rather than, as in liberal states, by state *fiat*. This has ensured that, rather than any significant move to *faire faire* in the work arena, new rules have continued to support *faire avec*.

In the welfare arena, enabling states' reform strategies divide between social-democratic and conservative welfare states. Scandinavian social-democratic welfare states did little to jeopardise their basic commitments to equality and universality of access. Benefits and services were maintained at a very high level of generosity despite across the board cuts in benefits, the introduction of user fees, and even some recourse to privatised pensions. Here the challenge is not poverty, as in Anglo-Saxon liberal welfare states, but rather in maintaining the welfare state at a high level (Scharpf and Schmidt 2000).

Reforms of Continental conservative welfare states have done more to jeopardise the traditional bases of the welfare state, and for good reason. Their grounding in the male breadwinner model, which expects full-time work over a lifetime to ensure a decent pension for the male worker and his spouse, is not suited to contemporary needs for greater labour market flexibility and demands for women's workforce participation. Reforms have for the most part been modest, although here too there have been increases in part-time and temporary employment and some partial privatisation of pensions. The main challenge for these enabling states is neither poverty nor sustainability but, rather, unemployment, since the structure of the conservative welfare state discourages the move to services (and part-time or temporary work) where growth in employment lies.

Generally speaking, then, enabling states have maintained their co-operative market interrelationships and generous welfare despite reforms. Scandinavian enabling states have maintained the highest rates of workforce participation, reasonably high labour mobility, active labour market policies, and comparatively low wage inequalities and unemployment. Many continental enabling states confront low rates of workforce participation, low labour mobility and increasing wage inequalities with high unemployment but not poverty. These general patterns, however, do not tell the whole story, since countries differ in trajectories and levels of reform success due to differences in political institutional capacity and discourse.

In Germany, governmental authority is dispersed and reforms must be negotiated among a wide range of actors. This is the result of corporatist relations with the social partners (business and labour) and the division of power with the *Länder*; the story has been one of little movement toward reform until very recently. Although economic vulnerabilities increased dramatically in the 1990s a result of the costs of unification as much as the competitive pressures of globalisation, the federal executive had little political institutional capacity to negotiate reform with business, which pushed for more far-reaching reforms, and labour, which resisted (Manow and Seils 2000).

This lack of political institutional capacity was exacerbated by the failure of the coordinative discourse among the federal government, *Länder* and social partners to produce any extensive agreements on reform. In the face of such failure, neither the conservative coalition government led by the Christian Democrats before 1998 nor the subsequent centre left coalition government led by the Social Democrats managed to construct a communicative discourse capable of reframing the terms of the coordinative discourse. What attempts there were mostly failed as, for instance, when Chancellor Schroeder sought to borrow the British discourse on the third way in summer 1999, switched to the French socialist discourse in the autumn before settling back into the traditional discourse by the end of the year. None of this did much for the government's reform effort. Only when the government made appeal to values of intergenerational solidarity in gaining agreement for a freeze on the rate of increase in pensions in 2000 did the discourse help (Schmidt 2002a, Chapter 6; see also Cox 2001). Generally speaking, what progress there has been since 2003 with Agenda 2010 and the Hartz III and IV reforms on pensions and unemployment pay, has occurred in the absence of much coordinative discourse and with a thin communicative discourse. These, however, benefited from Schroeder's consistency, finally, in sticking to the reforms despite major losses in the polls, as evidenced by a subsequent rise in popularity.

By comparison, the Netherlands has been the great success story, despite a multi-actor system in which negotiations are even more complicated than in Germany. The economic vulnerabilities of the 1970s and the collapse of the corporatist industrial relations system were background conditions to the introduction of flexibility into the labour markets in the early 1980s. This was made possible by the renewal of the social partners' political institutional capacity to negotiate co-operatively (Hemerijck, Visser and Unger 2000). Capacity was enhanced by a successful coordinative discourse among the social partners, the kick-start for which was the incoming Prime Minister Ruud Lubber's communicative discourse, which raised the credible threat of government intervention because his new conservative-liberal government was 'there to govern' (Hemerijck, Visser and Unger 2000; Schmidt 2000).

Reform in the 1990s of the Dutch welfare state, in crisis due to runaway costs and a disability system in which one in seven workers received disability pay, can be credited in large measure to the creation of a more single actor constellation. Coalition governments had the political institutional capacity not only to act (given a unitary state), despite the lack of participation of the social partners, but also to persist in the face of striking unions and even major electoral defeat in 1994 (Hemerijck, Visser and Unger 2000; Schmidt 2003). Here, while the government's single actor capacity explains its ability to impose reform, the government's communicative discourse explains both its 1994 electoral defeat and its subsequent 1998 landslide victory. The reforms instituted in the early 1990s because the Netherlands was 'a sick country' in need of 'tough medicine' generated increasing dissatisfaction that the discourse did little to address. The disastrous defeat of the conservative/liberal/left coalition can be attributed at least in part to the unbalanced, neo-liberal content of the conservative leader's electoral campaign discourse, which promised to freeze pensions for four years despite an electorate that was one-third elderly.[2] By comparison, the left-liberal coalition government's resounding electoral success in 1998 was due not only to the improved economic environment and to policies that produced 'jobs, jobs and more jobs' as promised but also to normative arguments. These expounded on the way in which government policies were safeguarding social equity even as they produced liberalising efficiency, for example, by attacking inefficient inequities such as paying disability benefits to the able-bodied (Cox 2001; Hemerijck, Visser and Unger 2000; Levy 1999; Schmidt 2000).

Following the economic crisis of the early 1990s Sweden showed similar single actor political institutional capacity to impose reform. The marginalisation of the social partners combined with unitary institutional structures and politically unified governments, enabled successive governments to enact labour laws and pension reforms largely without the co-operation of unions or business. The unions continued to have a de facto veto over certain kinds of reforms (Benner and Vad 2000; Iversen 1996). However, the case of Denmark shows that success is not entirely contingent on institutional structures that give governments the power to act on their own and on political interactions that consolidate governments' political unity. Denmark gained in its capacity to reform beginning in the 1980s not despite, but rather because of governmental disunity, which enabled reform after reform to be negotiated via ad hoc government coalitions that engaged in 'policy and party shopping' (Benner and Vad 2000; Schmidt 2003).

The contrast between Sweden and Denmark is enlightening. In welfare reform, Sweden as a single actor constellation was arguably as successful as the Netherlands in generating a communicative discourse for reform of the welfare state. In the face of economic crisis in the 1990s and in the absence of a coordinative discourse with the social partners, successive governments engaged in communicative discourses that spoke of the need for social solidarity and the acceptance of moderate cutbacks in the generosity of transfers (Rothstein 2001). Reforms were made more publicly acceptable even in the absence of a coordinative discourse by the fact that the government sought to consult widely in an open process of deliberation, where objections were heard and, if possible, incorporated prior to the decision. In the 1990s Social-Democratic governments consistently presented themselves as defending basic welfare state values of equality even as they cut benefits in order to 'save the welfare state'. Such a process has meant that Sweden has been unable to go nearly as far with reforms of the welfare state as Denmark, leaving its sustainability in question (Benner and Vad 2000). Danish discourse which justified reform by a greater focus on creating equity and efficiency meant that reforms could go deeper (Cox 2001; Schmidt 2000).

Enhancing state strategies

Countries with enhancing state strategies are characterised by 'state-enhanced market economies' which have evolved from the *dirigiste* capitalism of post-war France (Schmidt 1996, 2002a), the failed state capitalism of Italy,[3] or the developmental states of South Korea and Taiwan (Weiss 1999, 2003a; Woo-Cumings 1999).[4] In these countries, state strategies have been transformed, as the interventionist state of the post-war period which sought to organise inter-firm collaboration, direct business investment and impose labour management co-operation gave up on all of this as it liberalised, deregulated and privatised (Schmidt 2002a; Weiss 2003b). As a result, the formerly intervening state has taken on an enhancing role. Even as it seeks to create and preserve market institutions that locate decision-making power in companies, the enhancing state continues to intervene strategically to protect business and/or labour from the worst effects of markets, including trying to create something akin to the non-market coordination of the enabling states. Although the state has largely moved away from *faire* to *faire faire* and even, in some cases, to *faire avec*, it still retains more capacity and willingness to intervene than other kinds of state.

In the work arena, France and Italy have both moved very far in a *laissez faire* direction. Both continue to intervene much more than either liberal or enabling states. The French enhancing state continues to intervene strategically to bail out business or to 'moralise' the markets through rules that serve to protect labour and not just business. Privatisation, for example, was a highly state-controlled affair, as the state chose the group of hard core shareholders in order to provide stability and protect against takeovers. This is in contrast to liberal states in which privatised firms' shares were all simply floated on the stock markets (Schmidt 1996). Italy as well as Spain followed the French example (Della Sala 2004).

The French enhancing state's attempts to institute labour market coordination, or *faire avec* have ultimately led to much more *laissez faire* through the radical decentralisation of the labour markets, much as in liberal states such as the UK. The difference is that whereas the liberal state actively crushed the unions, the French enhancing state simply stopped organising wage bargaining (Schmidt 1996). Italy's enhancing state, by contrast, most notably engineered co-operative management-labour relations, or *faire avec*, that led to highly successful rounds of corporatist wage-bargaining and pension reforms in the 1990s (Ferrera and Gualmini 2004; Natali 2004).

Although Italy's reforms were modest, they were nevertheless milestones for a multi-actor state. Italy had long suffered from political institutional *in*capacity, given long-standing state paralysis and business and labour conflict that obviated any reform to speak of through the 1980s, despite deepening fiscal crisis (Ferrera and Gualmini 2004; Natali 2004). Italy's new reform capacity, however, resulted not only from political institutional gains following the collapse of the old party system and electoral reforms that reduced the amount of proportional representation but also from new discourse. Governments used the communicative discourse about European integration as their main rationale for change, with the external constraint involved in meeting the convergence criteria of the EMU (European Monetary Union) presented not only as a matter of economic necessity but also as a question of national pride. This Europe focused discourse acted as background to the more specific communicative discourse about the necessity of welfare reform. This discourse stressed a return to financial health and efficiency, to return to social equity, to end unfairness and corruption, and give 'more to the sons, less to the fathers' (Ferrera and Gualmini 2004; Radaelli 1998; Sbragia 2001; Schmidt 2000). In the mid-1990s, this communicative discourse complemented the coordinative discourse between the government and the unions, which also involved rank and file members in an extensive deliberative process culminating in a referendum to seal agreement on pension and workplace reforms (Baccaro 2000).

In single actor France, where one might have expected even greater political institutional capacity for reform than in multi-actor Italy, despite the institutional arrangements that gave the executive the power to impose change, welfare reform came significantly later. Governments of the left as much as the right, which had had little problem reforming the work arena by imposing monetarism, privatisation, deregulation and labour market decentralisation in the 1980s, had great difficulty with welfare reform (Schmidt 1996). Policies floated from the early 1990s by governments of the right proposing reductions in pension benefits, cost cutting in healthcare or partial privatisation of public services repeatedly provoked street protests. These culminated in the massive strikes against the Juppé government's social security reform bill that paralysed Paris and the provinces at the end of 1995. Only with the return of a government of the left in the surprise election victory of 1997 did welfare reforms proceed, albeit modestly, as the Jospin government began to negotiate with business and labour as opposed to simply trying to impose (Levy 2000; Schmidt 2002a: Chapters 4 and 6). Most significant, however, was the capacity of the Raffarin government to institute public sector pension reform, which the Jospin government didn't even try. This was related to Raffarin's ability to split the union opposition by buying off some unions through separate settlements while holding out against others (Natali and Rhodes 2004).

This historic lack of capacity with regard to welfare reform has much to do with the absence of a transformative communicative discourse in France. Beginning in 1983, successive French governments of left and right were eloquent on the necessity of neo-liberal reform, but did little more than vaguely proclaim the need to continue to protect national values of social solidarity and the obligations of the 'Republican State'. This worked so long as the welfare state continued to expand but not as of the early 1990s, when governments sought to institute major reforms in the welfare arena in response to continuing economic vulnerability and the need to meet the convergence criteria of the EMU. Time and again reform initiatives were proposed then withdrawn in the face of major protests by governments of the right which failed to speak to the reforms' appropriateness. The protests subsided and reforms proceeded only when the newly elected Jospin government in 1997 began a communicative discourse that argued that it was possible to reconcile neo-liberal policies with the values of social solidarity and even egalitarianism and redistribution. This it claimed to do by balancing economic efficiency with social equity. The methods used included, for example, privatisations to secure investment and jobs by involving the unions in negotiations, tax changes that provided for redistribution toward the poor without raising spending, and the creation of private pension funds administered by the social partners rather than private companies (Levy 2000; Schmidt 2000a). The relative lack of protest and the historically high popularity ratings of Prime Minister Jospin in his first three years in office attest to the success of the discourse as well as of the reform efforts. He did not, however, reform public sector pensions but did institute a coordinative discourse by way of a committee attached to the Prime Minister's office to build agreement on reform. Public sector reform was left to Raffarin, whose political institutional capacity was arguably enhanced by the previous decade's surfeit of communicative discourse about the necessity and appropriateness of reform.

Conclusions

State strategies, in short, started in different places, have taken different routes to adjustment, and have ended up in different places, with different continuing challenges with regard to work and welfare. This is due not only to the institutional legacies of the post-war period but also to the mediating factors which made some countries more vulnerable to the economic pressures than others and left some with less political institutional capacity to reform, whether because of opposing preferences or insufficiently legitimating discourses. Table 3.3 sums up just how different the success rates related to the differential impact of the mediating factors. What it shows is that lasting reforms generally require both significant political institutional capacity and transformative discourse, although sometimes a transformative discourse can facilitate reform even where there is little political institutional capacity, while political institutional capacity without a transformative discourse rarely produces lasting reform.

Notes

1 A telling contrast is with New Zealand, which resembled the UK in all mediating factors except that it lacked a persuasive discourse or any significant discourse that spoke to the appropriateness of reform. The result was a public revolt that led to a referendum which changed the very election system that had allowed the government the political institutional capacity to reform against the will of the electorate.

2 This is the view of Ruud Lubbers, the former Prime Minister, about the discourse of his successor, Brinkman. Conversation, Cambridge, MA, 1 May 2000.

3 Italy was the ideal-typically unsuccessful state. It had a paralysed state with runaway welfare costs and highly adversarial labour relations that did more to hinder than lead business and was incapable of controlling labour – such that the economy was 'state-led by indirection' (Schmidt 2002a: 109, 117) or a form of 'state-hindered' capitalism.

4 Most 'varieties of capitalism' scholars see either two varieties divided between LME and CME (Hall and Soskice 2001) or many (Crouch and Streeck 1997; Hollingsworth, Schmitter, and Streeck 1994). Those who see only two varieties tend to dismiss countries that don't fit as anomalies, as a geographically defined and indistinct 'Mediterranean capitalism', including Italy, Spain, Greece, and even Turkey (Hall and Soskice 2001: 21), or as stuck between Anglo-Saxon and Rhinish capitalism (Albert 1991). Instead, I see at least three varieties of capitalism, the third of which is 'state-enhanced' market economies (Schmidt 2002a: Chapters 3 and 4). A few scholars also note these three varieties, including Coates (2000) and Rhodes and Apeldoorn (1997) who describe a 'Latin' variety with a greater role for the state.

Table 3.3 Influence of various mediating factors for success of state strategies toward work and welfare

State strategies and legacies	Countries' main reform initiatives	Institutions		Political institutional capacity	Discourse		Reform success
		Single actor	Multi-actor		Coord-inative	Commun-icative	
Liberal states	US Reagan						
	work early 1980s		++	+	----	+++	++
	welfare mid 1980s		++++	--	----	+++	+
	US Clinton						
	work mid 1990s		+++	--	---	+	-
	welfare late 1990s		++++	+	+	+++	+++
	UK Thatcher						
	work 1980–87	+++		+++	---	+++	+++
	welfare 1985–90	+++		+++	---	+	+
	UK Blair						
	welfare 1997–2002	+++		+++	---	+++	+++
Enabling states	Netherlands work 1980s		++	---	+++	+	+++
	welfare 1994	+		++	+	--	+
	welfare 1998	+		++	+	+++	+++
	Germany						
	work/welfare 1990s		+++	+	-	--	--
	work/welfare 2003–		+++	+	--	+	+
	Denmark work/welfare 1980s–1990s		++	+++	+++	--	+++
	Sweden work/welfare 1990s	+		++	--	++	++
Enhancing states	Italy						
	work/welfare 1980s		++++	---	---	---	---
	Berlusconi 1994		+++	+	---	-	---
	Dini 1995		+++	+	+++	+++	++
	Berlusconi 2004	+		-	--	+	-
	France work 1980s	+++		++	---	+++	+++
	Juppé welfare 1995-97	+++		++	---	---	--
	Jospin welfare 1997–2002	+++		++	+	+++	+
	Raffarin welfare 2003	+++		++	-	++	++

References

Albert, M. (1991) *Capitalisme contre capitalisme*, Paris.

Baccaro, L. (2000) 'Negotiating pension reform with the unions: the Italian experience in European perspective'. Paper 12th International Conference of Europeanists, Chicago.

Benner, M. and Vad, T. (2000) 'Sweden and Denmark: defending the welfare state', in Scharpf, F. W. and Schmidt V. A. (eds), *Welfare and work in the open economy. Volume II. Diverse responses to common challenges*, Oxford.

Coates, D. (2000) *Models of capitalism: growth and stagnation in the modern era*, Oxford.

Cox, R. (2001) 'The social construction of an imperative: why welfare reform happened in Denmark and the Netherlands but not in Germany', *World Politics* 53.

Crouch, C. and Streeck, W. (eds) (1997) *Modern capitalism or modern capitalisms?*, London.

Della Sala, V. (2004) 'The Italian model of capitalism: on the road between globalisation and Europeanisation', *Journal of European Public Policy* 11.

Dobbin, F. (2002) 'Is America becoming more exceptional? how public policy corporatized social citizenship' in Rothstein, B. and Steinmo, S. (eds), *Restructuring the welfare state: political institutions and policy change*, New York.

Dore, R., Boyer, R. and Mars, Z. (1997) *The return to incomes policy*, London.

Esping-Andersen, G. (1990) *Three worlds of welfare state capitalism*, Cambridge.

—— (1999) *Social foundations of post-industrial economies*, Oxford.

Ferrera, M., and Gualmini, E. (2004) *Rescued by Europe? social and labour market reforms in Italy from Maastricht to Berlusconi*, Amsterdam.

Hall, P. A. and Soskice, D. (2001) *Varieties of capitalism: the institutional foundations of comparative advantage*, Oxford.

Hemerijck, A. and Schludi, M. (2000) 'Sequences of policy failures and effective policy responses', in F. W. Scharpf and V. A. Schmidt (eds), *Welfare and work in the open economy. Volume I. From vulnerability to competitiveness*, Oxford.

Hemerijck, A., Visser, J., and Unger, B. (2000) 'How small countries negotiate change: Austria, the Netherlands, and Belgium' in F. W. Scharpf and V. A. Schmidt (eds), *Welfare and work in the open economy. Volume II. Diverse responses to common challenges*, Oxford.

Hetzner, C. (1999) *The unfinished business of Thatcherism*, New York.

Hollingsworth, R., Schmitter, P., and Streeck, W. (eds) (1994) *Governing capitalist economies*, Oxford.

Howard, C. (1997) *The hidden welfare state: tax expenditures and social policy in the United States*, Princeton.

Iversen, T. (1996) 'Power, flexibility and the breakdown of centralized wage bargaining: the cases of Denmark and Sweden in comparative perspective', *Comparative Politics* 28.

King, D. and Wood, S. (1999) 'The political economy of neo-liberalism: Britain and the United States in the 1980s' in Kitschelt, H. *et al.* (eds), *Continuity and change in contemporary capitalism*, Cambridge.

Levy, J. (1999a) *Tocqueville's revenge: dilemmas of institutional reform in post-dirigiste France*, Cambridge.

—— (1999b) 'Vice into virtue? progressive politics and welfare reform in continental Europe', *Politics and Society* 27.

—— (2000) 'France: directing adjustment?', in Scharpf, F. W., and Schmidt, V. A. (eds), *Welfare and work in the open economy. Volume II. Diverse responses to common challenges*, Oxford.

Manow, P. and Seils, E. (2000) 'Adjusting badly: the German welfare state, structural change and the open economy', in Scharpf, F. W. and Schmidt, V. A. (eds), *Welfare and work in the open economy. Volume II. Diverse responses to common challenges*, Oxford.

Martin, C. J. (2000) *Stuck in neutral*, Princeton.

Natali, D. (2004) 'Europeanisation, policy arenas, and creative opportunism: the politics of welfare state reform in Italy' *Journal of European Public Policy*,11.

—— and Rhodes, M. (2004) 'Trade-offs and veto players: reforms pensions in France and Italy', *French Politics*, 2.

Pierson, P. (1994) *Dismantling the welfare state: Reagan, Thatcher and the politics of retrenchment in Britain and the United States*, Cambridge.

Radaelli, C. (1998) 'Networks of expertise and policy change in Italy', *South European Society and Politics*, 3.

Rhodes, M. (2000) 'Restructuring the British welfare state: between domestic constraints and global imperatives' in Scharpf, F. W. and Schmidt, V. A. (eds), *Welfare and work in the open economy. Volume. II. Diverse responses to common challenges*, Oxford.

—— and Van Apeldoorn, B. (1997). 'Capitalism versus capitalism in Western Europe', in Rhodes, M., Heywood, P., and Wright, V., (eds), Developments in *West European Politics 1*, London.

Rothstein, B. (1998) *Just institutions matter: the moral and political logic of the universal welfare state*, Cambridge.

—— (2001) 'Social capital in the social democratic welfare state', *Politics and Society* 29: 2.

Sbragia, A. (2001) 'Italy and EMU', in Green Cowles, M., Caporaso, J., and Risse, T. (eds), *Transforming Europe: Europeanisation and domestic change*, Ithaca.

Scharpf, F. W. (2000a) *Governing in Europe*, Oxford.

—— (2000b) 'Economic changes, vulnerabilities, and institutional capabilities', in Scharpf F. W. and Schmidt, V. A. (eds), *Welfare and work in the open economy. Volume I. From vulnerability to competitiveness*, Oxford.

—— (2002) 'The European social model: coping with the challenges of diversity', *Journal of Common Market Studies*, 40:4.

—— and Schmidt, V. A. (eds) (2000) *Welfare and work in the open economy: diverse responses to common challenges*, Oxford.

Schmidt, V. A. (1996) *From state to market? The transformation of business and government in France*, Cambridge.

—— (2000) 'Values and discourse in the politics of adjustment' in Scharpf, F. W. and Schmidt, V. A. (eds), *Welfare and Work in the Open Economy. Vol. 1: From Vulnerability to Competitiveness*, Oxford.

—— (2001) 'The politics of adjustment in France and Britain: when does discourse matter?', *Journal of European Public Policy*, 8:2.

—— (2002a) *The futures of European capitalism*, Oxford.

—— (2002b) 'Europeanisation and the mechanics of policy adjustment', *Journal of European Public Policy*, 9:6.

—— (2002c) 'Does discourse matter in the politics of welfare state adjustment?', *Comparative Political Studies*, 35:2.

—— (2003) 'How, where, and when does discourse matter in small states' welfare state adjustment?', *New Political Economy*, 8:1.

—— (2004) 'The European Union: democratic legitimacy in a regional state?', *Journal of Common Market Studies*, 42:4.

—— and Radaelli, C. (2004) 'Conceptual and methodological issues in policy change in Europe', *West European Politics*, 27:4.

Steinmo, S. (1994) 'Rethinking American exceptionalism', in Dodd, L. and Jillson, C. (eds), *The dynamics of American politics: approaches and interpretations*, Boulder, CO.

Visser, J. and Hemerijck, A. (1997) '*A Dutch miracle' job growth, welfare reform and corporatism in the Netherlands*, Amsterdam.

Weiss, L. (1999) 'State power and the Asian crisis', *New Political Economy*, 4.

—— (ed.) (2003a) *States in the global economy: bringing domestic institutions back in*, Cambridge.

—— (2003b) 'Guiding globalisation in East Asia: new roles for old developmental states', in Weiss, L. (ed.), *States in the global economy: bringing domestic institutions back in*, Cambridge.

Woo-Cumings, Y. (ed.) (1999) *The developmental state*, Ithaca.

Wood, S. (2001) 'Business, government, and patterns of labour market policy in Britain and the Federal Republic of Germany', in Hall, P. and Soskice, D. (eds), *Varieties of capitalism: the institutional foundations of comparative advantage*, Oxford.

Part II
The global neo-liberal challenge

4

Fractured capacity in regulating international labour standards: the perils of voluntary self-regulation and competition for moral authority

Austina J. Reed and Charlotte A. B. Yates

The consequences of de-territorialising national labour standards regulation

For all its promises for greater legitimacy, accountability and the general improvement of labour rights, we argue that the regulatory system of international labour standards falls short of its potential to protect workers worldwide from exploitation and poverty through rising labour standards.[1] The greatest challenge facing this system is what we will refer to as *fractured capacity* to implement and enforce compliance from its members around a core set of global labour standards. As the term fractured capacity would suggest, the inherent weaknesses in the system of labour standards regulation stem from the 'de-territorialisation' of labour market regulation. This is seen in the splintering of power and regulatory authority between competing spheres of public and private authority at multiple levels of governance and the general decline of national labour movements in a number of Western countries.[2]

Rather than seeing the state in retreat from labour market regulation, we argue that states have actively devolved authority for setting labour standards to other levels and types of governance. This devolution of authority includes shifting responsibility to supranational as well as sub-national governing institutions, at the same time as encouraging a greater role for private bodies, either to self-regulate or engage in new private forms of standard setting. The latter can be observed in the increasingly popular practice of voluntary self-regulation by multinational corporations to police their own behaviour in the employment relationship. When governments do intervene in labour standard setting, it has increasingly been to restrict labour rights and rollback state-based regulation of working conditions. These changes to the role of the state in labour market regulation have two implications. First, as state authority in labour standard setting is transferred to other institutions or jurisdictions there is a struggle for power, alongside competition for the moral authority to govern, and a fracturing of state capacity to establish and uphold certain labour standards. Second, changes in who governs and the manner in which labour standards are being implemented and enforced create a potential 'crisis of legitimacy' for the emergent system of labour regulation.

The materialisation of these trends, however, cannot be explained without looking at the changing balance of power in the global political economy associated with the diminishing power resources of national labour movements. The globalisation of production relations in which capital increasingly moves across national borders with fewer and fewer obstacles, as well as the internationalisation and privatisation of essential government activities to monitor employment conditions, together have undermined the place and role of organised labour movements. In those countries where Keynesian post-war settlements were entrenched, changes associated with globalisation have undermined the privileged status once afforded to national labour movements in policy making and labour standard setting. These trends have been reinforced by the explicitly anti-union initiatives introduced by neo-conservative governments in the United States, Canada, Great Britain, Australia and New Zealand (Fairbrother and Yates 2003).

It would be a mistake, however, to see this discussion only in terms of the implications for developed countries and their labour movements. For developing countries, the structural changes associated with economic globalisation have reinforced – if not magnified – the unequal power relationship between Northern and Southern countries and their respective national labour movements. Capital has tended to move from countries with strong labour market regulation and strong national labour movements to those with weaker labour market regulation and weaker national labour movements. Arguably, trade agreements signed between unequal economic partners, as is the case between Northern industrialised countries and newly industrialised or developing countries, further entrench these asymmetrical power relationships in the state system. As it relates specifically to the implementation and enforcement of international labour standards, arguably power lies with those states that determine exactly which labour standards are to be brought into these trade agreements or supranational governance initiatives, and these states overwhelmingly represent Northern developed countries' interests. The origins of the asymmetrical power relationships that exist in international labour standard setting practices are entangled in a complex web of unequal power relationships between Northern and Southern countries' interests, between their respective labour movements' interests, and between labour and capital interests more generally. The result is a tension between competing and overlapping interests that makes enforcing international labour standards difficult.

In the present system of international labour standards, this problem of a weakened domestic base for labour, coupled with the limited strength of international governance arrangements, translates into a kind of institutional mismatch between nationally-bounded labour movements and international labour initiatives. What we may be witnessing, then, is a 'scalar disjuncture' in the political organisation of the labour movement (Bronner 1997). As the functioning of the international labour standards system indicates, this disjuncture will remain unresolved so long as national labour movements face continued membership decline and associated losses of political influence at the same time that they must be prepared to fight on multiple fronts in the global political economy.

We suggest that the better answer for improving labour rights for all workers everywhere is found in the re-territorialisation of international labour standards through stronger state capacity and independent workers' organisations. A global platform of labour standards is most likely to succeed when the system is supported by the re-engagement of national governments and workers' organisations for the purposes of protecting and improving labour rights. To this end, the primary purpose of this chapter is to identify the principal sources of fractured capacity in the system of regulating international labour standards. By focussing this study on the structural weaknesses found in both existing and emerging models of labour standards regulation, we call into question the logic of relocating the jurisdiction of labour standard setting to the international level and the private sector. The first part of this chapter discusses briefly the conceptualisation of international labour standards and introduces the problem of a legitimacy crisis for the system of international labour standards regulation. We use different examples of the traditional, intergovernmental labour agreement to show just how little 'agreement' there is among states on matters concerning the design, implementation and enforcement of core international labour standards. The second part identifies the structural changes in both production and governance that are related to globalisation processes. It then explores the relationship between these structural changes and the practice of labour standard setting, thus demonstrating the origins of fractured capacity and its implications for achieving legitimate, effective labour standards regulation on a global scale. The third part returns to the question of how best to improve international labour standards. We argue that any study of international labour standards must be critical of the underlying power relationships that affect the setting and implementation of labour standards regulation. It follows that effective multilateral enforcement of labour standards, whether it occurs at the supranational level or within the private corporate domain, requires the re-engagement of the nation state, particularly among the developed countries like the United States and Canada, as well as strong, independent labour movements.

Fractured capacity and the 'crisis of legitimacy'

Since the creation of the World Trade Organisation in 1995, new concerns have surfaced about what constitutes the most appropriate jurisdiction for protecting and improving workers' rights. Both scholars and practitioners alike have pointed to the International Labour Organisation (ILO) Declaration on Fundamental Principles and Rights at Work as one of the defining labour standards models upon which all other subsequent initiatives should build. With its final adoption in 1998, the ILO Declaration was symbolic of the international community's renewed commitment to uphold and extend the core labour rights found in ILO Conventions. These principles include the freedom of association and right to collective bargaining, the abolition of forced or compulsory labour as well as child labour, and the elimination of discrimination in respect to employment and occupation (ILO 1998).

The ILO Declaration on Fundamental Principles and Rights at Work is one of several multilateral, intergovernmental initiatives that attempt to establish uniform labour standards and laws across national borders. Member countries of the European Union ratified the European Social Charter in 1961, which in effect requires of its members a commitment to a set of seven articles specific to labour rights.[3] In the case of the Americas, the primary example of a multilateral initiative is the North American Agreement on Labour Co-operation (NAALC).[4] Signed by Canada, Mexico and the United States in 1993, the four member countries of MERCOSUR have also experimented with drafting and implementing a core set of international labour standards which are specific to their region and their trade relationships.[5]

In addition to these multilateral initiatives forged between multiple countries, states have entered into bilateral trade agreements that include commitments to international labour standards. For example, Canada has been signatory to five bilateral or regional trade agreements, with four of them signed with countries in North, South, or Central America. Another eight are in various stages of negotiations. Like the NAFTA (North American Free Trade Agreement), Canada's trade agreement of 1997 with Chile includes a form of labour accord recognising the rights and interests of workers to safe working environments and grievance procedures. Likewise, the United States has signed trade agreements with Jordan in 2001, as well as with Singapore in 2003. What may in fact be most remarkable about a number of these bilateral treaties, like the one established between the US and Jordan, is the attempt to incorporate labour standards directly into the core provisions of the trade agreement, efforts that have been largely thwarted in many multilateral initiatives.

Most notable about these multilateral and bilateral labour agreements is the wide variation in the substance of their commitment to the core labour standards articulated by the ILO, as well as the range of institutional infrastructures put in place to implement and enforce these labour standards. For example, few of these multilateral and bilateral labour agreements contain commitments to freedom of association or collective bargaining. In turn, the lack of commitment to freedom of association or collective bargaining undermines one of the key institutional means by which labour standards have been upheld, namely the actions of independent trade unions. The result of this discrepancy in content, scope and structure is a multiplicity of very different agreements on international labour standards and overlapping memberships where states are involved in more than one of these different governance arrangements. As such, the crisis of legitimacy that we identify in the international labour standards system is characterised not by a vacuum of authority, as one might assume with the gradual pullback by states in labour market regulation, but rather by multiple voices of authority competing for legitimacy. Steffek has defined legitimacy as 'the phenomenon that a social order enjoys the prestige of being considered binding' (Steffek 2000: 5). According to Steffek, legitimacy involves both substantive (i.e. political) legitimacy and procedural (i.e. institutional) legitimacy. In international governance, substantive legitimacy is conferred when consensus, or agreement, is reached among members of an international institution over the content of rules or regulations and, thus, an implicit acceptance that peoples and governments will abide by and be held accountable to a set of agreed-upon rules and regulations. Procedural legitimacy rests on accepting the authority of the decision-making processes and institutions involved in making the rules. This second type of legitimacy is more likely conferred to those decision-making processes and institutions characterised by transparency, representativeness and accountability.

Largely absent from characterisations of legitimacy in international forms of governance is any notion of the link between effectiveness in governance (in this case the capacity to uphold minimum labour standards) and legitimacy, a linkage that draws our attention to the question of enforcement of international labour standards. One of the greatest weaknesses of the regulatory system is the lack of regulatory capacity or power to monitor and enforce compliance around agreed-upon labour standards. Thus, it is at the level of enforcement that many of the more substantively legitimate international labour standards are weak. Conversely, some of the less substantively legitimate standards generated by private bodies may have greater capacity for effective enforcement due to the overriding power of capital in shaping the relations between workers and managers. This disjuncture between different forms of legitimacy and effectiveness through enforcement contributes to the fractured capacity of the international labour standards system.

Legitimacy for an emerging international system of labour market regulation built on the core labour standards is undermined because the institutions that make up this system do not have the power to apply sanctions or coerce offenders. It is a system comprised of international bodies such as the International Labour Organisation, multilateral or bilateral agreements like the North American Agreement on Labour Co-operation, and voluntary self-regulatory instruments such as the corporate code of conduct. The regulatory mechanisms used by these institutions for monitoring compliance and disciplining violators of labour standards rely heavily upon shared norms and a willingness on the part of the participants in these various forms of governance (i.e. states and multinational corporations) to subject their own rules and institutions to international scrutiny and suasion (e.g. Weisband 2000). Legitimacy and enforcement of these labour standards, however, are impeded by three important factors: first, overlapping memberships for states in multiple labour standards agreements and in different supranational governance arrangements; second, mounting competition for moral authority in a situation of de-territorialised regulation; and third, weakened labour movements with declining capacity to uphold and defend labour rights.

Locating international labour standards in the global political economy: sources of fractured capacity

Our critique of the international labour standards system begins with the argument that the effectiveness of this regulatory system to protect and improve labour rights is inherently limited by a deep-seated inability, both politically and institutionally, to enforce compliance around a global platform of labour standards. We will refer to this particular limitation as one of fractured capacity (Sassen 1997). This image of fractured capacity suggests a fundamental break in, or splintering of, power and authority within the global political economy more generally. For the international labour standards system in particular, however, such fractured capacity has meant competition and disagreement between different regulatory bodies over the content of labour regulations, variable implementation and uneven enforcement of labour rights.

We theorise that the development of fractured capacity in this particular international labour standards system is emblematic of much larger, structural changes occurring to the global political economy, namely (1) the globalisation of production relations and (2) the internationalisation and privatisation of essential government activities.[6] Although much of the literature in global political economy posits a link between capital mobility, globalisation of production relations and the shift upwards to the supranational level for standards-making activity, there is less recognition of the way in which the restructuring of the state through international integration and privatisation impacts on the practices of designing, implementing and enforcing labour standards. It is all too often assumed that labour rights and standards remain a responsibility either of the nation state, or to be determined by the invisible hand of a deregulated market. What we are suggesting here is that the internationalisation and privatisation of government activities have opened up new political and discursive space for governments to seek new partners and agents in regulating the labour market. From this more general discussion, we can begin to identify some of the primary causes, or sources, of fractured capacity in the international labour standards system by framing them around the structural changes associated with globalisation processes more generally.

First, in an increasingly globalised world, there is a growing scalar disjuncture between the economic structures and processes of accumulation/production and the political structures and processes of collective action/representation (for a general discussion, see for example Brenner 1999; Herod 2001; Low 1997). For international labour standard setting and enforcement, this development plays out in terms of the institutional mismatch between nationally-bounded labour movements, many of which are in serious decline, and international governance initiatives.

Second, in an increasingly globalised world, there are multiple spheres of authority claiming power and legitimacy in the international system (Cutler *et al.* 1999). In the setting of labour standards, this development leads to fractured and competing spheres of authority between multiple agents of governance over which jurisdiction (or institution) is best placed to define and enforce legitimate labour standards.

Third, in an increasingly globalised world, there is an underlying shift towards the development of the competition state that more and more plays the role of political broker in negotiating the global flows of capital and goods (Cerny 2000). Arguably, this is at the expense of other goals such as strengthening state-based regulation of working conditions and labour rights (e.g. Mittelman 2000). The kind of public – private partnerships now being created between the competition state and multinational corporations signals a new phase in industrial relations that is reshaping the employment relationship between management and workers. In many instances, these partnerships have taken the form of multilateral, non-binding self-regulation.

The system is generally burdened by conflicts of interest between actors and their motivations for, or interests in, complying with a core set of international labour standards. But, as national labour movements decline in power, experience and reduced capacity for improving working conditions and labour rights, the result of these conflicts of interest and ensuing struggles over who sets labour standards is greater unevenness in standards setting and reduced likelihood that regulations and standards will meet the needs of working people. Moreover, the system of international labour standards regulation is characterised by overlapping memberships in multiple labour initiatives, and the very practice of enforcing compliance around international labour standards is intrinsically tied to both the actors that make rights claims and the processes by which these claims are made. Workers are faced with the dilemma of deciding which dispute mechanisms to access in order to have their concerns heard and rights violations resolved.

Scalar disjuncture between national labour, global capital and international governance

Whereas capital and states have developed the capacity for international coordination and action, unions are nationally bounded institutions with weak international coordinative institutions and capacity. This national-boundedness is in part a consequence of the post-war accord that encouraged the consolidation of national institutions of labour as a pillar of Keynesian demand-management. It is also a product of workers' boundedness to place and space as they live and work in communities with enduring social ties. This particular condition in effect reduces the capacity for unions to mobilise power and coordinate activities in the international arena and therefore to use effectively international institutions like the ILO or multilateral initiatives like the NAALC to influence supranational developments. Similar difficulties have also faced national labour movements in shaping and enforcing the voluntary, self-regulatory frameworks orchestrated by multinational corporations that are increasingly supported by governments like Canada and the US, for example.

The labour movement's limitations are compounded by declining memberships and, in many countries, anti-union measures undertaken by governments in their bid to entice investment. Of the three actors in the employment relationship, labour has experienced the most dramatic declines in its power resources. Union memberships in many countries in the North have stagnated or fallen, and the most significant of these declines has been registered in the Anglo-Saxon countries (Fairbrother and Yates 2003). In the United States, for example, the number of workers who belong to a trade union has fallen to its lowest percentage since the mid-1940s, and for the private sector in particular membership levels match those reported in the early 1900s (Greenhouse 2005). Simultaneously, unions and national labour movements in many countries have lost legitimacy even within their own national borders, a fact that contributes to reduced power and influence in the international governance arena.

The legitimacy and strategic capacity necessary to advance improvements in working conditions and labour rights at the international level are compromised by reliance on tripartite decision-making structures at a time of general weakening for unions. Tripartite structures, whether regional, national or international as we see in the ILO, guarantee a voice for workers in the decision-making process that underpins employment relations. But equal voice through equal representation in tripartite bodies does not guarantee equal power or influence over decision-making. The influence of any one party over another in this relationship is contingent on the power resources available to that party. When power declines, so too does the capacity to influence the outcomes of the decision-making process. The NAALC demonstrates this point all too well: In the several years following the implementation of the labour side agreement, no multinational corporations had participated in the public hearings to determine recourse for labour standards violations, despite the fact that they were named in the complaint. The case of Burma and its labour standards violations concerning forced labour provides another example of the importance of balance of power, and in particular the relative strength of corporate interests compared with labour's, in determining compliance with agreed upon labour standards. Despite multiple warnings from the ILO and various members of the international community representing workers' rights, as well as the willingness of countries to pursue trade sanctions against Burma, the number of corporations reported to have business dealings with the ruling junta or to have invested in the country has either stayed the same or increased during this time (Global Unions 2005). Such investment undermines measures taken by the international community to pressure Burma to comply with international labour standards, also sending a signal to other violators that such standards are weak.

The concept of scalar disjuncture helps us to begin to understand the origins of fractured capacity in the present system of international labour standards. Together, the general weakening and declining legitimacy of unions and the national-boundedness of workers' interests have fractured the capacity of the labour movement to uphold a system of international labour standards. Undoubtedly, international labour standards suffer because unions lack the capacity to play a strong role in negotiating and enforcing compliance with international labour standards. We would argue that the legitimacy afforded to international labour standards very much hinges on the legitimacy garnered by unions and national labour movements at home, that is on the national front. At the same time, we must be cautious about concluding that this limited capacity for sustained international collective action dooms labour to failure. Rather, work by Herod (2001) and others points to the continued capacity for labour to take effective collective action, often at the local level. Collective action in this form has been taken up by workers' organisations for the purpose of defending national or local standards, rather than international labour rights. This points to the continued importance of independent unions and national standards, a point to which we return in our conclusion.

Competing voices of moral authority across levels of governance

The system of international labour standards faces another of its more formidable obstacles to achieving both political and institutional legitimacy from the emergence of competing voices of moral authority across levels of governance. Democratic national governments have historically relied upon their moral authority, rather than outright coercion, to make and enforce laws and regulations. These national governments have been accorded legitimacy and a near monopoly on this moral authority to make the rules and enforce the regulations. In the international arena, no one set of institutions or practices have been able to garner such moral authority for their role in setting labour standards. Thus, there are three prominent sources of competition for moral authority, which undermine the political and institutional legitimacy of international labour standards.

The first source of competition over moral authority originates in competing national claims for the moral authority to shape the content of and advance the cause of a platform of international labour rights. Governments in many Western, advanced industrialised countries have tended to take the lead in championing the cause of improved labour rights everywhere. As such, these countries point to their historical leadership in establishing labour standards and rights for their own workers as a model for labour market regulation to be followed and emulated by less developed countries. For their part, governments of less developed countries claim that the West's championing of labour rights is nothing more than veiled protectionism. What follows from this is none other than a tendency to pit workers across geopolitical-ideological boundaries against each other. Indeed, the issue of protectionism and labour standards is one of the most glaring examples of the divide between workers and their governments which has continued to surface in debates over the merits of including labour standards in trade agreements.

The irony, of course, lies in the fact that many of the advanced industrial countries that champion the cause of international labour standards – in particular Canada, the United States and the UK – can be faulted for having undermined the legitimacy of international labour standards. They have done so by refusing to ratify ILO Conventions, or when they fail to respond to ILO investigations that find them in breach of conventions that they have endorsed. For example, although Canada and the US take the moral high road in their criticism of the lack of labour rights in Mexico and China, an examination of ratification of international conventions of labour standards offers some surprising results. Mexico has signed all but one of the eight core labour standards conventions, beginning in 1934, and the most recent being the elimination of child labour in 2000. Likewise, China has ratified one more labour convention than the United States, bringing its total to three, whereas the United States has only signed two conventions, both in the 1990s. Canada is positioned somewhere in the middle of these two groups, having signed five of the eight labour conventions, but not those related to freedom of association, the elimination of forced or compulsory labour and the abolition of child labour (ILO 2004). The fact that since 2000 two provincial governments in Canada have been named by the ILO as violators of international labour standards, but have failed to acknowledge the legitimacy of the ILO's findings, points to the deep disregard these governments have for international institutions and labour rights. This reduces the legitimacy of claims about the need for international labour standards and makes it that much harder to promote labour standards in countries like China when the so-called champions of labour rights fail to support these kinds of supranational initiatives at implementing and enforcing labour standards. Moreover, within their own jurisdictions, many Western industrialised countries may be held directly responsible for reversing a number of gains made by unions over the years in labour market regulation. The effect has been the gradual deterioration of labour standards, the dismantling of labour rights and often open government hostility to unions and their claims to the rights for representation in the employment relation-ship with business. When these same governments turn around and proclaim their commitment to international labour standards, their moral authority is reduced and the space is opened for alternative claims for the moral authority to act on labour rights.

The second source of competition for moral authority to define the terrain of labour standards comes from the rising prominence of neo-conservative ideas. Neo-conservatives put forth a particular model of labour market development in which the market (and not collective bargaining or socially-defined minimum labour standards) is the institution best able to determine the allocation of resources and rights. Neo-conservative ideas that espouse the rights and moral obligations of the individual, the efficiency of the free market in allocating resources and a puritan work ethic have become the foundation of the discourse around moral standards and regulation in the Anglo-Saxon liberal democracies, beginning with the elections of Margaret Thatcher and Ronald Reagan in Britain and the US, respectively. Neo-conservative logic is deeply embedded in various (Western-dominated) multilateral economic institutions like the IMF (International Monetary Fund) and World Bank, and structural adjustment programs are but one example of how the neo-conservative ideology has been introduced into the governing policies and practices of developing countries. In effect, neo-conservative ideas supplement those of neo-liberals, who also champion the role of the market in allocating resources. These neo-conservatives ideas are fundamentally at odds with international labour standards and human rights in two important ways. First, the neo-conservative doctrine of moral standards undermines collective rights by championing individual rights and responsibilities. Second, neo-conservative ideas doubt the need for a regulated minimum platform of labour rights and standards, preferring instead to see labour market outcomes as a reflection of individual effort, moral worth and market dynamics. Together, these developments undermine legitimacy for international labour standard setting practices because the neo-conservative narrative has usurped, and thus fractured, the political and discursive space in matters defining the relationship between rights and responsibilities.

The third source of competition over moral authority arises from the expanding domain of private authority, which increasingly overlaps and competes with that of public authority. Corporations have played a direct role in developing codes of conduct, often acting unilaterally in lieu of state regulation. Corporate codes of conduct and the notion of voluntary self-regulation are themselves nothing new. Their introduction into the wider system of international labour standards was first identified in the 1970s with the transnationalisation of production activities linking individual workplaces around the world in a dense network of supply chains (Dae-Oup 2004). The popularity and influence of the corporate code of conduct waned momentarily in the 1980s when corporations openly opposed any such development or adoption of uniform codes. By the mid-1990s, as a result of a resurgence in interest in voluntary self-regulation, the foundations underpinning the industrial relations systems of many Western industrialised countries showed signs of transformation with moves away from worker-led collective bargaining and state legislation and towards private monitoring mechanisms (Blackett 2001; Esbenshade 2001). We return to this point in the next section.

Legitimacy for international labour standards is undermined when the voice of private authority begins to supersede that of public authority. There is an inherent conflict of interest in firms regulating their own behaviour, with little or no involvement from civil society groups. Evidence of this is found in the selectiveness with which corporate designed codes of conduct use ILO standards as a model for their own. Noticeably absent from a number of these corporate devised codes of conduct is collective bargaining and unionisation rights. By this account, private authority poses a threat of diluting, rather than reinforcing, attempts to harmonise labour standards for the better. For the simple fact that there are more and more voices to listen to when it comes to educating oneself about corporate practices and their relationship to labour rights and working conditions, the danger lies in a kind of information overload so that fewer and fewer people may actually be tuning into these debates over the merits of international labour standards. More importantly, workers' access to effective dispute mechanisms in making rights-based claims to a fair wage and safe working conditions is made more difficult by the fracturing of regulatory authority and power, as well as the standards themselves, among several competing institutions with divergent interests and motivations. Under private codes in particular, defence of workers rights becomes entangled with consumer interest and activism. The paradox of private authority in the area of labour market regulation may very well be the development of 'active consumers' at the cost of 'active citizens', depending on how the general public views the credibility of these actions taken by private corporations and whether these actions eventually speak louder than those undertaken by national governments.

Public–private partnerships: towards privatisation and marketisation

The restructuring of the state during economic globalisation at the beginning of the twenty-first century has immense implications for the development of international labour standards. Under intense pressures to liberalise, deregulate and privatise essential government activities, for many Western countries the industrial welfare state has given way to the competition state (Cerny 1995; 2000). The competition state is characterised as a new form of state intervention in which one of the chief policy roles of the state is to promote economic competitiveness, innovation and profitability at home so as to improve overall competitive advantage in the global economy. The primary goal of the competition state, then, becomes one of providing a favourable business and investment climate for corporations. The logic behind this guiding principle suggests that if corporations are successful, then citizens and workers alike can expect trickle down effects to improve their economic and social well being. For labour market regulation in particular, the rise of the competition state does not mean the absence of government intervention, or the end of public services, but rather a shift in policy roles, goals and strategies from de-commodification to those based on the marketisation of state bureaucracies, public services and government enforcement mechanisms (Cerny 2000). As such, the state plays the role of both political broker and market actor in the employment relationship between management and workers, and the result of this development is an increase in the number of public–private partnerships created between state actors and corporations in the name of economic development. Evidence of these partnerships is observed in the types of employment services available to workers as well as the kinds of monitoring mechanisms used to enforce labour rights.

Government efforts to privatise various labour market functions are a particularly important entry point for private institutions into labour market regulation. The most dramatic example of this was seen in Australia's privatisation of its employment services. Argued by many as the single largest privatisation scheme ever, the decision in the late 1990s by the national government to hand over responsibilities for training, job placements and other previously government-led labour market activities marked a huge leap in private authority over labour market regulation. Private firms were offered bonuses for finding work for the long-term unemployed and were the gateway to access of education and retraining (Webster and Harding 2000). In Canada, similar trends have taken place with public institutions partnering with private temporary placement and training agencies to get the unemployed off public income support and back into the labour market, without regards to workers' skills, income sustainability of the job or ways in which family responsibilities may impact on the individual worker's ability to take up certain types of work (Stoutley and Yates 2004; Vosko 1998). The result is a growing role for private firms in implementing and enforcing labour rights, once again opening the door to competing voices for moral authority.

Likewise, government enforcement of labour rights is also being shaped by partnerships created between state actors and private institutions. The example of voluntary codes of conduct readily demonstrates the growing popularity of private monitoring schemes, allowing state investigations of labour abuses to be marketised by replacing them with NGO-based (non-governmental organisation) monitoring or contracting them out to accounting or compliance-consulting firms (Esbenshade 2001; O'Rourke 2003). The Canadian government, for example, renewed its commitment to support corporate responsibility initiatives, having published a set of guidelines outlining the features, benefits, drawbacks, conditions and processes for firms operating in Canada or abroad that seek to implement voluntary codes of conduct (Industry Canada 1998). The United States has pursued a similar course of action, with its announcement to promote 'Model Business Principles' for its corporations operating outside the US (Human Rights Watch). As well, the US government has launched the Fair Labor Coalition through which the Department of Labor is working together with corporations, public interest NGOs and activist shareholder groups to improve labour rights in the garment industry. Voluntarism in these instances is likely to take the form of paternalism, as Esbenshade (2001) has argued, because these private monitoring mechanisms do not allow workers to speak for themselves. Instead, the defence of their rights is intermingled with those of consumers, stakeholders, and public interest NGOs, which at first glance might not seem a negative development for labour standards. Closer scrutiny, however, reveals that in many instances the actual enforcement of workers' rights rises and falls depending on consumer whim and stakeholder interests. It is not a type of voluntarism based on empowering workers so that they may participate in collective bargaining or organise independent unions, but rather one based on dialogue between corporate headquarters, their suppliers, NGOs and state bureaucrats. The result has been to strengthen the power of capital, by expanding management prerogative, at the expense of workers' rights. This, in turn, reinforces power asymmetries between international capital and national labour movements.

These unilateral efforts at enforcing labour rights which partner individual corporations with their respective state bureaucracies are now being replicated on a grander scale, taking the form of multilateral, non-binding corporate responsibility initiatives. Two of the most well-known examples of multilaterally- endorsed codes include the UN Global Compact and the OECD (Organisation for Economic Cooperation and Development) Guidelines for Multinational Enterprises. Both of these corporate responsibility initiatives include recommendations for respecting labour rights but stop short of providing statutory enforcement or monitoring mechanisms. The most recent of these developments in multilateral public–private partnerships comes from the International Organisation for Standardisation (ISO) and its inclusion in the broader framework of Corporate Social Responsibility (CSR) (Gibbs and Yates 2004). Both the Canadian International Development Agency and the UK's Department for International Development, for example, have shown their support for these discussions (IISD 2004). Although these partnerships promise to include a more diverse group of interests and voices in the making of international labour standards, thereby expanding the institutional space where issues of corporate social responsibility arise, the danger to the broader system of labour market regulation is the act of substituting institutional legitimacy for substantive legitimacy. Furthermore, these agreements tend to use conciliatory language in reference to implementation practices and enforcement mechanisms, making the general request that corporations and governments respect tripartism and social dialogue between management and workers and any existing national legislation protecting labour rights. Thus, very few opportunities exist with these voluntary codes to expand the political and discursive space to include additional labour rights besides those already identified by the ILO.

Where next for international labour standards?

This chapter has demonstrated how and why the system of international labour standards suffers from a crisis of political and institutional legitimacy, by illuminating the major structural weaknesses in this system and by linking the source of these weaknesses to broader structural changes in the global political economy. We have identified at least three such structural weaknesses: namely, an institutional mismatch between nationally-bound labour movements, globally-oriented capital and international governance initiatives that protect labour rights; the competition between multiple actors for moral authority to set labour standards; and the privatisation of labour market activities and the marketisation of enforcement mechanisms through public–private partnerships created between state actors and private institutions.

With the adoption of the ILO Declaration and other multilateral labour agreements, as well as the growing popularity of voluntary, self-regulatory initiatives like the corporate code of conduct, consensus reached among members of the international community around, at the very least, the core labour standards would seem to signal a move in the direction of norm-setting and implementation. But as we have argued, the structural weaknesses identified in these different regulatory institutions are part and parcel of a larger problem, which is the lack of enforcement capacity or the inability to ensure compliance from signatories.

Fractured capacity, the splintering of power and regulatory authority between competing actors and levels of governance, suggests that a re-evaluation of the gains made in workers' rights in the environment of neo-liberal globalisation (i.e. political discourse and public policies supporting liberalisation, deregulation and privatisation) is both warranted and necessary. We have used the notion of fractured capacity to elucidate a few of the principal sources of conflict and power asymmetries in the wider system of international labour standard setting. These asymmetries contribute to tensions over issues of content and implementation between states, workers and management. Future efforts at analysing the effectiveness of the international labour-standard regime must consider the process of standard setting, as well as implementation, and enforcement capacity. As we have attempted to show with this concept of fractured capacity, it is critical to take into account the fundamental impact that power has in determining not only the actual content and scope of labour standards but also which players are likely to be present at the negotiating table and their capacity to shape these negotiations and effect compliance from members of the international community. Without including measures of power and power resources into our analysis, we risk missing important nuances in the developmental trajectory of international labour standard setting, which have resulted in variable implementation and uneven enforcement of even the most basic labour rights. These factors include, for example, the unequal balance of power between nationally-bounded labour movements and globally-oriented capital, which places labour at a distinct disadvantage in these international governance initiatives, as well as the converging interests of states and multinational corporations to pursue economic efficiency through different types of public–private partnerships all in the name of global competitiveness.

We are left to consider, then, prescriptions for action that would simultaneously revive national labour movements in their efforts to represent workers' rights and reintroduce political and institutional legitimacy back into the system of implementing labour rights. One such solution to move the present system forward is the re-territorialisation of labour market regulation. This would involve re-engaging national governments in labour standard setting, alongside a growing role for independent trade unions, which would give voices to and mobilise the power resources of the very workers most in need of the protections offered by labour standards setting initiatives.

Notes

1   Research for this paper has been funded by Auto21, a research Network of Centres of Excellence, Canada.
2   The term 'system' of labour standards regulation describes the horizontal and vertical linkages between different levels of governance, different models of labour standards setting, and the actors involved in the design, implementation and enforcement of labour standards regulation. The idea that a system of labour standards regulation exists, even at a very early developmental stage, is paramount to our argument that the practice of labour standards setting is characterised by overlapping jurisdictions and competing voices of authority. Rather than seeing these different institutions or practices as separate or distinct, our reference to 'system' seeks to capture the relational nature of regulating international labour standards between different actors and institutions at multiple levels of governance.
3   The seven articles outlining labour standards in the European Charter move beyond the principles outlined in the ILO Declaration to include rights to social security, social and medical assistance, social, legal and economic protection of the family, and protection and assistance for migrant workers and their families.
4   The NAALC identifies eleven labour standards, including those in the ILO Declaration, and stipulates that violators may be penalised with trade sanctions. The labour standards identified in the NAALC are, however, divided into three categories based on the severity of the penalty, which means that these labour rights are not given equal weight. For example, violations of the freedom of association or the right to collective bargaining would never result in trade sanctions, but rather only consultation.
5   The member governments of MERCOSUR have not agreed formally to enforceable labour rights or standards. Negotiations between government, employer and trade union representatives have fostered the development of an institutionalised consultative process, which has yielded the adoption of eleven ILO Conventions by all four countries.
6   The reference in this argument to both concepts, i.e. internationalisation and globalisation, as distinct processes is deliberate. The danger in making a distinction between the processes of internationalisation and globalisation is a kind of dualism, or false dichotomy, which misses the degree to which the structures underpinning these processes actually overlap and reinforce each other.

References

Blackett, A. (2001) 'Global governance, legal pluralism and the decentered state: a labor law critique of codes of corporate conduct', *Indiana Journal of Global Legal Studies*, 8:2.

Brenner, N. (1999) 'Beyond state-centrism: space, territoriality, and geographical scale in globalization studies', *Theory and Society*, 28.

Cerny, P. (1995) 'Globalization and the changing logic of collective action', *International Organization*, 49:4.

—— (2000) 'Political globalization and the competition state' in Stubbs, R. and Underhill, G. R. D. (eds), *Political economy and the changing global order*, Toronto.

Cutler, A. C., Haufler, V. and Porter, T. (eds) (1999) 'The contours and significance of private authority in international affairs', in *Private authority and international affairs*, Albany.

Dae-Oup, C. (2004) 'Demystifying corporate codes of conduct: Towards critical engagement with TNCs', in Asia Monitor Resource Centre (ed.), *A critical guide to corporate codes of conduct: voices from the South*, Kowloon, Hong Kong.

Esbenshade, J. (2001) 'The social accountability contract: private monitoring from Los Angeles to the global apparel industry', *Labor Studies Journal*, Spring.

Fairbrother, P. and Yates, C. (eds) (2003) 'Unions in crisis, unions in renewal?', in *Trade unions in renewal: a comparative study*, London.

Gibbs, H. and Yates, C. (2004) 'Mapping new forms of governance: the changing political landscape of labour markets in Ontario', Paper to the Annual meeting of the Canadian Political Science Association, Winnipeg.

Gill, S. and Law, D. (1993) 'Global hegemony and the structural power of capital', in Gill, S. (ed.), *Gramsci, historical materialism and international relations*, Cambridge.

Global Unions (2005) 'Companies linked with Burma', www.global-unions.org/burma/default3.asp (accessed 17 December 2004).

Greenhouse, S. (2005) 'Membership in unions drops again', *New York Times*, 28 January.

Herod, A. (2001) *Labor geographies: workers and the landscapes of capitalism*, New York.

Human Rights Watch (no date) 'Corporations and human rights', www.hrw.org/about/initiatives/corp.html (accessed 17 December 2004).

Industry Canada (1998) *Voluntary codes: a guide for their development and use*, Ottawa. http://strategis.ic.gc.ca/volcodes (accessed 17 December 2004).

International Institute for Sustainable Development (no date) *Process requirements for ISO CSR standardization*, www.iisd.org/pdf/2003/standards_process_framework.pdf (accessed 17 December 2004).

International Labour Organisation (no date) 'ILOLEX: database of international labour standards', www.ilo.org/ilolex/english/docs/declworld.htm (accessed 17 December 2004).

International Labour Organisation (1998) *ILO declaration on fundamental principles and rights at work*, Geneva.

Low, M. (1997) 'Representation unbound: globalization and democracy', in Cox, K. (ed.), *Spaces of globalization*, New York.

Mittelman, J. (2000) *The globalization syndrome: transformation and resistance*, Princeton.

Organisation for Economic Cooperation and Development (2003) 'The OECD guidelines for multinational enterprises: a key corporate responsibility instrument', *OECD Observer*, June.

O'Rourke, D. (2003) 'Outsourcing regulation: analyzing nongovernmental systems of labor standards and monitoring', *The Policy Studies Journal*, 31:1.

Reed, A. and Yates, C. (2003) 'The ILO declaration on fundamental principles and rights at work: the limitations to global labour standards', in Irish, M. (ed.), *The auto pact: investment, labour and the WTO*, The Hague.

Rhodes, M. and van Apeldoorn, B. (1998) 'Capital unbound? The transformation of European corporate governance', *Journal of European Public Policy*, 5:3.

Sassen, S. (1997) 'Informalization in advanced market economies', Issues in Development Discussion Paper 20, International Labour Office, Geneva.

Steffek, J. (2000) 'The power of rational discourse and the legitimacy of international governance', European Institute – Robert Schuman Centre working paper RePEc: fth:eurors: 2000–46.

Stoutley, A. and Yates, C. (2004) 'Structuring labour supply and demand in the auto parts industry: the role of temporary staffing agencies', working paper, McMaster University.

Vosko, L. F. (1998) 'Workfare temporaries: workfare and the rise of the temporary employment relationship in Ontario', *Canadian Review of Social Policy*, November.

Webster, E. and Harding, G. (2000) 'Outsourcing public employment services: the Australian experience', Melbourne Institute working paper no. 4/00. www.unimelb.edu.au/iaesrwww/home.html (accessed 17 December 2004).

Weisband, E. (2000) 'Discursive multilateralism: global benchmarks, shame, and learning in the ILO labor standards monitoring regime', *International Studies Quarterly*, 44.

5

Creating a labour dispensation for the twenty-first century: the case of South Africa

Darcy du Toit

Introduction

South Africa, an industrialised democratic state embedded in third-world society, is in many ways a crossroads of the globalised economy. It combines a powerful labour movement, enjoying an unequalled array of legal rights, with an assertive business sector seeking to compete internationally. Socio-economic policy has long been an area of contestation. While labour has called for greater state intervention to combat mass unemployment and poverty, business has pressed for greater market freedom as a precondition for growth. Government, since the advent of democracy in 1994, has sought to strike a balance between these (and other) concerns in accordance with a principle described as 'regulated flexibility'. This chapter focuses on the labour dispensation that has emerged from these competing pressures at the start of the twenty-first century.

The new century opened with protracted tripartite negotiations aimed at addressing the demands of business and labour while, at the same time, bringing the labour regulatory framework in line with the demands of global competitiveness. The outcome was a series of amendments to the relevant statutes that took effect in August 2002. This chapter will review the amendments, focusing in particular on the hotly-contested right of employers to dismiss workers for operational reasons. The changes enacted in this regard, I shall try to show, may be seen as a litmus test of the power balance between capital and labour, reflecting a new equilibrium between market regulation (worker protection) and managerial prerogative in the government's ongoing quest for stable market-based growth.

In conclusion, this chapter will briefly consider the so-called 'Polanyi problem' as a means of conceptualising the processes outlined above, as well as the continued validity of the notion of 'regulated flexibility' as a key feature of government policy.

The background

The transition from apartheid to South Africa's new democratic order has widely been acclaimed as a major political success story. Between 1990 and 1993, political parties representing almost the whole population joined forces in pulling the country back from the brink of civil war and enacting what is arguably the most democratic constitution in the world. Organised labour played a crucial role in the process, both in the struggle to end apartheid and in the battle for socio-economic transformation that followed (Godfrey 2003: 9–16). This was by no means accidental. Historically, apartheid was closely aligned with employers' demand for cheap and regimented labour while, at the same time, workers were (and are) closely integrated with the mass of the black population, millions of whom depend on the wages of workers in employment. As in Brazil, organised labour thus found itself thrust into the forefront of political struggle (Moody 2004). The 1970s saw the resurgence of an increasingly militant black trade union movement, combined with deepening divisions among employers and the ruling National Party. The outcome was a series of concessions to black labour, which saw the progressive recognition of all fundamental labour rights,[1] and the involvement of organised labour in national policy-making, well in advance of the advent of democracy in 1994.

Labour has continued to exert its influence no less vigorously since then. It has campaigned through policy-making institutions such as the National Economic, Development and Labour Council (NEDLAC),[2] as a member of the ruling 'Triple Alliance'[3] and as a driving force in various extra-parliamentary campaigns, while continuing to use the traditional channels of collective bargaining and industrial action.[4] The most intractable differences between the new government and its trade union allies have arisen around issues of socio-economic policy. By the time the African National Congress (ANC) came to power in 1994, it had retreated from its historical promise to nationalise the key sectors of the economy and committed itself to working within the framework of the globalised market economy. While its original platform, known as the 'Reconstruction and Development Programme' (RDP), had a strongly reformist emphasis, the macroeconomic strategy entitled 'Growth, Employment and Redistribution programme' (GEAR) adopted by the Department of Finance in 1996 has widely been criticised as 'pro-business'. Eight years later, the debate shows no sign of abating.

However, the issues are not as clear-cut as they may seem. At the level of policy there is a significant degree of consensus across the political spectrum. Critics of GEAR seldom challenge the underlying vision of market-based reform but, rather, the balance that has been struck; in particular, the commitment to privatisation and fiscal discipline at the expense of more expansionary policies. Another stabilising factor, to the surprise of many, has been the ANC's massive parliamentary majority. Given South Africa's traumatic historical divisions, and spared the need to engage in political trench warfare, its strategy has been one of inclusivity rather than confrontation. Much emphasis has been placed on involving (some would say co-opting) political opponents in government and organs of state (with a view to '[building] the sense of national unity, united action and the new patriotism' (Mbeki 2004). The outcome has been a highly-developed culture of conflict resolution, a tendency to seek negotiated solutions to problems and, in the area of law-making, procedures for seeking the broadest possible compromises.

Nowhere is this tendency more evident, and more problematic, than in the labour field. Labour law is ultimately concerned with the apportionment of power and resources between two social classes with opposing interests. While their relationship in the workplace embodies an element of co-operation, its distributive aspect is inherently adversarial. Laws that seek to regulate it must determine rights, duties and procedures that both sides will find acceptable at least for the time being. In this sense labour law is, and can only be, a compromise. The seemingly unifying right to 'fair labour practices', as enshrined in the South African Constitution (1996: s 23(1)), conceals the fact that 'fairness' will seldom mean the same for workers and employers. In practice it is a legal construct, not necessarily corresponding to either the worker's or the employer's idea of what is actually fair but, typically, embodying a carefully crafted balance between the two. 'Fairness' in this technical sense is the essence of labour law.

Fairness, however, presupposes a level playing field. In legal terms, the problem is that the inequality in bargaining power between worker and employer leaves no scope for genuine freedom of contract (Davies and Freedland 1983: Chapter 1). Labour law seeks to address the imbalance at two levels. First, it sets out to create an enabling environment for collective bargaining, thus allowing workers to bring their combined strength to bear on corporate employers and in other ways promoting what may be termed the socialisation of employment relations (Flanders 1968: 1). Second, it protects individual workers against the arbitrary exercise of managerial power, for example, unfair dismissal. The way in which it does this, however, is itself the outcome of contestation. The rights achieved by labour (mirrored in the corresponding limits placed on employers' power) may thus be seen as an indicator of the political power balance between capital and labour, setting the parameters for power play and the starting point in seeking further rights.

Nowhere is the legal compromise more fragile than in regulating the employer's right to dismiss workers for operational reasons and, conversely, the scope for labour to challenge the exercise of that right. This issue goes to the heart of the employment relationship. In cut-throat global markets, few things are more critical to employers than the right to shed labour which is considered uneconomical. Conversely, in a country with mass unemployment, few issues are more important to trade unions, and society in general, than saving jobs which can be saved. The careful balance struck by the Labour Relations Act (LRA) in 1995, as discussed more fully below, was perceived as being inadequate almost from the outset. This was manifested, for example, in the Presidential Summit on Job Creation held in September 1998 with the participation of organisations representing a wide spectrum of civil society. By 1999, the need to revisit the issue could no longer be postponed.

Regulated flexibility

In this chapter the term 'regulated flexibility' is used to describe the philosophy of the State in seeking to promote compromise between capital and labour. The term gained currency during the debate about the Green Paper that eventually became the Basic Conditions of Employment Act of 1997. The aim, it was said, was 'to balance the protection of minimum standards and the requirements of labour market flexibility' by means of two mechanisms: on the one hand, 'the protection and enforcement of revised basic employment standards' and, on the other, 'the establishment of rules and procedures for the variation of these standards'. Such variation, the Green Paper added, may come about through 'collective bargaining, sectoral determinations for unorganised sectors, administrative variation and individual contracts of employment' (Department of Labour 1996: par 4; Seftel and Bird 2001: 45).

The origins of the philosophy can be found the process leading up to the enactment of the LRA itself. Within three months of the election of the ANC-led government in 1994 a Ministerial Task Team was appointed to 'overhaul the laws regulating labour relations and to prepare a negotiating document in draft Bill form to initiate a process of public discussion and negotiation by organised labour and business and other interested parties' (Department of Labour 1995: 110). From the start, inevitably, the drafters were beset with opposing demands and objectives. Fundamental to the problems which had to be addressed, they argued, was the fact that previous legislation '[did] not take into account the objectives of the RDP' (Department of Labour 1995: 113). While the aim of the RDP was 'to avoid the imposition of rigidities in the labour market', it also promised to promote consultation, participation and capacity-building at all levels of governance along with a vision of 'industrial democracy' that would 'facilitate greater worker participation and decision-making in the workplace' (RDP 1994: pars 3.6.1, 3.11.4 and Chapter Seven). The draft Bill, on this basis, would seek 'to balance the demands of international competitiveness and the protection of the fundamental rights of workers' (Department of Labour 1995: 116).

These various aims are reflected in the stated purpose of the LRA 'to advance economic development, social justice, labour peace and the democratisation of the work-place' by, amongst other things, giving effect to employers' and employees' constitutional right to fair labour practices (s 1). The effect is that the LRA, in much the same way as the Basic Conditions of Employment Act (BCEA), sets out to 'balance the protection of [basic rights] and the requirements of labour market flexibility'. While collective bargaining (preferably at industry level) is the primary device for regulating the wage-work bargain, the protection of basic rights cannot be left to power play. Where basic rights are at issue, therefore, the Act creates mechanisms encouraging or obliging employers and unions to engage in consensus-seeking exercises in order to arrive at a mutually acceptable compromise. The dismissal of workers for operational reasons is such a matter par excellence.

The remainder of the discussion is divided into three parts. The first part looks at the relevant provisions of the LRA as enacted in 1995, prior to the amendments of 2002, as well as the reasons for the amendments. The second part examines the amendments. Finally, an attempt is made to situate the developments that have been identified within a broader framework and relate them to the theme of the chapter.

The law as it was: the problem

In legal terms, the topic under discussion translates into employees' right not to be unfairly dismissed (LRA 1995: s 185) versus an employer's right to dismiss employees for a 'fair reason' provided a 'fair procedure' is followed (LRA 1995: s 188). If both these requirements are met, a dismissal is said to be both substantively and procedurally fair. The LRA, in line with international labour law (ILO 1982), recognises three grounds which may give rise to a fair reason for dismissal: the employee's conduct; the employee's capacity and the employer's operational requirements. The present discussion is concerned with the third of these grounds.

Substantive fairness

To be substantively fair, dismissal must be based on 'operational requirements'. The term 'operational requirements' is defined as 'requirements based on the economic, technological, structural or similar needs of an employer' (LRA 1995: s 213). The meaning of the term is seldom in dispute. More often the question is whether the employer's reason for wishing to dismiss employees, while admittedly based on operational reasons, is sufficient to actually justify dismissal – in other words, 'fair'.

Two other provisions of the LRA qualify the meaning of 'fairness' in this context. The first is the requirement of procedural fairness as spelled out in section 189; the second is the prohibition of 'automatically unfair dismissals' contained in section 187. These will be looked at in turn.

Procedural fairness

When an employer 'contemplates' dismissing employees for operational reasons, section 189 states that it must 'consult' about a specified range of topics with the trade union or other representatives of the affected employees or, in the absence of any representative, the employees themselves.[5] Two of the mandatory topics of consultation are 'appropriate measures' to 'avoid the dismissals' or to 'minimise the number of dismissals' (LRA 1995: s 189(2)). This would seem to imply some limitation on the employer's discretion. While the Labour Appeal Court ruled, in a much-quoted decision, that dismissal for operational reasons need not be a measure of last resort only, it also accepted that it 'should at least not be the first resort' (*SACTWU* v *Discreto* 1998: par 41). 'The function of a court in scrutinising the consultation process', it was explained, 'is not to second-guess the commercial or business efficacy of the employer's ultimate decision (an issue on which it is, generally, not qualified to pronounce upon), but to pass judgment on whether the ultimate decision arrived at was genuine and not merely a sham'. This means not whether the employer's decision was 'the best decision under the circumstances, but only whether it was a rational commercial or operational decision, properly taking into account what emerged during the consultation process' (*SACTWU* v *Discreto* 1998: par 8). Although in later decisions this approach was criticised as being too 'deferential' to employers (*BMD Knitting Mills* v *SACTWU* 2000: par 19), it remained unchallenged until after the amendments of 2002.

Automatically unfair dismissals

A second limitation on management's right to dismiss for operational reasons arises from the prohibition of dismissal for reasons that are classified as 'automatically unfair'. Two of these reasons are especially pertinent in the present context:

(1) 'that the employee participated in . . . a strike or protest action that complies with the provisions of [the Act]'; and
(2) 'to compel an employee to accept a demand in respect of any matter of mutual interest between the employer and employee' (LRA 1995: s 187(1)(a) and (c)).

At the same time, the LRA expressly permits the dismissal of an employee taking part in a legal strike 'for a reason related to the employee's conduct during the strike, or for a reason based on the employer's operational requirements', provided such dismissal is substantively and procedurally fair (LRA 1995: s 67(5)).

These provisions draw a number of extremely subtle distinctions. Disputes often arise when employers seek to introduce operational changes which employees reject. In legal terms this gives rise to a 'dispute of interest' as opposed to a 'dispute of right'. The significance of the distinction is that, in principle, industrial action over a dispute of right is excluded (LRA 1995: s 65(1)(c)) whereas disputes of interest can, in the last resort, *only* be resolved by industrial action (unless the parties agree on an alternative method; for example, arbitration). By proposing operational changes the employer is, essentially, trying to persuade employees to agree to a change in their contracts of employment. Deadlock, in this scenario, signals a dispute of interest, allowing either party to resort to industrial action and, in terms of section 187, rendering it automatically unfair for the employer to dismiss the employees in an attempt to compel them to agree. Provided the statutory procedure is followed, moreover, any strike action taken in the circumstances will be legally protected. The dismissal of workers for going on strike under these circumstances will likewise be automatically unfair. While the employer's *operational requirements* may provide grounds for dismissal, therefore, a dispute about an employer's attempt to *introduce operational changes* is a 'dispute of interest' which cannot in itself justify dismissal, regardless of whether the employees resort to strike action.

The situation is transformed, however, if an operational change ceases being merely an 'interest' of the employer but is deemed to become an 'operational requirement' within the meaning of the Act. In this event, it follows, the employer is entitled to dismiss employees who refuse to comply with that 'operational requirement'. What started as a dispute of interest will thus have 'migrated' to becoming a dispute of right, pitting the employees' right not to be unfairly dismissed against the employer's right to dismiss them fairly (Thompson 1999: 755–6).

By the same token, 'operational requirements' in the form of workers' legitimate refusal to work on the employer's terms may justify dismissal even if the workers are taking part in a protected strike. In such a case the test is whether the strike itself or its consequences is the immediate reason for the dismissal. If the former, the dismissal will be automatically unfair; if the latter, it could potentially be justified on operational grounds (*SACWU* v *Afrox* 1999: par 30).

The problem

Against this background COSATU concluded that 'the provisions of the LRA have proven inadequate when it comes to preventing job losses'. Section 189, it argued, 'provides only for a procedure to be followed before retrenchments may take place. In many cases, even where the employer follows these procedures, it is apparent that the employer is simply 'going through the motions'' (Maenetje 2000: 1528). And by declining to 'second-guess' the employer's commercial rationale, it followed, the Labour Court, far from upholding substantive fairness, was doing little more than rubber-stamping the employer's decision to dismiss.

Employers had a radically different perception. From their standpoint 'the current system relating to retrenchments is cumbersome and uncertain, with a requirement of enterprise-level consultation, followed by statutory concilia-tion and thereafter resort to adjudication through the Labour Court, with this complete procedure taking up to two years in some cases to reach finalisation' (MLC 2001: 2).

This was the principal conflict which the amendments to the LRA, first mooted in 1999, set out to reconcile. The initial question was 'the extent to which the labour market legislative framework contributed to the achievement of government's economic and labour market objectives and to address any factors which could be seen to impact adversely on the imperatives of investment attraction and employment creation strategies' (Mdlalana 2000). As the debate unfolded, it turned into the most far-reaching revision of South Africa's labour laws since their enactment (Godfrey and Clarke 2002: 1–2; Le Roux 2000: 1), culminating in the threat of a general strike (Coleman 2001). The debate in its entirety falls beyond the scope of this chapter; only the changes to section 189 are discussed below. These, however, were seen by many as the key to the process as a whole.

The amendments to section 189: the solution?

COSATU's principal demands in relation to dismissals were twofold: first, compulsory third-party intervention in the event of deadlock in consultation over operational requirements dismissals and, second, a right to strike over the issue (Maenetje 2000: 1538–42; Van Voore 2002: 72–3). Both these demands were ultimately accepted by business and found their way into the amended sections 189 and 189A, although in qualified forms and with various checks and balances which, I shall argue, capture the essence of 'regulated flexibility'.

For present purposes the amendments may be divided into three categories: those aimed at making consultation more effective; those giving trade unions a right to strike against an employer's decision to dismiss; and those adjusting the dispute resolution procedure by separating disputes over procedure from those over substance.

Changes to the consultation process

The new section 189 formalises and regulates the consultation process to a significantly greater degree by introducing the following five changes. First, an employer who contemplates dismissals for operational reasons must now 'issue a written notice inviting the other consulting party to consult with it' and provide 'all relevant information' in writing (LRA 1995: s 189(3)). Second, in addition to the extensive list of topics on which the employer must disclose information, the new section 189(3) also requires disclosure of 'the number of employees employed by the employer' and 'the number of employees that the employer has dismissed for reasons based on its operational requirements in the preceding 12 months'. Third, in any dispute about the relevance of information required by a consulting party, the onus is now on the employer 'to prove that any information that it has refused to disclose is not relevant for the purposes for which it is sought' (LRA 1995: s 189(4)(b)). Fourth, the consulting parties are now charged to 'engage in a meaningful joint consensus-seeking process' (LRA 1995: s 189(2)). The phrase, inserted at the insistence of labour, reinforces the duty placed on management to 'consider' representations from the trade union side to avoid dismissals, thus reducing the scope for courts to place a minimalist construction on the duty. Fifth, if the union's representations are in writing, the employer's reasons for rejecting them must also be in writing (LRA 1995: s 189(6)(b)).

In addition, the new section 189A creates a number of routes by which outside facilitation can be invoked to augment the consensus-seeking process. Whereas section 189 applies to all dismissals on operational grounds, however, section 189A only applies to dismissals by employers with over fifty employees, and only if the proposed number of dismissals exceeds a certain threshold over a twelve-month period (LRA 1995: s 189A(1)). In cases of 'large-scale dismissals', three means of obtaining the intervention of a facilitator are available (LRA 1995: S 189A(3)–(4)). First, the employer may request the appointment of a facilitator by the Commission for Conciliation, Mediation and Arbitration (CCMA)[6] when giving notice of the contemplated dismissals to the consulting party. Second, consulting parties representing the majority of employees whom the employer contemplates dismissing may request the CCMA to appoint a facilitator; or, third, the parties may agree to appoint a facilitator.

This may be seen as another manifestation of 'regulated flexibility'. Rather than placing additional supervisory powers at the disposal of the court, the parties themselves are in the first instance encouraged to make the consultation process more effective and arrive at their own solutions within the statutory framework.

The right to strike

The idea of striking against an employer's decision to dismiss for operational reasons, though 'reluctantly' accepted by business (BSA 2001: 2), has given rise to questions. 'If new technology compels an employer to consider a reorganisation . . . with consequent retrenchments', as Van Voore points out, 'it is unclear how any amount of industrial action can change technological necessity' (Van Voore 2002: 83). As has been noted, however, operational requirements dismissals may be justified not only by 'necessity' but by any rational operational objective – for example, to increase efficiency. In such a case, the cost of industrial action may be a material factor in assessing the economic viability of the intended reorganisation.

The right to strike is, however, qualified in several ways. First, it only relates to the reason for dismissal and not to procedural fairness. Second, it is only available in relation to 'large-scale' dismissals. Third, it may only be exercised as an alternative to taking court action (see below); once employees or their representatives elect to go to court, therefore, the right to strike falls away. Finally, strike action is only permitted after the employer has given notice of dismissal – which, as a result of the various procedures laid down by section 189, is only possible after a minimum period of 60 days has elapsed since the employer's invitation to consult (LRA 1995: s 189A (7), (8) and (11). The effect is that strike action does not become permissible until, for practical purposes, the consultative process has been exhausted.

Finally, as noted already, an employer is expressly allowed to dismiss strikers for operational reasons even if their strike is legally protected. If the operational reasons relied on by the employer are found to be 'fair', in other words, they will also justify the dismissal of employees who challenge those reasons by means of industrial action.

Dispute resolution processes

It has been noted that, in disputes concerning the reason for dismissal ('operational grounds'), employees or unions may elect whether to resort to industrial action or (as before) refer the matter to the Labour Court. Should they choose the latter, the new section 189A(19) now directs the Labour Court to find 'that the employee was dismissed for a fair reason if:

(a) the dismissal was to give effect to a requirement based on the employer's economic, technological, structural or similar needs;
(b) the dismissal was operationally justifiable on rational grounds;
(c) there was a proper consideration of alternatives; and
(d) selection criteria were fair and objective.

This provision, however, does little more than restating the criteria which have been already been developed by the courts and suggests that disputes which go the route of litigation will continue to be dealt with much as before.

Conclusion

The amendments, in general, were hailed as a victory for labour (Coleman 2001). In the critical area of operational requirements dismissals, in particular, the amendments have extended additional protections to labour and, conversely, placed new checks and balances on the exercise of managerial power. There can be little doubt that the labour regulatory dispensation has been rendered more worker-friendly and that the labour movement emerged strengthened from the process. In contrast to the dominant trend internationally, trade union membership rose from 3,359,497 in 1999 to 3,939,075 by the end of the negotiations in 2001 (Godfrey 2003: 39). In conclusion, what has been termed the 'Polanyi problem'[7] (Munck 2004; Silver 2003) offers a framework within which to situate this phenomenon.

The starting point of Polanyi's theory is that labour, whilst a commodity or 'factor of production' subject to market forces, is 'not a commodity like any other. Rather, it is embodied in human beings who complain and resist if they are driven too long, too hard or too fast' (Silver 2003: 17). Productive human beings, at the same time, form the essence of society itself. This means that labour cannot simply be left to market forces; to do so would be to subordinate a vital part of society to laws of supply and demand which, without any form of regulation, would ultimately 'destroy humanity and transform the world into a wilderness' (Munck 2004). The result is what Polanyi termed a 'double movement': 'Each extension or deepening of the labour market is countered by mobilisation to regulate and constrain "the market for that factor of production known as labour power" through a variety of mechanisms including social legislation, factory laws, unemployment insurance, and trade unions' (Silver 2003: 17). Or, to put it differently: 'When the pendulum swings towards the commodification of labour, it provokes strong counter-movements demanding protection' (Silver 2003: 17). Though Polanyi developed his theory in the context of the nineteenth-century industrial revolution and the growth of the world market into the early twentieth century, it has also been used in explaining 'contemporary backlashes against globalisation' (Silver 2003: 18).

Even this brief characterisation suggests that the developments in South Africa, described above, may be a case in point. The opposing demands of business (less regulation) and labour (more regulation) at the outset may be seen as responses to the competitive pressures of global markets during the 1990s (Van Voore 2002: 72–73); MLC 2001: 2). Not surprisingly, negotiations about the amendments deadlocked at an early stage (Godfrey and Clarke 2002: 17). As the debate proceeded, however, it became apparent that the concerns expressed by labour struck a chord among broader groups in society. This exemplified 'backlash resistance to the spread of a global self-regulating market, particularly by working classes that are being unmade by global economic transformation' (Silver 2003: 20). This was reflected most strikingly in the fact that business, in the end, did not press home its initial demands but in the course of the negotiations, deferred to labour's position on most of the contentious issues (MLC 2001). This may be explained by the fact that, also from the viewpoint of business, economic growth is predicated on social stability; or, to put it in Polanyian terms, employers themselves may recognise the destructive effects of unleashing unmitigated market forces on South Africa's fragile socio-economic equilibrium. While seeking stability and avoiding confrontation may involve a cost, failing to do so is likely to prove more costly.

The amendments themselves may be seen as the ultimate manifestation of the 'counter-movement': Parliament, reflecting the broadest conglomeration of social interests, found it necessary to constrain the forces of the 'self-regulating market' embodied in management decisions to dismiss. Significantly, it chose to place the power to do so primarily in the hands of labour (in the shape of the consulting parties defined in section 189(1) of the LRA) rather than the courts.

At the same time, this outcome is entirely consistent with the underlying model of 'regulated flexibility'; indeed, the amendments reinforce it by creating additional processes for labour and management to engage in flexible problem-solving in an area where the law lays down general principles only. Collective bargaining in itself, with its built-in emphasis on adversarialism, is not a promising avenue for arriving at innovative answers. The new sections 189 and 189A, while creating scope for collective bargaining, underpin it with enforceable duties to make sure that the parties negotiate seriously, can hold each other to account and address all relevant issues. Industrial action is possible only as a measure of last resort.

What does this augur for the future? In the period since the amendments were adopted the courts have handed down a number of interesting decisions. In *Fry's Metals* v *NUMSA* the Labour Appeal Court emphasised that the LRA upholds an employer's right to dismiss 'without making any distinction between operational requirements in the context of a business the survival of which is under threat and a business which is making profit and wants to make more profit' (2003: par 33). Subsequently, in *CWIU* v *Algorax*, the same court held that 'the reason for the lawmaker to require [an employer to consider alternatives to dismissal] was to place an obligation on the employer to only resort to dismissing employees for operational requirements as a measure of last resort' (2003: par 70). On the face of it, this directly contradicts the ruling in *SACTWU* v *Discreto*. The seeming conflict can be reconciled on the basis that dismissal will be considered substantively fair if it represents the 'last resort' within a range of reasonable options to achieve a legitimate business aim; in other words, not only to secure the survival of the business.

These judgments, and some that followed (*NUMSA* v *Dorbyl* 2004; *FAWU* v *SA Breweries* 2004), seem important in two ways. On the one hand they reflect a greater willingness by the courts to engage with the question of substantive fairness, thus suggesting, possibly, a more rigorous approach in the future. While this may be seen as an indirect confirmation of the importance the issue has assumed, *Fry's Metals* also confirms the limits of the law in regulating the exercise of managerial discretion and, by implication, the primary role of labour (underpinned by legal rights) in doing so.

Against this background it may be expected that South Africa's labour dispensation will continue, for the foreseeable future, to be governed by the principle of 'regulated flexibility'. Organisational freedom and institutional leverage will continue to define labour's options in response to external threats. The 'counter-movement' of 1999–2001 gives an indication of the way in which future, possibly more serious, manifestations of global market pressures are likely to be met. While such resistance may not necessarily be equally successful, it does seem likely that any relaxation of market regulation in the future will take the form of procedures for negotiating exemptions rather than outright deregulation.

Notes

1   This took place mainly through the case law of the Industrial Court. Established in 1979 this introduced all the key principles of international labour law (often with reference to the Conventions of the International Labour Organisation) during the 1980s.

2 NEDLAC was established in 1994 as a multipartite council involving government, business, labour and community organisations in debating and seeking agreement on proposed labour legislation and changes to social and economic policy before being submitted to Parliament.

3 The Congress of South African Trade Unions (COSATU), the largest of the country's three trade union federations, and the South African Communist Party (SACP) are officially aligned with the ruling ANC, which won the May 2004 elections by a landslide 70 per cent.

4 All workers have the right to strike over job-related demands, subject to minimal procedural requirements (s64, LRA). Registered trade unions and trade union federations also have the right to embark on protest action (including the cessation of work) over socio-economic demands (s 77, LRA).

5 This includes a duty to disclose all relevant information on an extensive list of topics, subject to certain limits relating to confidentiality. The duty is discussed more fully in the context of the amendments to s 189.

6 The CCMA, roughly equivalent to ACAS in Britain, is the primary dispute-resolution organ in terms of the LRA.

7 Named after the economic historian, Karl Polanyi (1886–1964), author of *The Great transformation: the political and economic origins of our time* (London, 2001), to which the quotes refer.

References

Abedian, I. and Standish, B. (2002) (eds) *Economic growth in South Africa: selected policy issues*, Cape Town.

Baskin, J. (1991) *Striking back: A history of COSATU*, Johannesburg.

BSA (2001) Submission to Parliament on the amendments to the LRA and BCEA by Business South Africa (16–17 October) (unpublished).

Cameron, E., Cheadle, H. and Thompson, C. (1989) *The new Labour Relations Act*, Cape Town.

Coleman, N. (2001) 'Labour relations and basic conditions of amendment bills', *COSATU Parliamentary Bulletin*, no. 4 (November) at www.cosatu.org.za/parlbull/pb200111.htm.

COSATU (2001) Submission to Parliament on the amendments to the LRA and BCEA by COSATU (16 October) (unpublished).

—— (2004) *COSATU response to the president's state of the nation speech 6 February 2004* at www.cosatu.org.za/press/2004_1.

Davies, P. and Freedland, M. (1983) *Kahn-Freund's Labour and the Law* (3rd ed.), London.

Department of Labour (1995) *Explanatory memorandum to draft negotiating document in the form of a labour relations bill*, 10 February.

—— (1996) *Policy proposals for a new employment standards statute green paper*, 13 February.

du Toit, D. *et al.* (2003) *Labour relations law: a comprehensive guide* (4th ed.), Durban.

Flanders, A. (1968) *Management and unions*, London.

Gelb, S. (1991) (ed.) *South Africa's economic crisis*, Cape Town.

Godfrey, S. (2003) 'Continuity and change', in du Toit, D. *et al. Labour relations law: a comprehensive guide* (4th ed.), Durban.

—— and Clarke, M. (2002) 'The basic conditions of employment act amendments: more questions than answers', in *Law Democracy & Development* 1.

Grogan, J. (2003) *Workplace law* (7th ed.), Cape Town.

Howe, G. and Le Roux, P. (eds) (1992) *Transforming the economy: policy options for South Africa*, Durban.

ILO (1982) International Labour Organisation Convention on termination of employment 158 of 1982 at www.ilo.org/ilolex/english/convdisp1.htm.

Kraak, A. (1993) *Breaking the chains: labour in South Africa in the 1970s and 1980s*, London.

Le Roux, P. (2000) 'Proposed changes to the Labour Relations Act' *Contemporary Labour Law*, 1 (August).

Maenetje, N. H. (2000) 'Consultation versus negotiation in operational requirement dismissals: the COSATU proposals', *Industrial Law Journal (SA)* 21.

Mbeki, T. (2004) State of the nation address to the Houses of Parliament, Cape Town, 21 May.

Mdlalana, M. (2000) 'Briefing by the Minister of Labour, Mr Membathisi Mdladlana', 8 February at www.polity.org.za/html/govdocs/speeches/2000/sp0208.html.

Michie, J. and Padayachee, V. (1997) *The political economy of South Africa's transition: policy perspectives in the late 1990's*, London.

MLC (2001) Millennium Labour Council Agreement on the amendments (18 April) (unpublished).

Moody, K. (2004) 'Measures of resistance', in *New Left Review* 27.

Munck, R. (2004) 'Globalisation, labour and the Polanyi problem' at www.theglobalsite. ac.uk/press/402munck.htm.

Palmer, N., Niland, P. and Baker, J. (2004) 'An economic critique of the South African labour legislation' at www.ru.ac.za/academic/faculties/law/academic/Col%20Lab%20Essays/ Palmer.pdf.

Republic of South Africa (1995) *Labour Relations Act*, Pretoria.

—— (1996) *Constitution of the Republic of South Africa*, Pretoria.

RDP (1994) *White paper on reconstruction and development*, Cape Town.

Schrire, W. (ed.) (1992) *Wealth or poverty? Critical choices for South Africa*, Cape Town.

Seftel, L. and Bird, A. (2001) 'Labour market regulation and employment creation – the role of the Department of Labour', in *Rethinking South African labour law: burning issues in the world of work in the new millennium*. Proceedings of the 13th annual labour law conference, Durban.

Silver, B. (2003) *Forces of labour: Workers' movements and globalisation since 1870*, Cambridge.

Standing, G., Sender, J. and Weeks, J. (1996) *Restructuring the labour market: the South African challenge*, Geneva.

Thompson, C. (1999) 'Bargaining, business restructuring and operational requirements dismissal', *Industrial Law Journal (SA)* 20.

—— (2003) 'Retrenchments and restructuring', in Cheadle *et al. Current labour law 2003*, Durban.

Van Voore, R. (2002) 'The new retrenchment procedure: sections 189 and 189A of the LRA' 2002 *Law Democracy and Development* 71.

Cases cited

BMD Knitting Mills (Pty) Ltd v *SACTWU* [2001] 7 BLLR 705 (LAC).

CWIU and others v *Algorax (Pty) Ltd* [2003] 11 BLLR 1081 (LAC).

FAWU v *General Food Industries Ltd* [2002] 10 BLLR 950 (LC).

FAWU v *SA Breweries* [2004] 11 BLLR 1093 (LC).

Fry's Metals (Pty) Ltd v *NUMSA and others* [2003] 2 BLLR 140 (LAC).

NUMSA and others v *Dorbyl Ltd and another* [2004] 9 BLLR 914 (LC).

SACTWU and others v *Discreto (A Division of Trump & Springbok Holdings)* [1998] 12 BLLR 1228 (LAC).

SACWU and others v *Afrox Ltd* [1999] 10 BLLR 1005 (LAC).

6

Liberalisation and trade unionism in Mozambique

Beata Mtyingizana

Introduction

This chapter examines the evolving industrial relations system in Mozambique in the context of the double transition of political and economic liberalisation.[1] Focusing on the formal labour movement, the chapter explores whether liberalisation has created conditions where the unions can be more involved in the political and economic restructuring of society and the state, or whether it has led to marginalisation.

Studies of economic and political liberalisation demonstrate that labour's response varies from country to country and depends largely on the balance of forces that impinge on the exercise of state power (Beckman 2001). The impact of liberalisation on the least developed countries has received very little attention. This neglect is even more glaring with regards to Portuguese speaking African countries such as Mozambique. Analyses have concentrated on Mozambique's 'double transition' but have ignored its impact on labour. This study seeks to address this lacuna. Mozambique's dual transition embraced, first, a move between 1975 and 1994 from a capitalist and authoritarian Portuguese colonial state to a socialist and increasingly authoritarian independent state, then an authoritarian and increasingly capitalist state, and finally a democratic state and a market oriented economy (Pitcher 2002). Where Mozambique differs from other African experiences is the fact that Mozambique experienced a transition that did not involve a collapse of a regime. Instead, the ideology and institutions of the preceding period influenced the experiences of the succeeding period. Institutions, traditions and ideologies sustain the legitimacy of outdated authority relations allowing the persistence of aspects of the old regime into the new despite changes in economic and political power (Akwetey 2001). In Mozambique, features of the colonial and socialist regime remained embedded in the market economy and continue to influence interaction between the state and social actors.

Change in Mozambique should not be seen as a transition from one regime to another. Rather, it should be seen as a transformation-rearrangement that yields new interweavings of multiple social logics. This is a process of constant interaction between previous and emerging agents and organisational forces (Pitcher 2002: 7). The manner in which the colonial legacy continued to inform policy choices, state-society relations and economic outcomes after independence, is similar to the way in which the socialist period continues to inform processes that are undergoing transformation. As Beckman and Sachikonye argue, liberalisation has provided labour with scope for greater influence on the post-liberation development of labour regimes. In the case of South Africa, for example, legislative reforms and institutions of concertation introduced in the post-apartheid era were a way of recognising the special status that the labour movement acquired. Alternatively, liberalisation can see the reinforcement of state control of the unions (Beckman and Sachikonye 2001). Liberalisation in Mozambique has not yet led to the creation of a vibrant civil society capable of displacing or renewing of old institutions, nor has it facilitated capacity building to enable the development of an independent trade union movement. What has occurred is a transformative preservation in which there is a continuation of influences of the colonial and socialist period on the emerging market economy (Pitcher 2002: 27). The patterns of the past that ensured state control, subordination and prohibition of any resistance, remain embedded in the present, hampering the development of independent trade unions.

Historical background

Mozambique's recent history can be divided into two broad periods: the colonial and the Frelimo period.

The colonial period

Labour in this context refers to a working class but to speak of a working class as defined by Karl Marx in colonial Africa is misleading (Penvenne 1995). A definition of the African working class within a colonial context requires an examination of the workplace, the nature of workplace authority, employer and state practices that forge cultural and political hegemony and an exploration of the interrelations of the workers themselves (Freund 1988). The development of a working class in colonial Africa was not the result of alienation from the means of production. Alienation was the result of the gendered colonial labour policy pursued from the 1920s, that necessitated the kind of class relations that led working men, through production, waged work, workplace relations and working conditions, to see themselves as a working class. Penvenne further argues that the development of mutual support, credit, intelligence, friendship networks in their workplaces and urban neighbour-hoods also served as the basis for class formation. As workers developed strategies to advance and protect their interests against the employer and the capitalists who commanded special authority and privileges, they developed an African working class (Penvenne 1995).

The struggles and strategies of these working people begin with worker resistance to the colonial state-imposed moral obligation to work imposed by the *indiginato* regime. Though *Regime do indiginato* was already in practise, it was formally enacted in 1928 by the Salazar regime to reaffirm its hegemony over its subject population

(Isaacman and Isaacman 1983: 39). The *indiginato* was a body of labour legislation to regulate personal and labour relations with Africans promulgated by the colonial administration together with the employers. The system defined and treated Africans as lesser beings, particularly in the workplace and worked to ensure that a majority of Africans would be legally frozen into a subordinate race, class and cultural position. Under *Regime do indiginato* Africans were divided into two groups and classified either as *assimilados* or *indiginas.*

The *assimilados* were Africans that could read and write Portuguese, had rejected 'tribal' customs and were gainfully employed in the capitalist economy (Isaacman and Isaacman 1983). According to the Salazar regime, assimilation was the only way of civilising the 'natives'. It was portrayed as a policy of cultural give and take and by granting the Africans rights and obligations of a white Portuguese, it reflected the Portuguese' spirit of racial harmony and non-racial attitudes as it transformed '*natives*' into '*citizens*' (Serapiao 1979: 50). The *indiginas* were Africans who could not be classified as citizens as they did not meet the requirements as stipulated by the regime. They were the taxpayers, the labourers, producers within a traditional economy as well as a potential *assimilados. Indiginas* were subject to customary law and were directly ruled by a chief. The *indigina* was liable to a variety of services and was to acknowledge a general obligation to contract as a worker (Newitt 1981). Legislation on the moral obligation to work stipulated:

> All natives of Portuguese overseas provinces are subject to the moral and legal obligation of attempting through work, the means that they lack to subsist and to better their social conditions. They have full liberty to choose the method of fulfilling this obligation, but if they do not fulfil it, public authority may force a fulfilment. (Carter and O'Meara 1979: 58)

Force them they did. The basis for the enactment of the moral obligation to work legislation was forced labour, called *shibalo,* which came about as a result of slavery. The effect was that an overwhelming majority of African men were forced to work as contract labourers for at least six months a year, either for an employer or the state, to pay their taxes. Enforcement was by the passbook that recorded the last day of employment. The Portuguese' main need from Mozambique was raw materials and a labour force generated by coercion and exploitation (Abrahamsson and Nilsson 1995). The systems of *idiginato* and *shibalo* proved valuable for the coloniser as it guaranteed the African labour, whose value could most easily be realised (Newitt 1981).

Since Portugal was the weakest of the European powers, and had little capital to invest in Mozambique, the country remained underdeveloped and relied only on the crudest forms of labour exploitation to extract surplus value (Cheatham 1985; Isaacman and Isaacman 1983). These, methods increased the use of cheap labour and the export of workers to neighbouring countries. About 500,000 men were already working outside the country, and as weak Portuguese capital needed more cheap labour, the only choice was to increase the exploitation of labour and force the peasants to grow cash crops. The state control of labour tightened, making labour recruitment the central function of the colonial state. The *indiginato* regime was, therefore, nothing more than a reconfiguration of the forms and practices that characterised slavery. Even though slavery was abolished by law in the second half of the nineteenth century, the horrors of slavery and slave trading practices continued well into the 1960s (Carter and O'Meara 1979).

The Salazar regime could continue with coerced labour long after slavery was abolished because of the type of control it exercised. The Salazar regime's authoritarianism was not concerned solely with the repression of individuals per se, but also gaining and keeping control of institutions, the support of the armed forces and the bureaucracy to enable Portugal's underdeveloped economy develop from its colonial resources (Newitt 1981). It was out of this need that the *indiginato* policy became a perverted continuation of the harsh and exploitative practices of forced labour (Penvenne 1995). *Indiginato* was an institutionalisation and a legitimisation of practices characteristic of the slavery period through *shibalo*, a term that the Mozambicans used, to refer to work relations such as unpaid labour, coerced labour, ill-paid labour and slavery. The moral obligation to work and *shibalo* showed the fundamental role of the *indiginato* in making the transition from slaves to freedmen and from freedman to *indiginas* (Penvenne 1995: 4).

Workers tried, as early as in 1909, to resist *indiginato* and *shibalo*. In the rural areas the resistance saw workers' withholding their labour by fleeing to other neighbouring colonies. 'These flights' according to Isaacman and Isaacman, 'represented the harshest blow an individual peasant or rural labourer could strike against the productive demands of the colonial state' (Isaacman and Isaacman 1983: 64). Workers were successful in limiting the demands made upon them to a point at which the system broke down. The strategy of mass migration also had the effect of gradually raising wages (Newitt 1981). Colonial Mozambique was a police state. There was no freedom of speech, press or assembly. Opposition political parties and trade unions were illegal. Strikes were banned and Mozambican society was permeated by the secret-police who incarcerated and tortured opponents. African protests were vigorously and bloodily suppressed (Carter and O'Meara 1979).

Brutal repression did not silence the workers who voiced their grievances whenever an opportunity presented itself. Even though coercion and legislation served to discipline the labour force and undermined any worker action workers struck over wages, overtime, taxes and currency exchange. Ten strikes among African workers over wages were recorded between 1917 and 1925, but the details of the workers' organisation, activities or outcomes of those strikes remain fuzzy. The first strike over wages was initiated by the white Portuguese workers who were organised under União Ferroviário in 1917 (Penvenne 1995). White Portuguese workers formed the only trade union organisation in Mozambique at this time. Indifference and hostility accompanied explicit state prohibition of African trade unions from white trade unions to the needs of the African workers (Isaacman and Isaacman 1983).

Despite the racial and cultural prejudice of white trade unions, African workers supported the União Ferroviário's call for worker solidarity during the 1917 strikes only to realise that their support was expendable. This was more apparent when the government, in settling the 1917 strikes, excluded the African workers and União Ferroviário made no protest. The lack of solidarity displayed by União Ferroviário was shown when the government arrested and imprisoned more than four hundred African workers who had supported União Ferroviário in the 1917 strike (Penvenne 1995). White trade unions enjoyed a degree of state tolerance before the Salazar regime. By the 1930s however, the Salazar regime had dismantled all trade unions permitting only state-controlled corporate syndicates. Membership was open only to white Portuguese workers and the 'civilised', or second-class, assimilated citizens. These unions were integral to the fascist corporate state and were closely controlled by the government. Strikes were prohibited and the government reserved the right to dissolved them if it saw fit (Egerö 1987).

While the system of *indiginato* was intended to undermine indigenous cultures, it did not succeed completely. A large proportion of the African population qualified as *assimilados* and could belong to the state-controlled union, but they refused to join and retained a strong culture of their own (Serapiao 1979). There were pressures for Africans to search for genuine 'African-ness' among the African Mozambican workers. It was this need for a cultural revival that propelled Africans to organise and form an important sector of the emerging leadership of colonial resistance (Henriksen 1978; Newitt 1981). Another contradictory effect of *regime do indiginato* were that those Africans later constituted an important group of workers who resisted colonial rule in an effort to protect their interests as workers. *Assimilados* were not directly affected by the unjust labour legislation but as the law sought to subordinate African labour as a whole, it was met by sharp resistance from these workers (Penvenne 1995). These were office workers, merchants and proprietors who, under the leadership of João Albasini and his brother José Albasini collaborated, edited and directed the publication *O Africano* and its successor paper *O Brado Africano*, an organ of *Grêmio Africano*. They criticised *indiginato* as a racist, repulsive and humiliating legal concept that sought to exclude the majority of the population from upward mobility. The paper published extensive and supportive coverage of worker salary grievances, strikes, resistance to tax increases, demands for disability insurance, training and promotion.

The African middle class paid a price for resistance but because the group was divided over its own issues, the death of João Albasini weakened the leadership of this elite group over labour issues and the momentum they had under such leadership was never regained. In an effort to improve employment conditions and develop survival strategies for African workers under an oppressive colonial system and an exploitative capitalist system, workers organised themselves into the *União Africano* (African Union) for all African workers in Lourenço Marques (now Maputo). The union was eliminated before it got off the ground because workers lacked organising skills and the workers involved were limited in numbers due to the profitable practice of exporting workers. Furthermore, because Mozambique's development of a capitalist system was very slow, only a limited number of workers could be employed on a full-time basis (Isaacman and Isaacman 1983).

The Frelimo period

Pitcher argues 'the collapse of the Portuguese colonial regime triggered rapid social and economic change in Mozambique' (2002: 27) and on assuming power, 'Frelimo sought nothing less than to remake Mozambican society and economy' (Manning 2002: 50). The new regime began to intervene in the economy, nationalising large-scale industry with the result that state enterprises dominated almost every sector of the economy. Frelimo's nationalisation strategy was a result of the anti-colonial struggle, which was synonymous with the struggle against capitalism. Independence compensated for the failures of colonialism and socialism would eliminate exploitation (Abrahamsson and Nilsson 1995).

Frelimo saw itself as alliance of workers and peasants in Mozambique based on scientific socialism united in a struggle against exploitation. Saul, however, argued that Mozambique's attempted socialist project was 'both premature and wrong' because the country was seen, even by the Soviet Union, as a 'state of socialist orientation' whose social relations were too primitive to constitute a socialist society (1993: 58). Mozambique was one of many African countries that, after independence, found themselves faced with a dilemma. The dilemma was whether:

> to go the route directly prescribed by the classic definition of socialism or to chart the necessary compromises with the major global powers, class forces, the market, incentives and non-socialist relations of production (Munslow 1986: 3).

Frelimo's choice was the socialist route, which was, from the onset, laden with difficulties. There was no way that Mozambique could develop 'proper socialism'. Frelimo had no comprehension of what Marxism was and Frelimo lacked a Marxist party that would guarantee the active participation of the workers (Christie 1989). A transition to socialism can only take place in a society with a strong, organised working class seeking to transfer the ownership and control of production from private to public hands. There has to be modern industry with an immense productive capacity. (MacKenzie 1966). Failure to meet these requirements, means any attempts to construct a socialist society are doomed to failure. The construction of a socialist state is only possible through a revolution conducted by a strong, combative, self-conscious working class. The colonial legacy created and maintained economic and social structural conditions that prevented the development of a working class (Munslow 1986). Mozambique's socialist orientation was undermined by the absence of a strong working class and a weak industrial sector undermined by world recession. In 1982 alone, Mozambique's industrial output fell by 13.64 per cent (Munslow 1986). None of the countries added into the socialist camp after World War II experienced a socialist revolution. (MacKenzie 1966). These were societies where capitalism was weak, where the proletariat scarcely existed and where the revolution involved land-hungry peasants.

This neglects the importance of the revolutionary leadership and organisation as well as the constraints under which the peasants as a class operated. In the African context, peasants, the lumpenproletariat, migrant and permanent workers, all belong to and constitute the working class. Instead of generalising about the importance of the working class or the peasants, as 'the revolutionary class', it would be more useful to focus on 'the complex political, social, cultural and economic conjectures and historical processes of particularly societies' (Munslow 1986: 16). Any application of Marxist theory makes more sense if it is applied to the realities in Africa (Saul 1990). Mozambique attempted a leap into socialism. Through hasty efforts by the revolutionary movement to control state power and nationalise industry, socialise agriculture, abolish markets and plan the economy, Frelimo produced economic collapse and severe structural imbalances in the economy (Munslow 1986). Nationalisation accelerated the flight of the Portuguese which left tens of thousands of workers in construction and building, raw material industries, tourism, and even domestic servants, unemployed. Workers had no expertise to operate the abandoned enterprises and this was made worse by the colonial division of labour, which ensured that few African workers were skilled. The flight of the settlers shattered the economy and colonial society crumbled as doctors, lawyers, civil servants and shopkeepers disappeared. Colonial Mozambique appeared to have a large industrial workforce, but the vast majority of skilled workers were Portuguese and the minority of skilled African workers were employed in South African mines and factories (Hanlon 1984).

In the South African mines, Mozambicans constituted about 65 per cent of the foreign workers employed by the Chamber of Mines (First 1983). Many did not return home when their contracts expired. For instance, in Inhambane about 75,370 men left for the mines and only 43,885 returned home, this resulted in a serious net loss of population which hampered development and economic growth (Katzenellenbogen 1982). Frelimo's response to this was the *Grupos Dinamizadores (GDs)* (Dynamizing Groups) made up of ad hoc committees of eight to ten people set up in villages, urban neighbourhoods and workplaces. In factories, the GDs were set up to prevent further sabotage by the remaining settlers, to manage abandoned factories and to ensure control of the workers and the rest of the society (Hanlon 1984). The GDs were designed to extend Frelimo's political structure into every province and district and enforce state authority within society (Hoile 1989). Similarly, Hall and Young (1997) argue that the Frelimo government relied heavily on the GDs to keep the economy functioning at a minimum level as well as to enforce authority. In GD-managed enterprises, workers were organised into production councils. These were the major instruments to allow workers to combat 'indiscipline' and raise productivity and, in return, they reported to the Control and Discipline Committee. These can be seen as embryonic trade unions.

Production councils were not used to represent workers but as instruments of labour control on the part of the authorities. Frelimo remained doubtful of urban workers because, despite the claim that Frelimo was a worker-peasant alliance, it suspected urban workers of aiding the Portuguese war effort in return for higher wages (Hall and Young 1997). A good example was the Maputo dockworkers, the most organised section of workers during the socialist period. Frelimo remained deeply suspicious of demands for better wages and working conditions labelling them as 'opportunistic' and 'economistic' (Anon. 2003). The production councils, set up in late 1976, were converted into trade unions in 1984. Their role, however, was to ensure active and effective worker participation in the planning and control of production, ensure workplace discipline, and improve working and social conditions (Hanlon 1984).

Post-independence worker repression was common in Africa. Trade unions were invariably seen as potential rivals to the ruling party, which then sought to exert greater control over them. In those cases where the state saw itself as a natural patron of the working class trade union, functions were reduced to that of a transmission belt. Their main objective, as dictated by the state, was to ensure that production assisted the state's development (Freund 1988). When Frelimo created the Organisation of Mozambican Workers (OTM), its objective was to have a union movement that would enhance party/government control over wage earners. OTM would ensure docile support among wage earners for politically inspired programmes (Gumende 1999). OTM, the only federation permitted during the one-party years, was a federation of industrial unions created out of production council branches at firm and sector level. Membership was compulsory, with subscriptions being deducted from salaries.

OTM was the mechanism for mobilising workers' support for Frelimo, the vanguard party, on the Eastern European model. OTM's governing statutes stated that 'Frelimo . . . guides and directs OTM in all its activities' (Gumende 1999: 31). Only in 1990 did OTM begin to loosen its links with Frelimo. Since 1990 it has become a persistent critic of the government's economic policies (Hanlon 1991). This was made possible through the government's acceding to a more pluralistic approach to employment relations, which was triggered by the conversion to neo-liberalism (Gumende 1999; Pitcher 2002).

Liberalisation and contemporary industrial relations

Liberalisation was necessitated by the government's realisation that the country's development strategy had reached an impasse. The limitations of Frelimo's strategy became evident in the early 1980s. Agricultural policy absorbed virtually all state investment, co-operative farming and communal villages and the neglect of the 'family sector' caused severe social and economic disruption (Manning 2002). The economic crisis saw a fall in domestic production, the failure of agricultural modernisation, central planning and price-setting, and economic and military destabilisation. With the Soviet Union's inability to support socialist experiments in the Third World, socialist-oriented countries in the Third World were faced with having to fend for themselves (Cheatham 1985). Needing international disaster relief, international credits and debt rescheduling, Mozambique moved towards creating a market economy approved and underwritten by the International Monetary Fund (IMF) (Abrahamsson and Nilsson 1995). The government's restructuring of the economy accommodated the IMF's structural adjustment measures that were deemed essential for securing the country's macroeconomic stability and debt repayment (Africa Watch 1992).

Financial, monetary and trade policies were amended by privatisation, trade liberalisation, decreased state expenditure, deregulation of the labour market and reduced state-intervention in the economy. In 1984 Mozambique joined the IMF and the World Bank. In 1987, the first economic readjustment programme (Programma de Reabilitação Económica [PRE]) was introduced. The PRE's objectives were to revive domestic production, reduce financial imbalances, promote economic efficiency, eliminate the informal market and restore healthy financial relationships with commercial and financial partners. The IMF stipulated that this could only be achieved by the removal of price controls as an incentive for production, the adjustment of the terms of exchange, the reduction of public expenditure and privatisation. In 1989 the government adopted a policy on the transfer of ownership of state property. Two years later it developed a procedure for restructuring, transforming and resizing the state owned enterprise sector. This included privatisation and transfer of ownership. These measures were aimed at increasing enterprise efficiency and competitiveness through changing technologies, and modernising management techniques to increase productivity and attract national and foreign investment (Anon. 2003).

Privatisation and liberalisation in Mozambique have produced powerful private capitalist actors, which dominate particular sectors and determine patterns of production. Existing conflict of interests between and within the state, private sector and labour has produced policy incoherence, institutional paralysis and devastating economic results (Pitcher 2002). This is largely because the state mixed liberalisation with authoritarianism. At one point the state was accommodating and conciliatory, at another coercive and inflexible. In some parts of the country the state sought local compromises and employed ad hoc measures to rule, in other parts however, the state was unyielding, authoritarian and militaristic. The state 'continued to follow a socialist high-modern master plan to realise its objectives. At one moment, it responded to pressures from below by relaxing restrictions on trade, working together with private companies, or allocating land to small holders. Otherwise, it reinforced state participation in industry or increased its presence in the countryside' (Pitcher 2002: 106). In the end, the effects of a repressive authoritarianism created conditions for a transition towards a market economy and liberal democracy. Coercion only served to generate increased hostility and further undermine the state's legitimacy and where the state was more conciliatory, it helped to revitalise the private sector whose re-emergence further helped to erode the state's ideological and social foundations. The emergence of new guidelines governing private sector activity signalled a loosening of restrictions and a reliance on market principles (Pitcher 2002).

This marked a phasing out of the socialist period and a gradual move towards a market economy that later transformed the political environment through the establishment of a multiparty system. The multiparty system in Mozambique sought a balance between economic interests groups to counterbalance the tensions created by economic development. It also meant that the government had to encourage the formation of an institutional framework within which democracy could grow and be consolidated (Abrahamsson and Nilsson 1995). This required a significant altering of the nature of the state's economic and political power. It meant the government could no longer control the commanding heights of the economy, set exchange rates, subsidise consumption, or engage in detailed planning (Pitcher

2002). Instead, it had to incorporate broader interest groups in the population in decision-making, particularly for the purpose of maintaining state legitimacy and consolidating democracy. The industrial relations environment was tailored to serve this end. Industrial relations shifted from a unitary approach resting on rigid state controls and patronage of labour, to a pluralistic system that sought to accommodate the interests of the working class within the market economy. It is difficult to speak of a national industrial relations 'system' in Mozambique. There was an attempt to establish coherence at the national level but with little impact at the enterprise level. In large part, much of what purports to be a 'system' is a loosely connected set of weak industrial relations actors (Brookes, Webster and Wood 2004).

To understand Mozambique's industrial relations it must be located in the 'double transition' of the late 1980s and through the 1990s, a transition from authoritarianism to democracy, and from a closed economy to an open one (see Table 6.1).

The unitary industrial relations system

Mozambique achieved its independence at a time of global and regional economic and political reform. These reforms involved integration into the world economy through trade and investment, as well as a growing political consensus in favour of democracy and human rights. Mozambique was one of those newly independent states that sought to gain legitimacy and consolidate the newly acquired political power within a liberalised economic environment. This worked to undermine and weaken the state. In attempting to transform Mozambican society and a highly controlled economy that had been inherited from the rigidly authoritarian colonial state, Frelimo adopted a state-centred approach that weaved together nationalist, socialist and modernist ideas.

The industrial relations that existed at the time drew on the themes that the party had already developed for the whole society. Industry was central to the state's vision; it was the means whereby a worker's socialist identity could be forged. The

Table 6.1 The shift in industrial relations system

	State socialism	Market based
Economic policy	State intervention	Free market
Politics	Authoritarian	Multiparty elections
Industrial relations	Unitary system with one source of authority	Pluralistic system made up of sectional groups with divergent interests
Organisation of production	Centralised/monopolies import substitution	Flexibility/collective bargaining. Promotion of small, medium and micro enterprises
Wage system	Full-time permanent employment	Less full-time and more part-time, casual and informal jobs

state was actively involved in industrial relations, in coordination with the National Planning Commission. The Ministry of Industry and Energy identified branches of industrial activity, formulated production plans, management teams for each factory. The Ministry set production quotas for each enterprise, drew up budgets and accounts, promoted personnel, maintained equipment and saw to production needs. Workers were organized in such a way that not only furthered the government's socialist objective but also increased production (Pitcher 2002). Trade union organisation was not permitted and was regarded as an intrusion to the factory structure. At the shop-floor level, workers were organized by the GDs.

The GD's strategy was coordinated nationally. National and regional party activists ensured that the wishes of the party leadership were transmitted to the shop floor. However, due to the inability of the state to control members and their actions, the GD's performance was poor. GDs were not disciplined exponents of the party line and their activities often conflicted with the interests of the party. The government then supplemented them with the production councils, which were later complemented by the factory committee to correct production difficulties. Since there was no collective bargaining forum, the factory committee functioned as a bargaining forum. These consisted of the secretary and the assistant secretary of each production unit brought together to negotiate with management on behalf of the workers. The existence of any conflict of interest between workers and managers was minimised by ideologies that emphasised co-operation for the purpose of creating a new society. The role of managers was to satisfy the needs of the members. The structures that existed, particularly at the shop floor, helped to improve treatment in the workplace, contributed to the improvement of employment conditions by significantly reducing the level of exploitation that was so notorious during the colonial period. Some of the benefits included wage increases, subsidised transport, housing and food. Free health care, greater access to education as well as on-site day-care centres were provided. With 66 per cent of Mozambique's industry concentrated between Maputo and Beira the government was able to supervise production, monitor industrial activity and ensure compliance. Government officials were able to make surprise visits to factories, challenge worker indiscipline and exposed poor working conditions (Pitcher 2002).

The pluralistic industrial relations system

A pluralistic approach to industrial relations rests on the presumption that power will be distributed through processes of collective bargaining. Collective bargaining facilitates the development of conflict resolution mechanisms such as conciliation, mediation and arbitration (Bendix 2001). The emergence of a sound and effective industrial relations system depends on the organised representation of interests, meaningful social dialogue enhancing the independence and interests representation of the key actors, a coordinated bargaining process, and adequate mechanisms for dispute resolution (Webster, Wood and Mtyingizana 2004). To what extent has Mozambique created an effective industrial relations system?

The labour movement

The labour movement is weak and divided. Liberalisation meant trade unions were faced with the challenge of simultaneously assuming leadership of the workers within a market economy and changing their character and functions in a multiparty democracy. During this transitional phase, legislation guaranteeing various trade unions rights, independence and autonomy was passed. The law on trade union freedom permitted individual industrial union associations to become legal entities without being affiliated to a trade union federation. As a result certain trade union leaders claimed functional autonomy and in 1992, three trade unions representing workers in the hotel and tourism sector (SINTIHOTS), construction and mining sector (SINTICIM) and transport (SINTRAT) declared their independence from OTM. These formed an alliance called Sindicatos Livres e Independetes (Free and Independent Trade Unions [SLIM]) which in 1997 constituted itself as a trade union federation called Confederação Nacional do Sindicatos Independetes e Livres de Moçambique (National Federation of Free and Independent Trade Unions of Mozambique [CONSILMO]) (Anon. 2003). OTM, however, remained the largest federation. Of 20 trade unions, 14 are affiliated to OTM and four to CONSILMO with the other two (SNJ and SNPM/ONP) remaining independent (see Table 6.2). The breakaway from OTM was prompted in part, by the need to take full advantage of the liberal and democratic environment to create independent and democratic trade unions. CONSILMO criticised OTM for remaining too close to the ruling

Table 6.2 Unions in Mozambique by sector

Sector	Union	No. of members	Affiliation
Manufacturing	SINTIVEC	8,640	OTMS-CS
	SINTIAB	3,886	OTMS-CS
	SINTIME	6,913	OTMS-CS
	SINTIQUIGRA	6,923	OTMS-CS
Construction	SINTICIM	23,907	CONSILMO
Mining	SINTICIM	n/a	n/a
Transport	SINPOCAF	5,728	OTMS-CS
	SINPEOC	3,568	OTMS-CS
	SINTRAT	10,000	CONSILMO
Agriculture and forestry	SINTIA	13,431	OTMS-CS
	SINTIC	476	OTMS-CS
	SINTAF	15,531	OTMS-CS
Commerce and finance	SINTMAP	4,300	OTMS-CS
	SINITHOTS	18,410	CONSILMO
	SINECOSSE	9,225	OTMS-CS
	SNEB	3,803	OTMS-CS
Air transport and communication	SINTAC	5,911	OTMS-CS
State	SINAFP	4,116	OTMS-CS
Security guards	SINTESPGM	4,895	CONSILMO

Source: OTM-CS; CONSILMO.

party and for being 'a top-down federation' (Webster and Mosoetsa 2001). CONSILMO's objectives were justice, freedom and equality and the strengthening of the labour movement. This would be achieved by the democratisation of trade union structures and the promotion of the creation of national and autonomous trade unions to protect the individual and collective freedom (Anon. 2003).

Established in 1983, OTM is the oldest trade union federation in Mozambique and survived a socialist environment that did not permit trade union pluralism. The state enjoyed tight control over OTM, its leaders, ideology and practices, and its purpose was to control workers and production (Gumende 1999). Even though OTM proclaimed its independence from Frelimo in 1990, long after it was criticised for being a government union, it remained centralised with most top positions in the organisation's hierarchy occupied by Frelimo party loyalists. OTM leaders are criticised for not having emerged from the workers' ranks, but for being former student activist-cum-politicians whose social base has never been the labour movement (Gumende 1999). Faced with the need to demarcate themselves from the government and ruling party, and meet the challenges of liberalisation policies and a market economy, OTM constructed a new image and new capacities for intervening in the new market economy (Anon. 2003).

In 1995 OTM urged joint union action through the creation of Forum de Concertação Sindical (FCS, Coalition of Trade Unions). The FCS was intended to promote labour unity and to coordinate trade union action. OTM aimed to promote and consolidate class consciousness and solidarity amongst the workers in the struggle for better living conditions, justice and social progress (Anon. 2003). OTM set out to coordinate and provide assistance to its affiliates, represent them in tripartite forums and participate in the development of policies that affect the workers and the trade union movement. Both OTM and CONSILMO share similar policies. The differences between them seem largely historical. Both are represented on the tripartite Comissao Consultiva Do Trabalho (CCT, Consultative Labour Commission) and meet beforehand in a day-long forum, funded by the Friedrich Ebert Stiftung (FES), to develop a common strategy (Webster, Wood and Mtyingizana 2004).

The employers' association

Employers associations are weak and undeveloped. The principal association is the Confederação das Associações Económicas de Moçambique (CTA, Confederation of Business Association of Mozambique), a confederation of sixty-four affiliates (CTA interview, November 2003, Maputo). CTA is an intermediary between the state and the private sector and meets regularly with the Prime Minister. CTA represent fifty-three business associations and participates in eleven ministry economic groups (CTA interview, September 2003, Maputo). CTA believes it has enjoyed a good relationship with government, which welcomes dialogue. Government has formally stressed its support to CTA in the promotion of public-private sector consultations. CTA believes it has good relations with the unions and is involved in a similarly constructive social dialogue with them (Webster, Wood and Mtyingizana 2004).

However, CTA feels that labour law is too protective of workers. It is seeking legislation to increase flexibility making it easier to dismiss a worker and complain of the difficulty of contracting foreign labour. CTA voiced its discontent publicly after failing to persuade the government to approve a 10 per cent allowance for each firm for the contracting of labour (CTA interview, November 2003). CTA believes that the courts are not working efficiently and that it can take as much as five years to resolve a dispute unless one is 'well-connected', meaning the courts favour those who are willing to pay bribes. In the case of employers, the bribe would keep the case in court and for the employees it would lead to an earlier hearing. CTA argued that the court system was so bad that it was no longer regarded as a problem. If it took 524 days to hear a case, CTA believes the legal framework has in effect collapsed (CTA interview, November 2003). There is also a National Chamber of Commerce (NCC) with 350 members. They have close bilateral links with South Africa, the United States and Brazil. As with CTA, the NCC believes that labour law is too rigid and protective of workers (NCC interview, November 2003).

The Department of Labour

During the socialist period in Mozambique, the Department of Labour set wages centrally. Since the opening up of the economy, the department has played a less interventionist role. Indeed it is weak and under-resourced, lacking the capacity to ensure compliance (Department of Labour interview, September 2003). It is located on the sixth floor of a dilapidated and dingy city-centre building with no lights and a lift that has not worked for the past decade (Department of Labour interview, July 2004).

There is no separate labour court system to deal with labour related issues, and companies are effectively free to ignore labour rights. Of the 15,000 cases taken to court every year, only 200 or 300 are dealt with. A separate labour court system has been proposed but nothing has yet happened, though a process of labour law reform is under way (Webster, Wood and Mtyingizana 2004). Under the Ministry of Labour is a Labour Inspectorate, charged with ensuring compliance with the 1998 Labour Law. The Inspectorate answers directly to the Minister and its responsibilities as stipulated in Articles 207 and 208. These involve inspection and ensuring compliance with labour legislation as well as reporting any verified violations to the relevant authorities of the state (Anon. 2003).

Many employers escape the 1998 Law's provisions by employing day labourers, or subcontracting to outside service providers 'that are indifferent to the law' (Levy 2004: 3). Day labourers do not receive paid leave or other benefits and can be instantly dismissed. The enforcement of workers' rights under the constitution and labour legislation is very uneven owing to infrastructural limitations, corruption and decisions made by officials (Webster, Wood and Mtyingizana 2004). The Labour Inspectorate itself is often described as dysfunctional and corrupt. There have been numerous reform proposals but nothing has been done. The most frequent complaints are from the shop-steward committees who state that the Labour Inspectorate does not even inform them of any follow ups regarding reports of irregularities lodged with it (Anon. 2003).

Social dialogue and tripartism

CCT was established in 1994 to bring together representatives of the state, employers and unions. The main purpose of CCT is promoting dialogue and securing social agreement in matters related to economic, social and labour policies (Levy 2004). It is located in a room in the Department of Labour and meets twice a year to discuss socio-economic issues (Webster, Wood and Mtyingizana 2004). This suggests a somewhat minimal role. While government is expected to play the role of a mediator between employers and trade unions in the CCT, it is criticised for disadvantaging labour. Not only is the state the largest employer in the country, but also some of its political leaders are entrepreneurs representing their interests within the state (Anon. 2003). The labour movement's top priority in the CCT is to present a coherent and united position as a social movement. Yet critics have charged that CCT is 'essentially a smokescreen for government, business and international financial institutions', masking the latter's real control of the economy (Webster, Wood and Mtyingizana 2004: 31). On a more positive note, there is a shift to a direct and co-operative relationship between labour and management, and a disposition to identify priorities and negotiate solutions directly without the mediation of the Ministry of labour (Levy 2004). While the CCT is, theoretically, both an advisory group and a negotiating forum on a broad range of issues, including wages and prices, training, occupational health and safety and social security, in practice, the main issue is the annual negotiation of the national minimum wage (Levy 2004).

IMF pressure had resulted in the minimum wage for non-agricultural private sector workers being reduced in real terms from $38 month in 1987 to a low of $18 in 1993, although it was subsequently allowed to slowly recover (Mozambique Peace Process Bulletin 8/2000). In 2000, the threat of a general strike forced the government to agree to an increase in the minimum wage of 30 per cent, with the rider that it could only afford to pay its employers 26 per cent, bringing the minimum wage to $33 per month (AIM Reports 9/1/2001). The fact that OTM seemed both willing and capable of organising a general strike represented a new assertiveness by organised labour (Mozambique Peace Process Bulletin 8/2000). This strike signifies a degree of labour independence for labour but there are those who believe that unions can use tripartite negotiations to demonstrate the unions' independence of government. Both trade union federations have admitted to a limited capacity to develop collective bargaining strategies and to extend bargaining in tripartite forums. This is largely confined to a limited number of professional union employees with capacity to analyse the socio-economic and political situation, a capacity that could help unions to develop more appropriate strategies.

Co-operation with, and assistance from, other labour movements has made it possible for some union leaders to receive training and advice on, for example, union leadership, collective bargaining and social tripartite dialogue, which proved to be of assistance in capacity building for union leadership in Mozambique (Anon. 2003). Links with trade unions in South Africa in particular have also become increasingly significant for labour in Mozambique. An umbrella coordinating body for unions in southern Africa, the Southern African Trade Union Coordinating Council (SATUCC), was launched in 1983. OTM is affiliated to the Council.

Contacts between unions operating in the region tend to be at the regional level. There are few, exceptions are MOZAL and Shoprite, of significant contacts at the grassroots level (Miller 2004). Grassroots links were established between workers in MOZAL and their counterparts at Hillside Aluminium in Richards Bay, South Africa after a lengthy strike at the MOZAL plant in 2000. The strike grew from a demand of Mozambican workers to be paid in United States dollars at South African wage rates. After pressure on MOZAL management, both union and management visited the Richards Bay plant. This led to a Mozambique-South Africa worker exchange in November 2001 between the three Billiton Smelters in southern Africa (Webster, Wood and Mtyingizana 2004).

Along with many of its counterparts in the other SADC (South African Develop-ment Community) states, OTM is a member of the International Confederation of Free Trade Unions (ICFTU). Meanwhile, SINTICIM has good relations with a number of individual COSATU affiliates, including NUM, BICAWU and NUMSA (Webster and Mosoetsa 2001).

Collective bargaining

Collective bargaining is relatively new to Mozambique. It was first introduced in terms of Decree 33/90 of 24 December 1990; the terms and provisions of the decree were incorporated into the 1998 Labour Law (Gumende 1999: 49). The Constitution of the Republic of 1990 prohibits involuntary servitude and provides workers with a right to a fair wage, to rest and holidays as well as a safe and healthy working environment (Webster, Wood and Mtyingizana 2004). It further guarantees the dignity and the protection of labour, and the protection of the rights and dignity of working women. Labour rights also comprise freedom of association, for both employers and employees (Article 89), it guarantees free exercise of trade unions activity within the company or establishment (Article 95) and independence and autonomy of trade unions association (Article 98). Unions have the right to organise, to belong to a trade union, and to strike. Lockouts are prohibited and workers may only be dismissed if due legal procedures are followed (Levy 2004). The right of association, specifically mentioned in Section I and II of Chapter III of the Labour Law, protects the interests of both employers and employees. In collaboration with the state, both employers and the employees prepare labour legislation, develop and execute policies pertaining to labour, employment, vocational training and development, production, salaries, and health and safety at work. The right of association also encourages the right to collective bargaining by government, employers and employees associations through the tripartite forum, the CCT.

The Labour Law (Article 106) states that the purpose of collective bargaining is to establish and stabilise collective employment relations. It sets to regulate mutual rights and duties of both the employers and the employees bound by individual employment contracts. The process of collective bargaining also provides an environment for the regulation of the dispute resolution process. The 1998 law permits plant and sector bargaining, although the bulk of collective bargaining takes place at enterprise level. Only in the banking sector (SNEB), which represents about

16 per cent of firms, does bargaining occur at the industry level. There is no effective coordination of enterprise and sector level bargaining in Mozambique.

Identified as some of the obstacles to a coordinated bargaining process are the shop stewards' lack of training, low economic growth, high inflation and employer resistance. Employers often do not disclose true information about company economic performance and do not comply with the existing agreements (Anon. 2003). Indeed only 42 per cent of respondents felt that managers bothered to comply with the terms and conditions of union recognition agreements that provide for collective bargaining. Firms practising collective bargaining are ones with the strongest interest in supporting a minimum wage and the tripartite Labour Commission's activities in order to discourage 'free-riding' (Webster, Wood and Mtyingizana 2004).

Dispute resolution

A 'court of competent jurisdiction' may only adjudicate individual disputes. Collective disputes may be dealt with through arbitration, with the Minister of Labour naming the arbitrator. In the case of disputes involving essential services and cases of disputes involving workers in Free Processing Zones, arbitration is compulsory and regulated by Decree no. 75/98 of 12 October (Webster, Wood and Mtyingizana 2004: 62; Anon. 2003: 20). The 1992 Labour Courts Law provides for district and provincial labour courts to deal with 'labour questions as well as those arising from occupational illness and workplace accidents' (Levy 2004: 6). Procedures are simpler than in normal courts to make them more accessible to workers and are required to promote conciliation prior to adjudication. However, the labour courts have yet to be established. In the interim, separate labour sections exist in both the Beira and Maputo provincial courts. These courts have a backlog of cases, which favours the well connected. In 2002 for example, of the 336 registered labour conflicts (155 individual and 181 collective), only 79 had been processed a year later. The remaining 180 were referred to court while the remaining 77 were still being negotiated (Anon. 2003).

The government has formally ratified ILO Conventions 87 and 98, guaranteeing freedom of association and the right to collective bargaining. State employees are excluded from some elements of the 1998 Labour Law that define the right to freedom of association and from collective bargaining (UNI 2001). The ILO Committee of Experts on the Application of Conventions and Recommendations (CEACR) has concluded that the penalties levied against employers in cases where the 1998 law has been violated are insufficient. While employees' jobs are protected when they fall ill, they do not have to be paid sick leave (Levy 2004). Whilst the core ILO Conventions 100 and 111, dealing with discrimination and equal remuneration have both been formally ratified by the government, discrimination on gender grounds remains widespread, and parts of the constitution and workplace codes weaken employee rights (Webster, Wood and Mtyingizana 2004). ILO Conventions on child labour (138 and 182) and Convention 29 on Forced Labour have yet to be ratified. The legislation of the late 1970s and 1980s, which reintroduced the forced labour practices of the colonial labour, notably the forced cultivation of cotton, remain on the statute books but in practice, forced cultivation been abandoned.

Conclusion

An effective industrial relations system in Mozambique is still being developed. A representation gap is emerging between unions in the workplace as well as a failure to represent the growing number of workers in the informal economy. Employers can avoid the law with impunity. Clearly there is a need for an effective mechanism where both parties can test whether employment practices are fair. While bargaining at enterprise level is emerging it is not coordinated with the broader collective bargaining process at the national level. Furthermore, while an institution to facilitate social dialogue, the CCT, has been created, it is ineffective.

Liberalisation has had far-reaching implications for labour. Privatisation has resulted in powerful private capitalist actors dominating particular sectors and determining patterns of production. Conflicts of interest between and within the state, private sector and labour have produced policy incoherence, institutional paralysis and economic difficulties. Restructuring has involved a deregulation of the labour market to make room for a much more flexible labour market required for business expansion and economic growth. Compared with the rest of Southern Africa, Mozambique offers a much more flexible labour market, with fewer labour regulations, weaker and less militant trade unions, and lower wages. Employers, however, are seeking even greater flexibility.

Employment security is not the only problem facing workers. Privatisation has necessitated reductions in government spending on health and education. Cutbacks have also meant that large job losses in the public sector leave the costs of reproducing labour power in the hands of the wage earners whose real wages have been dramatically reduced. As costs rise, so does the cost of schooling and health provision and as wages are insufficient to pay rent and meet food and clothing bills, other means of earning income become essential, and this fuels the growth of the informal sector.

The informal sector mainly consist of women who struggle to survive in the liberalising economy (Virreira 2000). Survival strategies adopted by these women are a form of capital accumulation influenced by certain forms of mutual aid inspired by lineage and community level values and forms of solidarity (Casimiro 1998). While Mozambique's unions struggle to reach out to more marginal categories of labour, ASSOTSI is an organisation recruiting street traders in the informal sector and has managed to develop a relationship with OTM. It has an estimated membership of 50,000 of which 4,000 are drawn from market traders.

The impact of liberalisation in Mozambique has been contradictory. On the one hand, it has opened up opportunities for the creation of a democratic society that would enable independent unions to emerge. Labour has been able to use these opportunities to increase its bargaining power through active participation in political reform and broader democratic alliances. On the other hand, however, liberalisation has eroded the union's material base as wage earners face a sharp decline in their bargaining power. This widens the scope for ignoring labour's political claims and unions are increasingly seen as both irrelevant and as obstacles to development. Furthermore privatisation has led to cutbacks in state expenditure increasing the costs of social services for the working poor placing the burden of restructuring on poor households.

Notes

1   The full results were analysed in Brookes, M., Webster, E. and Wood, G., Residual unionism and renewal: organised labour in Mozambique, presented at the conference on Labour Movements in the Twenty-First Century, 1–3 July 2004. Sheffield, United Kingdom.

References

Abrahamsson, H. and Nilsson, A. (1995) *Mozambique: The troubled transition*, London.
Africa Watch Report (1992) *Conspicuous destruction. War, famine and the reform process in Mozambique*, New York.
AIM Reports (2001) Maputo.
AIM Reports (2003) Maputo.
Akwetey, E. (2001) 'Trade unions and democratisation. A comparative study of Zambia and Ghana', in Beckman, B. and Sachikonye, L. M. (2001) *Labour regimes and liberalisation: The restructuring of state-society relations in Africa*, Harare.
Anonymous (2001) *Mozambican Criticised over labour rights violations* www.icftu.org/displaydocument (accessed June 2004).
—— (2003) 'Contingent identity and socialist democracy in the port of Maputo', Unpublished.
Beckman, B. (2001) 'Who's civil society? Trade unions and capacity building in the Nigerian textile industry', in Beckman, B. and Sachikonye, L. M. (eds), *Labour regimes and liberalisation: the restructuring of state-society relations in Africa*, Harare.
—— and Sachikonye, L. M. (2001) *Labour regimes and liberalisation: the restructuring of state-society relations in Africa*, Harare.
Bendix, S. (2001) *Labour relations, a conceptual analysis. Industrial relations in the new South Africa*, Kenwyn.
Brookes, M. Webster, E. and Wood G. (2004) 'Residual unionism and renewal: organized labor in Mozambique', presented at the conference Labour Movements in the Twenty-First Century, 1–3 July. Sheffield.
Carter, G. M. and O'Meara, P. (1979) *Southern Africa: The continuing crisis*, Bloomington.
Casimiro, I, (1998) 'Women's empowerment and organisation in Mozambique', in Cruz Maria e Silva, T. and Sitas, A. (eds), *Gathering voices: perspectives on the social sciences in Southern Africa*, Madrid.
Cheatham, M. W. (1985) *Constructive management in Mozambique, 1980–1984: The accord of Nkomati*, Oregon.
Christie, I. (1989) *Samora Machel: A biography*, London.
Egerö, B. (1987) *Mozambique: A dream undone. The political economy of democracy, 1975–84*, Uppsala.
First, R. (1983) *Black gold: The Mozambican miner, proletariat and peasant*, Sussex.
Freund, B. (1988) *The African worker: African society today*, Cambridge.

Friedrich Ebert Stiftung (2004) *A survey of trade unionism in contemporary Mozambique*, Maputo.

Giddens, A. (2001) *Sociology*, Cambridge.

Gumende, A. (1999) 'Industrial relations in a restructuring economy: implications for corporate strategy and human resource management in Mozambique'. Unpublished MBA dissertation, Nottingham Trent University.

Hall, M. and Young, T. (1997) *Confronting the leviathan: Mozambique since independence*, London.

Hanlon, J. (1984) *Mozambique: the revolution under fire*, London.

—— (1991) *Mozambique: who calls the shots?*, London.

—— (1996) *Peace without profit*, Oxford.

Henriksen, T. H. (1978) *Mozambique: a history*, London.

Hoile, D. (1989) *Mozambique, a nation in crisis*, London.

Isaacman A. and Isaacman B. (1983) *Mozambique: from colonialism to revolution*, Harare.

Katzenellenbogen, S. (1982) *South African and Southern Mozambique: labour, railways and trade in the making of a relationship*, Manchester.

Levy, S. (2004) *The legal and administrative framework for labor relations in Mozambique*, Maputo.

MacKenzie, N. (1966) *Socialism*, London.

Manning, C. L. (2002) *The politics of peace in Mozambique: post-conflict democratisation, 1992–2000*, Westport.

Miller, D. (2004) 'The regional claims of workers in post-apartheid Southern Africa: A case study of Shoprite, a retail multinational, in Zambia and Mozambique', PhD John Hopkins University, Baltimore.

Mozambique Peace Process Bulletin 8/2000 (2000) Maputo.

Munslow, B. (1986) *Africa: problems in the transition to socialism*, London.

Newitt, M. (1981) *Portugal in Africa: the last hundred years*, London.

Penvenne, J. M. (1995) *African workers and colonial racism: Mozambican strategies and struggles in Lourenço Marques, 1877–1962*, London.

Pitcher, A. (2002) *Transforming Mozambique: the politics of privatisation*, Cambridge.

Saul, J. (1990) *Socialist ideology and the struggle for Southern Africa*, Trenton.

——(1993) *Recolonisation and resistance in Southern Africa in the 1990s*, Trenton.

Serapiao, L. B. (1979) *Mozambique in the 20th century: from colonialism to independence*, Washington D.C.

United Nations Industrial Development Organisation (2001) *Mozambique public–private sector dialogue*, www.unido.org/ (accessed May 2004).

Virreira, S. (2000) *Political power and female protagonism*, Maputo.

Webster, E and Mosoetsa, S. (2001) *Connecting and disconnecting: an introductory review of labour in selected SADC countries in the era of globalisation*, Johannesburg.

—— Wood, G. and Mtyingizana. B. (2004) 'A survey of industrial relations practices in Mozambique'. Unpublished Paper.

Interviews

CTA (Federation of the Mozambican Economics Association). Jose Figueiredo, 4 September 2003, Frederico Sitoe, 3 November 2003.

DLM (Department of Labour-Mozambique). Dr Emmanuel Jonas, 4 November 2003, Dr Paulo Mole, 5 September 2004.

NCC (National Chamber of Commerce of Mozambique). Manuel Noticio, 4 November 2003.

7

Relations between capital and labour in Turkey: from neo-liberalism to democratisation

Nazım Güveloğlu[1]

Introduction

The period after the 1980 military coup in Turkey has been marked by transformations in many areas, including capital-labour relations. The coup ended the widespread labour militancy of the 1970s and initiated a new period in Turkish political history, a period marked by restricted and constrained politics dominated by a neo-liberal economic agenda. Since the late 1990s, what has changed is not the neo-liberal economic orientation of the civilian governments but the prodemocratic political agenda supported by virtually all political actors in Turkey. Associated with the country's possible accession to the European Union, the democratisation project started in the late 1990s and accelerated at the beginning of the twenty-first century.

This chapter discusses the implications of democratisation and neo-liberalism in Turkey on class relations. The chapter briefly discusses the national and international contexts followed by an outline of general political economic processes taking place throughout the capitalist world to define the Turkish case. Finally, the Turkish case will be analysed. Jessop's conceptualisation of 'hegemonic projects' will be employed particularly in order to establish the links between the democratisation project in Turkey and the process of 'radicalisation of bourgeois democracy'.[2] The chapter concludes that the democratisation project in Turkey has implications broader than establishing hegemony.

The nexus of the national and international contexts

The realist approach to international relations conceives of the nation state as an entity, which has an ontology distinct from other nation states. Such an attitude, taking the nation state as the sovereign authority of its territory, conceives of the relations involved in and among the societies of various territories through the relations between nation states. Although the concept of nation state corresponds to a meaningful level of analysis, taking it as an entity distinct from other nation states is misleading. Such a conception takes the relations between the nation states as external relations, and conceives of international relations as the relations between distinct subjects. However, the social relations involved in and between different territories cannot be reduced to relations between nation states, because the nation state is not a homogeneous entity representing a homogeneous unity of society located in a territory. Capitalist society, with its class contradictions, is not a homogeneous unity that can be represented by a unique will. These class contradictions involve relations that go beyond the limits that can be understood in terms of nation states.

The national and international contexts are internally related to each other and the social relations involved in the national and international contexts are the counterparts of the same ontological whole.[3] This is the nexus of the national and international contexts. The nation state is not a thing in itself but a field of social relations, of class struggles. These social relations and processes, which constitute the nation state, themselves involve the international context. It is necessary to deal with the international dimensions that class struggles involve; likewise, it is necessary to analyse historical processes according to their implications for the international context.

Defining the national context in internal relations with the international context does not mean that the nation state is a meaningless concept. The nation state is the form in which the state is organised in contemporary capitalism. The need for such a conception does not arise from the popular argument that 'the nation state is withering away'. There are aspects of social reality that can only be grasped through external relations among nation states. Such a relational approach searches for the aspects of social reality, which is not explicable, and is sometimes masked by, the notion of nation states. The following analysis of the relationship between advanced capitalist countries and the 'less developed' countries depicts the matrix of social relations and historical processes in which Turkey is located. In order to understand the historical specificity of the neo-liberalisation process and democratisation in Turkey, it is necessary to analyse the historical processes and relations that makes this project viable and necessary.

The radicalisation of bourgeois democracy and neo-liberalism

Recent decades have witnessed changes in the form of regime in many 'less developed' capitalist countries, typified by 'the third wave' of democratisation (Huntington 1991). However, the emerging regimes in these countries are often regarded as deficient. Schmitter (1994) argues that some regimes are neither authoritarian nor democratic. The *dictablanda* is 'a hybrid regime that combines elements of autocracy and democracy', and the *democradura*, is a 'persistent but unconsolidated democracy' (1994: 59 and 60). This conception of hybrid regimes underlies many approaches in the democratisation literature (Case 2001; McFaul 2001; Shevtsova and Eckert 2001).

Cammack (1998) argues that changes in the form of regime leads to a specific type of democracy. This 'state orchestrated electoralism', or 'state-managed democracy', is much more compatible with neo-liberalism, which Cammack sees as capitalism's current form, than is liberal democracy. States of this type, such as Malaysia and Mexico, give great competitive advantage to their bourgeoisie. It is because of this that Cammack argues regime change is likely to be towards state-managed democracy, which is 'possibly the only viable form of democracy' (1998: 262).

As regards the Western countries, there are developments and tendencies, which may be seen as deviations from traditional liberal democracy. The political structure of the European Union is problematic in terms of liberal democracy since it involves a highly bureaucratic apparatus (the European Commission) and a powerful Executive (the European Council) with a very weak Parliament (Carchedi 2001). The European Constitution approved this institutional structure, rather than changing it. The party leadership becomes more important than before within a political environment in which American-type electoral campaigns become predominant, paralleling a weakening of party membership and activism (Sussman and Galizio: 2003). Kennedy and Joseph (2001) argue that the developments in the British Labour Party aim at a 'partyless formation' under the control of party leadership. The implications of this go beyond the party itself, signalling a 'longer-term transformation of British political structures' in which 'a new type of governmental machinery' would develop. The impact of neo-liberalism on political structures accorded 'closely to the requirements of neo-liberal economic management, while drawing upon developments in the wider global environment' (2001: 267). This chapter departs from Cammack's approach to focus on aspects which are characteristic of liberal democracy. Change will be explored in terms of their linkage with the characteristics of bourgeois democracy. In order to construct an account of the interconnections between neo-liberalism and changes in the form of regime, the basic features of the neo-liberalisation will be sketched out and their regime implications assessed.

As the symptoms of the end of the period of welfare capitalism materialized in the late 1970s and early 1980s, it became common to talk of a new era of capitalism. Thatcher and Reagan initiated neo-liberal market-oriented economic policies under the political designation of the New Right and neo-liberalism has since become increasingly dominant in advanced capitalist countries. The economic programmes conducted in the less developed countries under the guidance of the International Monetary Fund (IMF) and the World Bank have taken neo-liberal principles as the major source of reference, expressed by the Washington Consensus. In the advanced and the less developed capitalist states a process of neo-liberalisation process has been taking place.

Panitch argues that globalisation, conducted under the aegis of the New Right, built upon neo-classical economics. The New Right purported to reduce the state's role in the domestic and international economic spheres but in practice the New Right involved the active role of states in promoting globalisation and the balance of class forces (1998: 13). The first New Right programme was carried out in Britain by the Thatcher government. For Jessop, Thatcherism 'combined a distinctive "two nations" authoritarian populist hegemonic project, a centralizing "strong state" project, and a neo-liberal accumulation strategy' (2003: 4). This had a number of elements. First, liberalisation promoted free market competition as the most efficient basis for market forces; second, deregulation gave economic agents greater freedom from state control and legal restriction; third, privatisation, reduced the public sector's share in the provision of goods and services to business and community alike; fourth, the (re-) commodification of the residual public sector promoted the role of market forces directly or through proxies; fourth internationalisation encouraged the mobility of capital and labour, stimulated global market forces and imported more advanced processes and products into Britain as a means of economic modernisation; and finally reduced direct taxes expanded the scope of markets through enhanced investor and consumer choice (2003: 5).

These elements of the New Right in Britain have been influential in other advanced capitalist countries, albeit in varying degrees, so the above is a good illustration of the general character of neo-liberalisation. While the Reagan government in the USA had similarities to Thatcher's policies, Germany has been far more reluctant to embrace neo-liberalism. However, the dominant process in advanced capitalism has been towards the implementation of neo-liberalism. In less developed capitalist countries the neo-liberalisation has been carried out with the guidance of the IMF and the World Bank via the Washington Consensus. John Williamson, the originator of the concept, says that he used 'Washington Consensus' to refer to 'the lowest common denominator of policy advice being addressed by the Washington-based institutions to Latin American countries as of 1989' (2000: 251). The elements of this 'consensus' are: first, fiscal discipline; second, the redirection of public expenditure toward activities offering high returns and improved income distribution, such as primary health care, primary education, and infrastructure; third, tax reform to lower marginal rates and broaden the tax base; fourth, interest rate liberalisation; fifth, competitive exchange rate; sixth, trade liberalisation; seventh, liberalisation of inflows of foreign direct investment; eighth, privatisation; ninth, deregulation to abolish barriers to entry and exit; and tenth, secure property rights (Williamson, 2000: 252–3). These constitute the dominant neo-liberal economic agenda throughout the capitalist world in recent decades. Yet, the second one stands out since 'the least progress had been made in . . . redirecting public expenditure policies' (Williamson, 2000: 253). The similarity of the framework drawn by the Washington Consensus to the above listed elements of Thatcherism is striking.

From the aspect of labour relations, neo-liberalisation involves significant changes. First, deindustrialisation weakened the strongest and most militant trade unions; second legislation was passed directed at strike action and collective bargaining; third, there was a general de-legitimisation of corporatism and tripartism; fourth, the flexibilisation and deregulation of labour markets was promoted; and finally 'welfare-to-work' strategies were developed (Jessop 2003: 10–11).

Depoliticisation of economic management

Neo-liberalisation involves changes in the form assumed by the separation of the economic and political realms. Poulantzas employs the concept of 'form of state' to understand the modifications in the relationship between the political and economic realms (1975: 148). Neo-liberalisation involves transformations related to the form of state, analysed by Burnham as the 'depoliticisation of economic management'. Burnham argues that the late 1980s had established a 'depoliticised form of economic management', succeeding the 'politicised form of economic management' of 1945–76. Depoliticised economic management is defined as 'the process of placing at one remove the political character of decision making' (2001: 128). Depoliticised management involves 'the reordering and reassignment of tasks from the party in office', 'moves to increase accountability, transparency and external validation of policy', and 'the acceptance of binding rules (constrained discretion) limiting government room for manoeuvre'; and it has such characteristics as 'relaxation/abolition of direct controls' over the economy, 'decentralisation and devolution of policy making', 'privatisation, deregulation and the recomposition of management hierarchies within states', and 'downgrading of income policies' (2001: 131). Burnham stresses that depoliticisation should not be taken to mean the removal of politics, political power or influence from the economy. Depoliticisation is 'a governing strategy and, in that sense, remains highly political' (2001: 136). As a governing strategy, depoliticised management provides governments with room for manoeuvre reducing the risk of being directly affected by economic crises, and reasserts the 'operational autonomy' of the political executive (Burnham 2001: 131). A move towards depoliticised management became possible as a result of developments such as higher unemployment rates in a more 'flexible' labour market, reduced control over movement of capital and the integration of financial markets. Burnham's conceptualisation of depoliticised economic management has increasing applicability to the whole of the capitalist world. International agreements such as GATG, GATS and TRIPS are good examples of 'constrained discretion' because they bind national governments in many aspects of domestic and international economic affairs. Although these do not deny the importance of the nation state, they obviously entail a reduced role in economic policy making. This development does not mean that the state is deprived of all forms of intervention. The point is that, although authority is transferred from publicly elected governments to autonomous institutions, the functions of the latter are an aspect of the state. These institutions serve to exclude representative government from economic policy making. The state still intervenes in economics but takes the form of excluding 'the people' from economic policy.

Capitalism is built upon the separation of the economic and political. Class exploitation in the economic field does not necessarily involve direct political mediation. It is different from feudalism, for example, which requires direct involvement of political power in the economy. The primary specificity of bourgeois democracy as a form of regime arises from its separation of the economic and political, though the form of separation assumes changes in time and geography. Separation creates opportunities for preserving and reproducing the domination of the bourgeoisie. Its specific institutions and mechanisms such as a national parliament, general elections and competing political parties have established the hegemony of the bourgeoisie. Such institutions and mechanisms have frequently served to contain movements and political projects that oppose the class domination of the bourgeoisie.

Neo-liberalisation has significant implications for bourgeois democracy as a form of regime. Since, via the depoliticisation of economic management, production relations become increasingly independent of the representational politics, and the separation between the economic and political deepens and widens. The separation of the economic and political is characteristic of capitalism, however, social democracy and welfare capitalism were still bourgeois democracy, leaving governments room for determining economic policy for redistributive purposes. Parallel to this deepening, the dynamics of neo-liberalisation extends the domination of the bourgeoisie in the economic. Major changes occur in the political realm. Non-economic issues, such as cultural, religious, national, ethnic and gender identity, security and terrorism gain increasing importance (Güveloğlu 2004). Although these have ties with economics, economic issues are presented in the form of non-economic topics.

Bourgeois democracy reproduces the deepening of the separation between economic and political realms in such a way that creates new opportunities for the reproduction and extension of bourgeois domination. What the 'radicalisation of bourgeois democracy' indicates is this process. Changes in democracy and class relations do not bring about a form of regime distinct from liberal democracy. On the contrary, the radicalisation of some basic characteristics of liberal democracy, as Meiskins Wood argues, 'if we are confronting the "End of History", it may not be in the sense that liberal democracy has triumphed, but rather in the sense that it has very nearly reached its limits.' (1994: 55).

Briefly stated, the process of radicalisation of bourgeois democracy involves the following dynamic. There is a decreased role for representational institutions such as parliament and political parties in economic policy, and the strengthening of the executive and bureaucracy as a result of transfering authority to autonomous regulatory authorities. Parallel to the strengthening of the executive, the party political elites are strengthened and class-based politics are downgraded thereby increasing the importance of non-economic issues in politics, such as cultural and identity politics. The corollary of the rise of identity politics is the decreasing importance of social justice politics and social and economic rights. Politics changes in such a way that promotes indirect association with the electorate through advertisement-like electoral campaigns. Radicalisation weakens other classes vis-à-vis bourgeoisie in their capacity to effect or change the characteristics of bourgeois domination within bourgeois democracy. The Turkish democratisation of the late 1990s occurred in the framework of such a process.

The Turkish case

After the 1980 military coup, the growth of neo-liberalisation began to determine the dynamics of the Turkish political economy. Military rule adhered to a neo-liberal economic framework, the origins of which can be seen in the civilian government preceding the coup, known as the *January 24 Decisions.* The policies related to the Decisions had little chance of being implemented in the pre-coup political context, and the coup was functional in giving a start to the neo-liberal economic reforms. Under the economic programmes conducted under the guidance of the IMF and the World Bank, successive civilian governments have remained loyal to the neo-liberal economic orientation. The major transformations relating to the form of state have taken place in the Turkish case through the neo-liberalisation process. The most remarkable are the major privatisations in many economic sectors. The central bank is the sole autonomous authority of monetary policy, an example of governing authority being transferred to 'autonomous regulatory authorities' which has occurred in many aspects of economic management, together with measures taken against the rights and status of the working class.

International agreements have been effective in Turkey in promoting neo-liberalisation. Turkey's signature of GATS has formed the basis of excluding the state as a service provider from the service sectors, including health and education, (Güzelsarı 2003). The regulatory reforms implemented in Turkey under the guidance of the OECD (Organisation for Economic Cooperation and Development) have been aimed at 'providing the good functioning of the market economy'. This meant that state would be subordinated to the market in a way that worked to the disadvantage of labour (Bayramoğlu 2003: 151). The economic programmes implemented in the 1980s and 1990s disregarded social justice and, as a result, the income gap between the upper and lower segments of society widened.

Political and hegemonic dimensions

While neo-liberalisation followed a consistent path after the 1980 military coup, the relations between capital and labour in terms of hegemony has not been straightforward. Despite advancing neo-liberalisation and the anti-labour orientation of the economic policies, there was almost complete docility on the part of the masses in the 1980s, in contrast with the period before the coup. No doubt, military repression involving the detention of hundreds of thousands of people and the prohibition of many organisations, including the political parties, was a primary reason for this situation. There was some small-scale opposition, but it had no influence on critical segments of society. Some mass worker movements occurred at the end of the 1980s but the basic concern of these movements was the level of wages rather than a demand for widespread change in political and economic conditions. As a result there was a suitable environment in the 1980s for the implementation of neo-liberal policies.

According to Yalman (2002), the post-1980 period in Turkey was marked by a change in the form of state, which had a clear authoritarian character guaranteed by the new Constitution put into effect by the military. The hegemonic strategy at the core was putting an end to class-based politics and accompanying this process was the restructuring of the state. While analysing the ideological and political aspects of the period, Yalman makes frequent references to the Thatcherite New Right because of its relevance to the Turkish case, such as the promotion of authoritarian individualism, and the rhetoric of 'There Is No Alternative' (Yalman 2002). Similarly, Tünay (2002) uses the 'Turkish New Right' to characterise the civilian government following military rule. He analyses the period in terms of hegemonic projects but arrives at a different conclusion from Yalman. According to Tünay, the Turkish New Right's two-nations hegemonic project failed because of the narrowness of the 'first nation' upon which its ideology was based, in contrast to the 'second nation' which included the masses.[4] However, Yalman (2002) argues that the post-1980 market ideology has been far more successful than any other attempt in Turkish history to promote value change because many of its elements have been internalised by large sections of society.

The Turkish experience of the 1980s illustrated the possibility of constructing new class hegemony under an authoritarian state by means of an ideology that extolled the market. At the same time the dependence of the bourgeoisie on the state was perpetuated. This could be described as a 'passive revolution', which aimed at depoliticisation (Yalman 2002: 48). Considering the wide range of transformations conducted and the radical difference of the dominant ideology compared with the 1970s, there are few reasons to doubt that bourgeois hegemony was successfully accomplished in the 1980s. This can be seen in the radical change of attitudes towards the market achieved in this period, which is still effective at the beginning of the twenty-first century.

By the late 1980s, the PKK (Kurdistan Workers' Party) movement in the southeastern part of the country was the primary determinant of Turkish politics. The dramatic consequences of the associated armed struggle and the perceived danger of territorial separation formed the basis of a powerful upsurge in nationalism throughout the country. After a decade of depoliticisation, which started with the coup, a process of politicisation occurred under the influence of politicians, bureaucrats and secret services.[5] Some activities of the armed forces and police were kept out of civilian control grounded in the 'low intensity war' between the Turkish state and the PKK. Until 1998, when Abdullah Öcalan, the leader of the PKK, was arrested and the PKK agreed to a ceasefire, political life in Turkey remained dominated by these national issues.

Another major development in the 1990s was the resurgence of political Islam. The rise of the Welfare Party (RP), an Islamist party in the mid-1990s took place at the same time as a decline in the parties of the centre. The party emerged as the leader in the 1995 elections by collecting 21 per cent of the votes and became the biggest element in a government coalition with the centre-right True Path Party (DYP). The rise of the Islamic party was accompanied by the spread and exposition of the Islamic lifestyle in society, especially in the suburbs and in the peripheries of the metropolitan cities. Under such circumstances, the secular character of the state was seen as under serious threat. In the meeting of the National Security Council on 28 February 1997 the representatives of the armed forces expressed the military's 'worries' about Islam. The subsequent period became known as 'the process of February 28' and resulted in the resignation of the government and later the closure of the Welfare Party by the Constitutional Court. The rise of political Islam has also been used in this period as a justification of the need to achieve Turkey's alignment with the West and accession to the EU.[6]

A new hegemonic project: democratisation and accession to the EU

By the end of the 1990s, attitudes towards the regime began to change. Criticisms of the 1982 Constitution, for example, became increasingly common. In 1995, TOBB (Union of Turkish Chambers and Stock Exchanges), a semi-official organisation of all businessmen in the country, published *The South-Eastern Report*. The report proposed extra-military solutions to the problems in the southeastern region and exceeded the usual limits of criticism at the time about this issue. In 1997 TÜSIAD (Turkish Industrialists' and Businessmen's Association) published a report which gave a detailed account of the democratic deficits in Turkey and proposed solutions. Remarkably, the demand for change and democratisation came primarily from business organisations, which, hitherto, had been very reluctant to support such demands.

In December 1999, Turkey's candidacy for EU membership was approved at the Helsinki summit of the European Council. This was characterised as one of the most important developments in Turkish history. It marked a certain change in the aura of politics. Meeting the requirements of accession to the EU is presented as a great national project. In this context, a 'democratisation project' started in Turkey with the declared aim of meeting the Copenhagen political criteria. A new hegemonic project came on the agenda, based on this democratisation project and accession to the EU.

Characteristics of the democratisation project

TÜSIAD, the organisation of major businesses in Turkey, has been a supporter of the democratisation project and has published numerous reports supporting the process (1997; 1999; 2001a; 2001b). These reports are of significance because, first, they represent the views of the most influential organisation of big business in Turkey; and second, there has been strong correspondence between their policy suggestions and the policies pursued in Turkey's democratisation.[7] TÜSIAD's support for democratisation is shared by other nationwide business organisations, albeit with varying degrees of emphasis (Önis and Türem 2001).[8] Although TOBB supports the project, it has been less vocal since its *Southeastern Report*. Önis and Türem observe that TISK is quite passive and focused on collective bargaining and labour relations, while supporting the democratisation project and EU membership (2001: 102).

MÜSIAD's case is somewhat different from the others. Formerly it had been against Turkey's accession to the EU and democratisation, but after the process of February 28 mentioned above, it radically changed its attitude (Önis and Türem 2001: 101). Meral Aksener, then the Minister of Internal Affairs, argued that the February 28 process had dimensions which went beyond merely preserving the secular character of the state, as had been proclaimed by the military. Accordingly the process involved the realisation of the interests of a section of capital which had lost the ties with the state that it developed in the import substitution era (Düzel 2003). Aksener indicates the section that is usually assumed to be represented by TÜSIAD. Interpreting the February 28 process as a direct reflection of the struggle between this section of capital and the section assumed to be represented by MÜSIAD would be misleading. Nevertheless, the process had remarkable implications for the conflict between these sections. After February 28, MÜSIAD became a proponent of accession to EU, and prominent politicians known to have been involved in political Islamist circles became advocates of accession to the EU and democratisation. This change, a consequence of the pressure from the military, should still be considered in terms of a struggle of hegemonic strategies within the capitalist class.

Önis and Türem rightly argue that while all the four business associations have supported the democratisation project, they have tended to interpret democracy as 'better governance'; 'a precondition for reaping the benefits of market-driven globalisation' (2001: 103). Their observations parallel those of Tülin Öngen (Aren et al., 1997) and Filiz Zabcı (2000) who believe that the support of TÜSIAD for democratisation was instrumental. Önis and Türem observe that none of the organisations care much about the 'civil and human rights' dimension of democratisation. Although all, except TISK, have published reports proposing the improvement of democratic standards, none have been willing to do more (Önis and Türem 2001: 104, 114). In cases of violation of these rights, for example, in the press and mass media none of the organisations responded with significant action. However, this does not change the fact that TÜSIAD and other business organisations have actively supported the democratisation project with publications and public declarations.

There has been a significant overlap in the contents of TÜSIAD's reports, European Union documents (e.g. European Council 2001, 2003), national programmes and reforms undertaken by the Turkish government. The democratisation reform agenda focused on topics such as freedom of expression, freedom of association, torture and pre-trial detention, capital punishment, legal redress against violations of human rights, cultural rights, and the National Security Council and state of emergency. The dominant approach has been to regard democratisation as merely a political process with only indirect linkages to economic matters (Güveloğlu 2003). Democracy has been constructed around the concepts of 'rule of law' and 'individual liberties'. The latter has been narrowly defined through civil, political and cultural human rights, while social and economic rights have been overlooked. The way that 'the Kurdish question' is handled in the TÜSIAD reports is a good example of this approach. Although admitting that '"the Kurdish question" also had social and economic causes', these causes are not dealt with since 'the subject [of the first major report on democratisation] does not cover social and economic fields.' (TÜSIAD 1997: 169). Attention is paid merely to the cultural and political aspects of 'the Kurdish question' and the socio-economic dimensions are excluded from the democratisation report. This attitude defines the logic of the reforms expected by the EU and government regulations made in response to this. The democratisation reforms have been based exclusively on political and cultural rights.

Economic issues are handled separately from issues related to democratisation in other publications and reports of TÜSIAD. How these economic reports deal with the problem of unemployment present another illustration of the conception of economic and political separate realms. The solution for unemployment and related social issues lies in economic policies, which may indirectly increase employment opportunities by economic growth, reducing the labour costs and flexible employment practices but not, for example, public investment or redistribution policies (TÜSIAD 2002: 234–5). There is an assumption that unemployment can be solved through market mechanisms facilitating the employment of more people.

On 17 December 2004, the European Council decided to start the negotiation phase of the accession process with Turkey with the observation that the country has fulfilled the requirements of the Copenhagen political criteria. The expectations of the Union had been satisfactorily met. However, democratisation cannot be conceived of simply as the imposition of a structural template on Turkey by the EU. The project has been accompanied by a radicalisation of bourgeois democracy at the nexus of the national and international contexts. In other words, 'the European Union' is not external to 'Turkey' and the relationship should not be understood in terms of the 'effects' of an entity named 'the European Union' on a distinct entity named 'Turkey'. Rather, the phenomenon involves dimensions where national and international contexts appear as the counterparts of the same ontological whole. This nexus is characterised by the process of radicalisation of bourgeois democracy in the 1980s and 1990s.

It is true that large sections of society have consistently supported the democratisation project and accession to the EU. However, as Jessop argues, the class character of a hegemonic project depends not on the 'a priori class belonging of its elements or any self-professed class identity of its proponents. It depends instead on the effects of pursuing that project in a definite conjuncture' (1990: 217). The radicalisation of bourgeois democracy, on which the hegemonic project is based, is a process that reproduces and extends bourgeois domination. Support for changes in the form of regime should not be seen simply as a compromise granted to the subordinate classes in order to pre-empt opposition arising from the social consequences of neo-liberal economic programmes. The changes in the form of regime, especially changes related to democratisation, have broader implications than merely gaining the consent of the masses. Such changes as the enhancement of liberal individual rights and the promotion of the rule of law have gone hand in hand with the neo-liberal transformation of the state. Just as the development of 'the rule of law' protects the citizens against the state, for example, it also neutralises class-based laws and regulations, and guarantees the government's detachment from economic intervention. As much as the civil and political rights are acknowledged and promoted, the notion of freedom becomes defined hegemonically within the narrow limits of these rights, and social and economic rights are omitted. Again, cultural rights are acknowledged but the social problems are detached from their socioeconomic background and defined in terms of their cultural dimensions.

This hegemonic project has provided many advantages to the bourgeoisie in a process of changes related to the state form and form of regime. Even if these positive results had not been achieved, the project could still be seen as successful since, as Gamble (1984) argues, the success of a hegemonic project is related to the social endorsement and sharing of its objectives and priorities, rather than their actual achievement. Jessop defines three dimensions on which the construction of a successful hegemonic project and the realisation of it depends; first, 'integration of strategically significant forces as subjects with specific interests'; second, 'formulation of a general, national popular project'; and third, 'specification of a "policy paradigm" conflicts over competing interests and demands can be negotiated without threatening the overall project' (1990: 209). When the hegemonic project is evaluated in these terms, it appears successful in all three aspects. The second condition, the formulation of a national popular project, is realised by accession to the EU and democratisation. Within the frame of this formulation, assigning specific returns to significant forces satisfies the first condition. Rights and status of the workers, for example, would be raised to the European standards, investment would create new job opportunities, small and middle scale businessmen would have new opportunities in a wider market; and individuals would have more liberal rights. The policy paradigm, the third dimension of success, is constructed in such a way that locates a single issue directly in relation to EU accession and democratisation. A popular motto used to condemn the practice of an individual or institution shows how all political issues are related to this hegemonic project: 'If this mindset persists they will not accept us into the EU'.

This hegemonic project fulfils all the requirements of a successful project. It should be seen as a one-nation hegemonic project aimed at, and to a great extent realised, encompassing the whole of society. It did not address any 'second-nation' questions.

Conclusion

Turkey's candidacy for EU membership and the democratisation project are the counterparts of a hegemonic project which has become dominant in the 1980s and 1990s. A particularly important feature of this hegemonic project was that it was accompanied by the increasing predominance of neo-liberalism and changes to democracy throughout the capitalist world. The democratisation process in Turkey occurred in a process in which major changes in the state form and regime occurred in such a way that deepened the separation of the economic and political realms and extended the class domination of the bourgeoisie. The hegemonic project, a one-nation type, has been successful, gaining the consent of large sections of society.

The overall process cannot be conceived in terms of the 'effects' of an external actor on Turkey. Rather, the process should be considered as being realised at the nexus of the national and international contexts. The process involves both national and international dimensions where these two constitute the counterparts of the same ontological whole and cannot be separated. Developments in the Turkish political economy have been a product of a dynamic that has national and international dimensions. The radicalisation of bourgeois democracy is the major process that has shaped this dynamic.

The 'unexpected progress' of democratisation in Turkey in recent years is closely related to the class interest of the bourgeoisie. The conception of 'democracy' envisaged and largely achieved is a specific one based on the expansion of political and cultural rights rather than economic or social rights. This is the underlying reason behind the controversies over whether Turkey has become 'really democratic'. The answer lies as much in the changing frame that defines this 'really democratic' democracy.

Notes

1 This chapter draws on Güveloğlu (2003 and 2004). I am grateful to Galip Yalman, who supervised the original Ph.D. thesis, for his criticisms and suggestions. Any remaining errors are my responsibility.

2 Jessop argues that class struggles should be examined in terms of competing hegemonic projects (1991: 344). The hegemonic project of the dominant class entails changing the 'formal unity' of the state apparatus to a 'substantive unity' to overcome conflicts between various branches of the state in a way that reproduces the system of political domination (1990: 210).

3 The definition of internal relations followed here is based on Ollman (1993). There are other conceptions (Sayer 1992) but Ollman's establishes a well-defined framework that takes the notion of internal relations as an ontological category.

4 The difference between 'one-nation' and 'two-nations' hegemonic projects is that a one-nation hegemonic project aims at an expansive hegemony encompassing the whole of society. The latter aims at 'a more limited hegemony concerned to mobilize the support of strategically significant sectors of the population and to pass the costs of the project to the other sectors' (Jessop 1990: 211).

5 After 'the Susurluk accident' Tansu Çiller, then the Prime Minister, used the expression: 'The one who shoots and is shot for the country are both honourable'. This was interpreted as supporting those engaged in these activities (Oktay 1996).

6 The Justice and Development Party (AKP) is composed of the cadres of the Welfare Party and has become one of the strongest supporters of the democratisation project and Turkey's EU accession. Major reforms have taken place under the AKP whilst the party has been reconstructing its identity to distance itself from political Islam. Tayyip Erdogan, the leader of the party, defines it as conservative democratic.

7 As Ayse Bugra notes of the 1997 report, TÜSIAD's democratisation reports do not disclaim responsibility for the views of the reports' authors (Bugra 1998: 527). On the contrary, in the foreword the TÜSIAD Board of Directors endorsed the report's proposals.

8 The membership of these organisations, TÜSIAD, MÜSIAD (Independent Industrialists' and Businessmen's Association), TOBB, and TISK (Turkish Employers' Confederation) are not mutually exclusive.

References

Aren, S. *et al.* (1997) 'TÜSIAD raporu üstüne tartisma', *Marksizm ve Gelecek*, Bahar 1997.
Bayramoglu, S. (2003) 'OECD Türkiye Raporu üzerine elestirel bir çözümleme', *Praksis*, 9.
Bugra, A. (1998) 'Class, culture and state: an analysis of interest representation by two Turkish business associations', *International Journal of Middle East Studies*, 30.
Burnham, P. (2001) 'New Labour and the politics of depoliticisation', *British Journal of Politics and International Relations*, 3:2.
Cammack, P. (1998) 'Globalization and the death of liberal democracy', *European Review*, 6:2.
Carchedi, G. (2001) *For another Europe: a class analysis of European economic integration*, London.
Case, W. (2001) 'Malaysia's resilient pseudodemocracy', *Journal of Democracy*, 12:1.
Düzel, N. (2003) 'Interview with Meral Aksener', *Radikal*, 18 September.
European Commission (2003) 'EU enlargement – a historic opportunity', http://europa.eu.int/comm/enlargement/intro/criteria.htm (accessed 10 March 2003).
European Council (2001) 'Council decision of 8 March 2001 on the principles, priorities, intermediate objectives and conditions contained in the Accession Partnership with the Republic of Turkey', *Official Journal of the European Communities*, 24 March.
—— (2003) 'Council decision of 19 May 2003 on the principles, priorities, intermediate objectives and conditions contained in the Accession Partnership with Turkey', *Official Journal of the European Communities*, 12 June.
Gamble, A. M. (1984) 'This lady is not for turning: Thatcherism mark III', *Marxism Today*, June.
Güveloğlu, N. (2003) 'A democratisation project in the age of neoliberalism: the historical specificity of the TÜSIAD reports', Master's thesis, Middle East Technical University, Ankara.
—— (2004) 'Demokrasinin neo-liberal çagda geçirdigi dönüsümün siyasal partiler üzerindeki etkileri', *Praksis*, 12.
Güzelsari, S. (2003) 'Küresel kapitalizmin anayasası: GATS', *Praksis*, 9.
Huntington, S. P. (1991) 'Democracy's third wave', *Journal of Democracy*, 2:2.
Jessop, B. (1990) *State theory: putting the capitalist state in its place*, Pennsylvania.
—— (1991) 'On the originality, legacy, and actuality of Nicos Poulantzas', *Studies in Political Economy*, 34.
—— (2003) 'From Thatcherism to New Labour: neo-liberalism, workfarism, and labour market regulation', http://www.comp.lancs.ac.uk/sociology/soc131rj.pdf (accessed 28 August 2003).
Kennedy, K. and Joseph, J. (2001) 'The erosion of party politics in Britain', *New Political Science*, 23:2.
McFaul, M. (2001) 'A mixed record, an uncertain future', *Journal of Democracy*, 12:4.
European Union (2003) National Programme for the Adoption of the Acquis, http://europa.eu.int/comm/enlargement/turkey/pdf/npaa_full.pdf (accessed 10 January 2004).
Oktay, A. (1996) 'Tarih ve siyaset', *Milliyet*, 5 December.
Ollman, B. (1993) *Dialectical investigations*, London.
Önis, Z. and Türem, U. (2001) 'Business, globalization and democracy: a comparative analysis of Turkish business associations', *Turkish Studies*, 2:2.
Panitch, L. (1998) 'The state in a changing world: social democratizing global capitalism', *Monthly Review*, 50:5.

Poulantzas, N. (1975) *Political power and social classes*, London.

—— (2000) *State, power and socialism*, London.

Sayer, A. (1992) *Method in social science: a relational approach*, London.

Schmitter, P. C. (1994) 'Dangers and dilemmas of democracy', *Journal of Democracy*, 5:2.

Shevtsova, L. F. and Eckert, M. H. (2001) 'Russia's hybrid regime', *Journal of Democracy*, 12:4.

Sussman, G. and Galizio, L. (2003) 'The global reproduction of American politics', *Political Communication*, 20:3.

Tünay, M. (2002) 'Türk yeni saginin hegemonya girisimi', *Praksis*, 5.

TÜSIAD (1997) *Perspectives on democracy and democratisation in Turkey*, TÜSIAD, Istanbul.

—— (1999) *Perspectives on democratisation in Turkey – progress report 1999 – Executive Summary*, Istanbul.

—— (2001a) *Perspectives on democratisation in Turkey – progress report 2001 – Executive Summary*, Istanbul.

—— (2001b) *'Perspectives on democratisation in Turkey' and 'EU Copenhagen political criteria' – views and priorities*, Istanbul.

—— (2002) *Türkiye'de isgücü piyasası ve issizlik*, Istanbul.

Williamson, J. (2000) 'What should the World Bank think about the Washington consensus?', *The World Bank Research Observer*, 15:2.

Wood, E. M. (1994) 'A tale of two democracies', *History Today*, 44:5.

Yalman, G. (2002) 'The Turkish state and bourgeoisie in historical perspective: a relativist paradigm or a panoply of hegemonic strategies?' in N. Balkan and S. Savran (eds), *The politics of permanent crisis: the state, class and ideology in Turkey*, New York.

Zabci, F. Ç. (2000) 'Küresellesmenin demokrasi makyaji', *Mülkiye*, 24:220.

8

Strange company? Organised labour and the politics of liberalisation in India

Michael Gillan

Introduction

In 2001–3, the Government of India, in response to intensified demands from both domestic and international capital, attempted to advance India's programme of economic liberalisation by launching a 'second generation' of economic reforms. In particular, the government signalled that there would be action in the controversial policy areas of public sector 'disinvestment' and the comprehensive restructuring of labour regulation. The rationale for this agenda was explicit: the need to pursue totemic neo-liberal goals such as 'labour market flexibility' in order to attract greater levels of foreign and domestic investment and to promote 'international competitiveness' in the context of India's intensified integration with the global economy.[1]

This chapter examines the political response of major national trade union organisations to these initiatives, arguing that central Indian trade union organisations have mounted defensive and selectively coordinated campaigns that have been relatively successful in delaying the implementation of 'second generation' labour market reforms. In particular, the chapter will detail, through a narrative strategy, the interventions of central trade unions in regard to several policy announcements. In 2001, the National Democratic Alliance (NDA) government, led by the Hindu nationalist Bharatiya Janata Party (BJP), signalled an intention to introduce a series of changes designed to reshape employment security provisions for workers in the organised sector[2] and to intensify a program for divesting central government controlled enterprises. In mid-2002, the Second National Commission on Labour, formed by the NDA-BJP government in 1999 to set out a comprehensive agenda for 'reforming' labour regulation, delivered a report that also recommended changes to the entitlements and security provisions of organised sector workers. Each major policy reform initiative was met with effective resistance from central trade union organisations which were able to utilise the coalitional nature of the government and their own institutional linkages to national politics to delay or derail the implementation of these reform drives.

The labour movement in India confronts new waves of management-driven flexibility initiatives at enterprise level and an increasingly hostile institutional and policy environment. These developments are facilitated by a reoriented state, all of which signals that while central trade unions continue to defend formal legislated rights, there is a discernible weakening of trade union vitality and political agency at the grassroots (Roychowdhury 2003). Moreover, while the institutional linkages between central trade unions and major political parties in India offer inroads into national policy making processes, these affiliations can also pose acute political dilemmas. In particular, this chapter will consider the rise of the right wing Hindu nationalist affiliated Bharatiya Mazdoor Sangh (BMS) as one of India's largest (officially recognised) central trade unions and the strategic role that this organisation played in opposing various aspects of the NDA-BJP liberalisation program. The institutional and political influence of the BMS during the term of the NDA-BJP government (1999–2004) at times placed Left trade union organisations in 'strange company' in responding to liberalisation. An effective response must include a clear commitment to ideological and organisational renewal, with a particular emphasis upon trade union organisation among 'informal' sector workers.

The politics of economic liberalisation in India

In 1991, a Congress party government presided over a decisive shift in India's economic development strategy. It accepted an IMF (International Monetary Fund) sponsored loan and embarked upon an accompanying programme of economic liberalisation. Among other policy measures, the liberalisation programme signalled the gradual removal of protectionist trade barriers, the deregulation of domestic production, the promotion of foreign investment and the pursuit of long-term policy goals such as financial sector restructuring, governmental fiscal restraint and public sector 'disinvestment' (Jenkins 1999). Following on from tentative moves towards liberalisation in the 1980s, the new programme, in total, represented a historic move way from the interventionist Nehruvian 'nation-building' economic paradigm of the post-independence era.

After the 1991 General Elections and the launch of the liberalisation programme, three major political formations alternated in government. The first of these was a Congress government led by Narasimha Rao, which managed, through a range of pragmatic political manoeuvres, to serve a full term in office from 1991 to 1996. The most prominent feature of this government's term were the aforementioned economic liberalisation initiatives and the ongoing electoral decline and organisational decay of the Congress party (Yadav 1999). After a fleeting, ill-fated attempt by the Hindu nationalist BJP to assume power after the 1996 national elections, the Congress government was succeeded by a 'United Front' coalition of (primarily) regional parties between 1996 and 1998. Notably, despite internal organisational divisions and squabbling over central government economic and political concessions, the United Front continued, and, in many ways, intensified the process of economic liberalisation initiated by the Congress party.

After the collapse of the United Front government, several of the regional political forces formerly contained within this coalition transferred their support to a more accommodating and seemingly centrist BJP. As a result, two successive national elections in 1998 and 1999 saw the BJP, in alliance with a number of smaller parties and regionally based politicians, emerge as a new governing national coalition (Gillan 2001). After 1999, the BJP was able to stabilise this government, although the relatively fragile and diverse nature of the coalition meant that it was susceptible to sectional and regional demands and that its agenda for governance was constrained in significant ways (McGuire 2002).

Aside from the rise of the BJP, one outcome of the decline of the Congress party has been a trend towards 'regionalisation'. As a result, it is at this level that changing patterns of political and economic competition are taking place (Rangarajan 1999; Yadav 1999). In particular, under the new policy paradigm of liberalisation, State control over investment and production has eased a situation that has intensified competition between different states competing for foreign and domestic investment (Rudolph and Rudolph 2001). As noted by Lloyd and Susanne Rudolph, this led to media 'iconisation' of individuals such as Chandrababu Naidu, the former chief minister of the southern state of Andhra Pradesh (Rudolph and Rudolph 2001) known for his populist style, technocratic posturing and commitment to neo-liberal economics. The implications for labour of the reorientation of the State are often starker at a regional level as state governments, including ostensibly social democratic/communist governments in several regions, seek to create 'investment friendly' business climates by promoting stable patterns of industrial relations and 'flexible' labour markets.[3]

Overall, although the relative pace of reform has varied, every successive central government has, in a range of ways, extended and deepened the process of global integration. Despite obvious instabilities in terms of party political regimes, there has been a remarkable degree of *stability* in terms of the broad direction of economic policy (Gillan 2001). In large measure, this has reflected the gravitation of each successive government to the largest and most powerful sections of domestic capital and an influential, and largely urban, upper middle class population who have mobilised behind the liberalisation programme.[4] At the same time, there has also been evident debate and political resistance by the labour movement to specific liberalisation policy measures. These include reduced State subsidies and fiscal restraint, regulatory restructuring (particularly in key sectors such as power and insurance), public sector disinvestment and industry wide tariff reductions (Jenkins 1999). The multiparty, multi-regional and, at broader level, multi-class nature of national governance and coalition politics in India allows for some capacity for organised actors to intervene in policy formation and implementation, although the fragmented nature of this resistance has acted against a more fundamental shift in state policy objectives.[5] Notably, however, the results of the 2004 general elections in India revealed an apparent popular backlash against neo-liberal policy settings, particularly at regional level, which at least offer the possibility of a partial reorientation of State developmental and policy priorities (Chandrasekhar 2004).

Flexibility frustrated? Regulatory restructuring and 'second generation' labour reforms

The most striking contextual feature of labour relations in India is the enormous size of the informal or 'unorganised' sector, with only around eight per cent of workers in India falling within the purview of the formal economy. The structure of the labour market, in the context of retreating state intervention and intensified competition, thus applies unique pressures on workers and trade union representatives within the organised sector who seek to defend their relatively (as compared with unorganised sector workers) regulated and protected status (Breman 1999: 34–7).

These pressures have intensified with a general employment crisis in the 1990s. Although unemployment and underemployment are regionally differentiated and while there has been an expansion in private sector employment, large-scale closures in the public sector and limited growth in manufacturing and agricultural jobs has consigned millions in the labour market to unemployment or intermittent forms of casual or part-time employment. Overall, the annual average rate of employment growth between 1993 and 1994 and 1999 and 2000 fell to 1.07 per cent (from 2.7 per cent between 1983 and 1993–94) with 26.58 million officially unemployed persons at the end of the same period (Muralidharan 2003).

Clearly, moves to sell off or close so-called 'sick' (loss making) public sector enterprises are one of the features of the liberalisation programme with the greatest implications for workers in the organised sector. Throughout the 1990s, there were attempts by various national coalition governments to address this issue by signalling a range of closures, launching voluntary retirement schemes (VRS) to escape legal restrictions on retrenchments, and by decentralising managerial structures and, accordingly, the bargaining process (Bhattacherjee 1999). Nonetheless, the fate of the public sector enterprises has continued to generate intense political controversy and restructuring or closures were delayed by internal divisions within the BJP led coalition government and external criticisms over the pace and scope of the process (Mayer 2002). In this respect, the relatively high level of unionisation in public sector enterprises and strategic sectors of the economy have allowed trade unions to continue to exert influence in delaying and directing the reform process. At the same time, there has also been an evident structural shift in terms of bargaining relationships and the vitality of collective actors with the onset of liberalisation.[6] Increasingly, management has taken the initiative and demonstrated greater autonomy and enhanced power in various industries and at workplace level in driving changes to work practices. A growing number of workdays have been lost through managerial lockouts rather than union initiated strike actions (see Table 8.1).

Managers in the organised sector have also pushed for enhanced 'flexibility' at enterprise level by outsourcing a greater proportion of production to the informal sector and small to medium enterprises. This trend has been particularly evident in labour intensive industries and companies operating in the consumer non-durable

Table 8.1 Days lost to strikes and lockouts (in millions)

Year	Public sector	Private sector	Strike	Lockout	Total
1991	4.14	22.28	12	14	26.43
1992	1.92	29.23	15	16	31.26
1993	2.29	18.01	6	15	20.30
1994	1.32	19.67	7	14	20.98
1995	4.79	11.50	6	11	16.29
1996	3.15	17.13	8	12	20.28
1997	2.18	14.79	6	11	16.97
1998	7.58	14.79	9	13	22.06
1999	1.18	25.61	11	16	26.79
2000	10.68	18.08	12	17	28.76
2001	2.02	21.74	6	18	23.77
2002 (Provisional: Jan.–Sept.)	0.19	6.02	1.40	4.82	6.21

Source: Government of India, Ministry of Labour, Annual Report 2002–3.

sector (Bhattacherjee 2001). Flexibility measures, while far from uniform in terms of their frequency and implementation, have included labour hire via intermediaries in order to escape restrictive aspects of labour law, and new contract provisions increasing managerial discretion. These include wage freezes for limited employment guarantees, agreements to suspend industrial action, and productivity-linked wage agreements (Sen Gupta and Sett 2000: 148–9; Venkata Ratnam 1995: 288–9).

The dichotomy between organised and unorganised workers, a general employment crisis, public sector restructuring, initiatives to enhance managerial prerogative and the structural position of trade unions and trade union federations are at the heart of the contemporary debate over the reform of the legislative framework of labour relations in India. The debate has produced a range of policy proscriptions, from a radically deregulated, decentralised and individualised form of enterprise level bargaining to the introduction of a semi-autonomous industrial relations commission to balance conflicting interests and oversee a common national regulatory framework (Sen Gupta and Sett 2000).

The underlying justification and rationale for these changes is the imperative of intensified global and domestic competition, and the concomitant neo-liberal demand for increased labour flexibility. Domestic capital is far from monolithic in its response to liberalisation. A significant section of industrial capital, for example, demanded a phased integration into the global economy to allow for the necessary 'breathing space' to secure competitive parity (Lakha 2002). Nevertheless, there is a notable degree of consensus as to the broad thrust of economic policy, a consensus that is particularly evident in the area of industrial relations and labour regulation. In particular, leading industrial houses and employer lobby groups (Confederation of Indian Industries, Federation of Indian Chambers of Commerce and Industry) have sought to advance an agenda for re-regulating labour relations and employment security provisions (Muralidharan 2003). While capital has made numerous advances in its pursuit of flexibility gains and restructuring initiatives within the organised sector, at a formal level these gains have largely failed to translate into a restructured regulatory framework and a faster pace of public sector disinvestment (Mayer 2002). As Roychowdhury notes there are apparent tensions given 'a legal framework that continues to protect labour, while political-economy realities underlie a certain disempowerment of organised labour' (2003: 32).

Central trade unions: campaigns, strategic coordination and political imperatives

Historically, the provisions of colonial labour legislation allowed for union proliferation and fragmentation in India and the need for access to state institutions and political patronage at both regional and central level fostered close linkages between national trade union federations and major political parties (Bhattacherjee 1999, 2001). The All India Trade Union Congress (AITUC) and the Centre for Indian Trade Unions (CITU) are two of India's largest, although regionally concentrated, trade union bodies and have direct institutional linkages with India's two main communist parties – the Communist Party of India and the Communist Party of India (Marxist). The Indian National Trade Union Congress (INTUC) is closely linked to the Congress party and, in line with Congress economic policy, has adopted a more accommodating position on issues related to economic restructuring (Bhattacherjee 2001). Finally, the aforementioned BMS is affiliated with Hindu nationalist politics and has offered both support for the BJP as the political wing of the wider movement and, as later sections will discuss, pointed criticism of the economic policy approach adopted by the BJP in government (Gillan 2001). Candland has noted that 'the principal source of the political strength of the Indian trade union movement – its relationship to the major political parties – is also its principal source of shopfloor weakness' (2001: 85). Indeed, the collective response of central trade unions to the liberalisation programme has been characterised by union fragmentation at enterprise level that often works to the advantage of management and ongoing political rivalry at a national level.

The Left central trade unions (CITU, AITUC, Hind Mazdoor Sabha (HMS)) have banded together under the organisational umbrella of the 'Sponsoring Committee of Trade Unions' to campaign against liberalisation (*The Hindu* 1 January 2001). However, INTUC and the BMS have consistently avoided strikes and joint campaigns. In part, these strategic responses mirror party alignments, adjustments and compromises at a national level in a time of coalition building politics. Despite historic divisions, the left/social democratic parties and unions have found it necessary to find some ground for co-operation to survive as actors in national politics. The two major parties and their trade union affiliates, in seeking to become pre-eminent, project their separate political character and organisational identity (Muralidharan 2003). At the same time, the extent of the neo-liberal policy offensive against organised labour has also made necessary a greater degree of coordination between the central trade unions since the 1990s. This has been particularly evident in regard to combined lobbying activity on restructuring and disinvestment in public sector enterprises and central government policy settings. As later sections will discuss, such lobbying activities and concerted central trade union campaigns have been relatively successful in achieving short-term delays in the realisation of restructuring initiatives. Nonetheless, even the public statements of trade union leaders convey a sense of fighting a somewhat desperate rearguard action since 1991 to delay and reshape privatisation initiatives and regulatory restructuring. According to Gurudas Das Gupta, general secretary of the AITUC, while the general political climate for trade unions is 'hostile':

> The attack has intensified but the resistance has also increased. We have not been able to reverse the policies, but some decisions of the government have been put on hold. The privatisation of NALCO [National Aluminium Company] has been deferred; the Bill proposing the dilution of government stake in banks has been deferred; and the proposed Bill for the privatisation of the existing coal mines has also been stalled.

Such defensive campaigns since the 1990s have been based largely around the ability of trade union organisations such as AITUC and CITU to mobilise members for mass demonstrations, engage in limited strike actions and to utilise India's news media to exert pressure on government. Possibly the most impressive example of direct mobilisation was a one day strike against privatisation and the government's labour policy held in April 2002 in which millions of public sector employees and workers from ports, insurance and banking industries participated across the nation (*The Hindu* 17 April 2002). While such mobilisations have been important demonstrations of strength, several union leaders also recognised a general failure to extend their activities into the informal/unorganised sector and to coordinate resistance given the plurality of representative trade union organisations. (There is a move to dilute labour laws, 2003.)

Moreover, the organisational affiliations and ideological character of the Hindu nationalist aligned BMS also pose an intrinsically *political* dilemma for the broader labour movement in seeking to develop an appropriate response to liberalisation. Indian trade unions are often depicted as isolated or weakening in their influence and membership growth, bur the BMS has made gains in both respects over the last two decades. Controversially, it secured official recognition as India's largest national trade union centre. There is a paucity of detailed information as to the organising and recruitment strategies, membership structure and sectoral spread of the BMS and these matters require further empirical research.[7] While there is likely to have been considerable over-reporting of growth, the general membership of the BMS appears to have grown substantially during the 1990s, a trend very much in accordance with the rapid growth in the membership of the BJP and affiliated Hindu nationalist organisations throughout India. The BMS claims its membership more than doubled between 1990 and 2002 (to a total of 7.6 million members) and that the number of its local union affiliates increased from around 3,000 to 5,000 during the same period.[8]

The BMS is unique in that it is embedded in the Rashtriya Swayamsevak Sangh (RSS), an organisation that coordinates a broad 'family' of Hindu nationalist organisations in civil society.[9] The BMS originated from the strategic decision of the RSS to launch several organisations in the 1950s in order to expand the scope of Hindu nationalist influence in public life. By the 1990s, the BMS had developed a membership base among central and regional government employees (particularly in BJP-ruled states) in the insurance, banking and defence sectors, and with workers in mining and engineering enterprises, typically within the public sector (Saxena 1993). Throughout the 1990s and into the twenty-first century the BMS has further extended its influence across a number of sectors and regions. Growth has been, in part, facilitated by the deepening political and institutional influence of the BJP and the RSS at the Centre and in a number of key states in Northern India.

Direct linkages between the RSS and the BMS are apparent in the ideological and policy formulations of the latter organisation. BMS draws on organicist notions of 'integral humanism' developed by the RSS and that the nation, defined in ethno-religious terms, precedes 'sectional' interests including both labour and capital. As a result, the BMS has traditionally rejected 'conflict based' understandings of society and has typically been reluctant to join in industrial action or sustained militant workplace activity. The BMS explicitly rejects the idea of class conflict. This is depicted as a 'foreign' ideology, instead espousing the need for a mutual recognition of 'dharma' (duty) in the workplace and an imagined future of industrial harmony through shared belief in Hindu nationalist ideology, national unity and constructive co-operation between labour and capital (Saxena 1993). The reluctance of the BMS to become involved in a joint action with other trade union centres is also, in part, an indication of the intense ideological aversion on the part of the BMS and the RSS to the Indian Left. The BMS's paternalistic conceptualisation of labour relations and organicist understanding of Indian society are also evident in its official policy pronouncements. Indeed, many of these positions appear to endorse the notion of trade unions as willing participants in 'enterprise partnerships' that ultimately work towards the greater good of the Indian (Hindu) nation.[10]

While the BMS prioritises the need for productive co-operation with national capital, its official policy positions differ markedly on the question of the role and spread of foreign capital within India's economy and society. Indeed, the BMS's misgivings on this question are clearly related to the fact that the presence of foreign investment and employers erodes the very foundations of the formerly discussed notion of an 'industrial family' where sectional interests are dissolved in the face of a resurgent and transcendent Hindu nation. These tensions have also been evident in relation to the BJP, which has pursued a strong neo-liberal economic agenda in government.[11] Both the RSS and affiliated organisations such as the BMS were prominent in an economic nationalist, *swadeshi* (self-reliance) campaign. This opposed the cultural and economic consequences of foreign investment, external economic intervention and the 'consumerist' culture of the West as represented most visibly by the market penetration of multinationals in the consumer goods sector. These campaigns often appeared to contradict the BJP's call for a 'balance' between the demands of the global economy and the gradual development of domestic industrial and economic capacities, a tension which sharpened once the BJP came to power in the late 1990s.[12] Between 2000 and 2003 the divergent views of the BMS and the BJP on liberalisation initiatives were even more evident, a divide that, as the following sections will show, did not preclude the former from using its embedded place within the Hindu nationalist organisational network to influence policy outcomes.

Proposed labour law amendments, 2000–1

In 2000, the NDA-BJP government, and in particular, the Ministry of Finance headed by Yashwant Sinha, signalled an intention to forward the labour 'reform' agenda by forming a working group to draft changes to laws regulating the status of contract labour in the organised sector. The existing provisions of the Contract Labour (Prohibition and Regulation) Act (1970) were designed to abolish contract labour in many jobs and regulate contract labour employment where abolition was not possible. In practice the Act was rarely enforced. However, industry and employer groups demanded that the Act be amended to legitimise the use of contract labour and to abolish provisions that an employee working for a period of 240 days must be absorbed as a permanent employee by the relevant enterprise (*Business Standard* 27 September 2000). With widespread speculation that the government would accede to the demands of industry lobbyists, central trade union organisations combined in a joint delegation to the prime minister. They argued against the replacement of permanent workers with contract labour and for the proposition that contract workers in 'core' areas of production should continue to have some prospect, at least in principle, of gaining permanent status (*The Hindu* 16 August 2000). More specifically, the central trade unions united in demanding extensive consultation rights on the issue of contract labour laws, and their interventions were apparently successful in removing the issue from the immediate policy and legislative agenda of the government in 2000.

In early 2001, Finance Minister Sinha used a Budget speech to reactivate labour reforms by announcing a range of labour law amendments that were depicted as the main components of 'second generation reforms'. Sinha's Budget speech claimed that amendments were necessary to 'address the issue of rigidities in labour laws' and align them with a 'new economic environment' (*The Statesman* 1 March 2001). The speech included proposals to amend the Industrial Disputes Act (IDA) to free up legislative restrictions pertaining to lay-offs, retrenchments and enterprise closures. In particular, Sinha proposed to limit requirements for notifying and obtaining permission from government in order to engage legally in enterprise closure. In this regard, Chapter 5B of the IDA was to be amended to lift the 'ceiling' at which these requirements would come into effect from enterprises with 100 or more workers to enterprises with 1,000 or more workers. Additionally, Sinha proposed the repeal of the Sick Industries and Companies Act (SICA) in order to facilitate greater flexibility in seeking closures and signalled the government's support for the extension of Voluntary Retirement Schemes to facilitate the restructuring of the public sector (*The Statesman* 1 March 2001). In all, these announcements were very much in line with the policy agenda of business lobby groups and the recommendations of the pro-business Economic Advisory Council (*Business Standard* 8 February 2001).

The public response of the central Trade Unions was uniformly vitriolic with the BMS, CITU and HMS labelling the proposals as 'anti worker' and as affording employers virtually unlimited capacity to drive through enterprise closures and retrenchments (*The Statesman* 1 March 2001). There was also evidence of inter-union coordination of the political response to the proposals with S. Reddy, the President of INTUC, claiming that joint discussions were held as to the possibility of forging a unified campaign to defeat the Budget proposals (*The Hindu* 2 March 2001). Ultimately, however, while there was evident ongoing strategic coordination in regard to lobbying activities, CITU and the 'left' trade union centres campaigned under the name of the 'National Platform of Mass Organisations' while INTUC and the BMS ran separate campaigns.

The BMS campaign against the 'Budget' amendments was particularly strident. Despite the extensive and overt lobbying pressure brought to bear by large domestic capital to secure the amendments, there was a very clear emphasis in the BMS campaign on the role of foreign capital – a stress that was entirely in accord with its focus on *swadeshi* economics. In the build up to a mass rally in New Delhi to protest against the government's economic policies, BMS leaders referred to a 'complete sellout to multinationals' and the role of the World Trade Organisation (WTO) in facilitating factory closures, retrenchments and privatisation (*The Times of India* 21 March 2001). These themes were reiterated at the mass rally on 16 April 2001, with Dattopant Thengdi, the founder and senior leader of the BMS, announcing a 'mass movement' against the WTO, the Fund-Bank and the central government for its 'anti-national and anti-people policies' (*The Hindu* 17 April 2001). In addition to referring to the finance minister as a 'criminal', Thengdi issued a direct challenge to the BJP led government stating that 'we will oppose the Government, which opposes the interests of the nation, people and its workers. We oppose multinationals. We will oppose the Government which support multinationals' (*The Hindu* 17 April 2001).

The intensity of this criticism from within the Hindu nationalist 'family' of organisations had an immediate political impact with the Prime Minister, A. B. Vajpayee, forced to defend publicly the reform programme (*The Statesman* 18 April 2001). Moreover, reports of a meeting of the parliamentary wing of the BJP suggested that party members became alarmed by these developments and pressured the finance minister to develop 'people friendly' policy signals (*The Statesman* 18 April 2001). By May 2001, *The Times of India* noted that the government had failed to table the proposed amendments and 'now appeared to be soft-pedalling labour market reforms' (*The Times of India* 1 May 2001). There were clear divisions within Cabinet ranks. The Labour Minister S. Jatiya reported to favour delaying the amendments, suggesting that there would be no changes to the IDA or the Contract Labour Act without extensive consultation with trade unions through tripartite bodies and direct dialogue (*The Hindu* 13 May 2001). Notably, these conciliatory gestures came after a joint meeting between Jatiya, Vajpayee, and central trade union leaders (BMS, CITU, HMS, AITUC, INTUC) (*The Hindu* 13 May 2001).

The effect of the BMS campaign and pressure from within the Hindu nationalist fold was also evident. Vajpayee met senior RSS leaders (H. V. Seshadri and M. G. Vaidya) to discuss the party's concerns about the damaging public attacks on serving ministers (Sinha) and the mass campaign launched against the government's economic policy (*The Statesman* 17 May 2001). At the same time, the BMS campaign continued unabated. The BMS President, H. Dave, served notice of an (unusual) intention to strike should the government open up defence industries to foreign investment. He predicted that the NDA-BJP government 'would fall under its own weight' if it continued to pursue 'anti-national' and 'anti-labour' policies (*The Times of India* 17 May 2001). The cumulative effect of these interventions was evident at the 2001 Indian Labour Conference, an annual tripartite forum. Here, despite the public defence of the need for labour reforms, central trade union leaders received an assurance that amendments to the IDA and the Contract Labour Act would not be introduced in the forthcoming session of Parliament. Moreover, in accordance with their demands, the BMS indicated that the implementation of amendments was to be suspended until the findings of the Second National Commission on Labour were released (*The Hindu* 19 May 2001).

The Second National Commission On Labour report (2002)

In seeking to advance reforms, the BJP-led coalition government formed the Second National Commission on Labour (henceforth NCL) in 1999 as an advisory body to advance a comprehensive agenda for labour in India. The formation of this body, only the second such national commission since independence, reflected both the need to gain practical policy suggestions and to serve strategic political interests by distancing the government from the process of formulating specific policy recommendations (Rajalakshmi 2002a). Nonetheless, there was considerable controversy over the membership composition of the NCL, which was heavily weighted towards BJP sympathisers drawn from industry and civil society (*The Times of India* 20 May 1999). Left unions complained of their exclusion and INTUC demanded (and subsequently was granted) representation on the commission along with the BMS. Notably, the NCL also included a representative from an informal sector organisation (Ela Bhatt, the founder of the Self Employed Women's Association) (*The Hindu* 4 November 1999). This was a highly strategic inclusion given that differences in status and social protection between organised and unorganised sector workers was a crucial component in the public legitimation of a 'reform' agenda.

As such, the stated objective of the NCL was to develop a series of policy objectives that would allow for rationalising labour laws in the organised sector and extending minimum employment protection in the unorganised sector. An overriding concern for the NCL was to consider the implications of 'globalised' economic development in India and recommend specific policy measures to facilitate enhanced competitiveness. According to the NCL report's terms of reference there was a need to consider:

the globalisation of the economy and liberalisation of trade and industry; the rapid changes in technology and their consequences and ramifications; the effects that these changes were likely to have on the nature and structure of industry, on methods and places of production, on employment and the skills necessary to retain employability and mobility; and the responses that are necessary to acquire and retain economic efficiency and international competitiveness.

While the report also recognised the need to 'ensure a minimum level of protection and welfare to labour' (Second National Commission On Labour 2002a: 6). The priority on restructuring labour regulation to facilitate competitiveness was clear.

The final recommendations of the NCL report were handed down in June 2002. The NCL report suggested the rationalisation and consolidation of the existing legislative framework into a single 'Labour Management Relations Law'. Specifically, this would entail the consolidation of a complex web of law largely inherited from colonial rule under the Trade Unions Act (1926), Industrial Employment Act (1946) and the Industrial Disputes Act (1947) (Second National Commission On Labour 2002b: 38).

As expected, the most contentious changes signalled by the report were changes to existing legislative restrictions on retrenchment procedures and requirements for central government approval for enterprise closures. In particular, the implications of the NCL report recommendations were that government notification would only be required in rare circumstances and would only apply for a limited duration in enterprises employing three hundred or more workers (National Commission On Labour 2002b: 43–5). In relation to the stalled 2001 'Budget' amendment proposals, this was a more moderate position yet trade unions estimated that the new ceiling would exclude around sixty per cent of workers in organised sector enterprises from the provisions (*The Economic Times* 30 June 2002). Moreover, in terms of retrenchment procedures, the report recommended that restrictions on the basis of enterprise size and type should be removed, allowing for virtually unrestricted managerial prerogative to lay off workers at enterprise level (Second National Commission On Labour, 2002b: 44).

The report also recommended a 'flexible' approach to weekly working hours and fixed holidays. It drew a distinction between the deployment of labour in 'core' and 'non-core' activities, arguing that competition and seasonal fluctuations in demand required the use of temporary or outsourced labour, which could then legally be used to meet non-core demands (Second National Commission On Labour 2002b: 47–8). Not surprisingly, the problem of distinguishing between what were core and non-core activities was evaded, although, given increasing outsourcing to the informal sector and casualisation, the recommendation appeared to be a partial legitimation of already common practices in many enterprises (Rajalakshmi 2002a).

The report supported an ongoing role for trade unions in collective bargaining but envisioned a more constrained and defined role for unions as workplace intermediaries. The report suggested that the new legislative framework contain provisions and procedures for the appointment of approved 'negotiating agents'. These required the support of sixty-six per cent of all employees to entitle a union to act as a single negotiating agent to bargain with management and settle industrial disputes at enterprise level (Second National Commission On Labour 2002b: 41). The existing legislative framework was regarded as facilitating union proliferation (but not necessarily recognition from employers), and thus the NCL report suggested that unions must have at least ten per cent of all employees as members in order to represent workers in various forums. Significantly, the report also suggested new measures designed to limit the ability of unions to launch legal strike actions, including the introduction of strike ballots (Second National Commission On Labour 2002b: 40). The implications of these recommendations were that the legitimacy of limited collective bargaining and union representation at enterprise level would continue but that union operation and agency would be curtailed in relation to management prerogative.

In terms of the stated requirement to ensure a 'minimum level of protection and welfare' the report recommended that contract workers should be afforded permanent status after a period of two years. It stipulated that export processing zones should not be exempted from the reconstituted labour legislation – recommendations that drew praise from otherwise harsh critics (Rajalakshmi 2002a). Moreover, in accordance with the terms of reference, the report found that various 'social security' measures (health and pension benefits) should be extended to the unorganised sector, although the funding, implementation and enforcement of these minimal welfarist protections was largely unexplored (Second National Commission On Labour 2002b: 74–5).

In sum, the NCL report represented the most comprehensive proposal for restructuring the legislative framework of labour relations in India in the post-independence era. While recognising the legitimacy of collective bargaining and the need for minimal protections, the broad thrust of the report was squarely in line with neo-liberal economic orthodoxy and employer demands for greater labour flexibility at enterprise level in meeting the imperatives of international competition. Accordingly, the BJP-led coalition government warmly received the NCL report with the labour minister and the prime minister supporting the broad reform agenda laid out by the report. Claiming that workers interests would be 'safeguarded' while meeting the demands of industrial efficiency and global competition (*The Hindu* 30 June 2002), the government signalled an intention to move forward reform legislation based on the NCL in the next available session of parliament (*The Telegraph* 10 September 2002).

In response, leading central trade union organisations such as the CITU and the AITUC responded with intense hostility to several of the recommendations of the NCL report. In line with past campaigns, they concentrated their opposition on the proposed changes to employment security protections and the legitimation of the use of contract workers in core and non-core areas of production (AITUC 2002). These criticisms were echoed by significant sections of the Congress party aligned with INTUC, despite the fact that the INTUC president, S. Reddy, was a prominent member of the commission and an advocate of the broad thrust of the proposed reforms (Second NCL Report Submitted 2002). The sharpest, and for the BJP-led government, the most politically uncomfortable, attack on the NCL report came from BMS trade union leaders who described the report as 'anti-labour'.

Indeed, while the BMS also participated in the NCL it insisted on attaching a detailed rebuttal of the major findings and recommendations of the report in a formal 'note of dissent' (Rajalakshmi 2002a).

Contestation over the NCL reform agenda was also a prominent feature of the 2002 Indian Labour Conference. While tripartism in India has been historically characterised as 'atrophied' (Venkata Ratnam 1995) the Indian Labour Conference serves as a symbolic annual meeting point at which the largest industry groups and employer federations discuss labour issues with leading trade union centres and the central and regional state bureaucracy. The 2002 Labour Conference was characterised by an unusual degree of acrimony (Rajalakshmi 2002b). While the government and employer confederations attempted to shift the NCL reform agenda to the forefront of debate and urged participants to support new flexibility provisions, the major trade union bodies united to insist that a separate tripartite meeting would be required to consider the recommendations.

In the year after the NCL and the Indian Labour Conference, the major left trade union centres intensified their mass based political campaigns and industrial actions against the government's restructuring agenda. They organised; for example, a mass march on the national parliament in February 2003 and a one-day strike in May (*Businessline* 3 February 2003; *The Times of India* 22 May 2003). While the BMS refused to support these actions and remained somewhat distanced from other labour organisations, it continued to denounce and lobby against the major features of the proposed reform agenda. Again, the cumulative effect of these campaigns resulted in an implicit understanding that legislative amendments and the implementation of the NCL would be suspended until the conclusion of the 2004 general elections.

Conclusion

In 2000–3, the renewed efforts of the BJP-NDA government to introduce policy changes in order to advance labour market flexibility goals largely failed to translate into substantive action. The labour movement in India was thus relatively successful in obstructing a radical restructuring of labour regulation for organised sector workers. Direct political linkages between unions and major national parties are a potential source of influence over the actual implementation of policy. Trade unions have also been able to exploit the fact that the multiparty character of coalition government creates political vulnerability to coordinated campaigns on controversial aspects of the liberalisation agenda – particularly in regard to employment security issues. This can be interpreted as evidence of the success of central trade union organisations as political agents (separately and collectively).

At a broader level, however, many of these initiatives were more likely delayed rather than decisively defeated and the apparent success of such campaigns at national level often masks the eroding position of trade unions at enterprise level, particularly in public sector units (Roychowdhury 2003). While the defensive nature of such campaigns are doubtless a matter of necessity, imperatives to develop and project coherent policy alternatives to the neo-liberal consensus and to reclaim a degree of strategic advantage through organising and campaign offensives are perhaps lost. This is most evident in relation to expanding the presence and relevance of established trade unions among informal sector workers. As Jan Breman (2001) has noted, the failure to organise the unorganised has been a 'historic blunder' on the part of an overly bureaucratised and static trade union movement in India, a failure that now haunts the attempts of organised sector workers to defend their basic employment and security entitlements.

The need to engage in defensive 'rear-guard' actions and coordinate lobbying activities perhaps neglects the serious political and organisational implications of the membership growth of the Bharatiya Mazdoor Sangh among organised (and, purportedly, unorganised) workers and its increasing institutional influence through a representative role within tripartite bodies. On the one hand, the BMS appeared to play a significant role in delaying and mediating state policy initiatives. On the other, the BMS remains an intrinsically ultra-nationalist trade union that is historically averse to industrial conflict and committed to enterprise partnership (with domestic capital). It is also organically linked to the network of social and political organisations that make up the Hindu nationalist movement in India.[13] Clearly, there has been a link between the rise of the BMS and the centrality of the Hindu nationalist movement to a reoriented state in the 1990s. The 2004 general (Lok Sabha) elections, however, weakened the structural influence of the BJP and the broader Hindu nationalist 'family', and may allow an opportunity for the labour movement to present a more cohesive and conjoined political challenge to both authoritarian-communal politics and neo-liberal policy prescriptions.

The defeat of the BJP-NDA in that election was also especially significant for the labour movement in that the polls resulted in the defeat of several prominent pro-reform governments in southern India (most notably, in Andhra Pradesh).[14] The hitherto moribund Congress Party was unexpectedly swept back into national office in May 2004 through an effective strategy of forging electoral alliances with regional parties, thereby benefiting from anti-incumbent voter sentiment in several key states.[15] After the election a new 'United Progressive Alliance' (UPA) coalition government was formed by the Congress. Crucially, the new government relied on parliamentary support from the major parties of the Indian Left, the Communist Party of India (Marxist) and the Communist Party of India, which nonetheless did so from 'outside' by refusing to participate directly in the new government. The results of the 2004 elections, therefore, appear to have not only averted the reforms to labour law previously proposed (and postponed) by the BJP-NDA but created some space, particularly for Left trade unions, to shape policy agendas in national politics. This was evident in the post-poll period. Unions and the Left influence was exercised in relation to both desired (an employment guarantee scheme, strengthening tripartite consultation, guaranteeing the right to strike) and undesired (reformulated 'flexibility' initiatives; public sector privatisation; interest rate reductions for employee provident funds) policy agendas.

However, Jenkins (1999) has argued that India's liberalisation program advanced in the 1990s in spite of varying political configurations. This has been achieved by competition between the states within the Indian federation and by a 'politics of stealth' in the introduction and political representation of reforms. The UPA government has periodically provided public reassurances and signals to the markets that the liberalisation programme will proceed, an approach likely to create tension with the Left and coalition partners over the implementation of the Common Minimum Programme (CMP) (Tripathi 2004). Tactically, the challenge confronting the labour movement may not be the central trade unions' capacity to defeat the 'second generation' of liberalisation. Rather, the main challenge may be the unions' capacity to mediate and delay the 'reform' process to create the necessary space to reconstruct a stronger movement capable of challenging the foundations of the neo-liberal consensus.

Notes

1 Typical of neo-liberal advocates of 'reform' is the view that for India to become 'an attractive destination for FDI [foreign direct investment] and a major platform for labour-intensive manufacturing exports, reforms in labour laws and exit policies are extremely essential' (Bajpai, 2002).

2 Hensman (2001: 6–7) defines the organised sector in India as denoting 'enterprises covered by the Factories Act, which applies to units with electrical power employing ten workers or more, or units without electrical power employing twenty workers or more.' Informal sector workers include a 'small proportion of genuinely self-employed persons' while the majority work for others as rural labourers or contingent labour in urban areas. There are a large number of workers in both the organised private sector and public sector. Those hired through a labour contractor are informal and are unprotected by labour legislation.

3 Moreover, the reorientation of the State is also evident in terms of judicial activism. In particular, a judgement of the Supreme Court in 2003 questioned the fundamental nature of the right to strike under the Indian constitution. Notably, the relevant judgment pertained to a decision by the government of Tamil Nadu to dismiss thousands of public sector employees after the passage of a controversial Tamil Nadu Essential Services Maintenance Act (TESMA) in that state (Venkatesan 2003).

4 As Achin Vanaik (2004) has noted, the orientation towards this 'mass elite' was evident in the BJP/NDA government's 'India Shining' campaign for the 2004 Lok Sabha elections.

5 For Jenkins (1999) federalism and the fragmented nature of the polity allowed for a relatively effective strategy of 'reform by stealth'.

6 Bhattacherjee (2001: 259) has indicated that trade union membership as a percentage of non-agricultural labour fell from 6.6 per cent in 1985 to 5.5 per cent in 1995, and union membership in the organised sector fell from 26.5 per cent to 22.8 per cent during the same period.

7 Saxena (1993) provides one of the few existing studies of the BMS while general studies on the rise of the Hindu nationalist movement in India (Anderson and Damle 1987; Jaffrelot 1996) provide only limited analysis of its historical development and founding leaders.

8 The BMS website (www.bms.org.in/home.htm) (accessed 10 January 2004) also provides details of the reported growth of the union at regional level. The BMS claims to have gained membership in Uttar Pradesh, Madhya Pradesh, Gujarat, Rajasthan, areas that have been bastions of Hindu nationalist politics. There are also claims of rapid growth

in southern and eastern states that have traditionally been dominated by Leftist parties and trade unions.

9 The Hindu Nationalist 'family' (Sangh Parivar) revolves around the Rashtriya Swayamsevak Sangh (RSS), a highly disciplined cadre based organisation that is built around thousands of locally based *shakhas* (units) for recruitment and ideological and physical training throughout India. In addition to the RSS there are a myriad of affiliated organisations including the Vishwa Hindu Parishad (VHP), the Bajrang Dal and the Akhil Bharatiya Vidyarthi Parishad (ABVP).

10 BMS website (www.bms.org.in/home.htm) (accessed 10 January 2004).

11 Nonetheless the BJP has occasionally supported the notion that domestic industry should be allowed a period of 'breathing space' before being exposed to international competition. In this, the party reflected the views of a powerful contingent of domestic industrial houses, often referred to as the 'Bombay club', who complained of an unequal playing field for domestic capital in relation to foreign competition (Gillan 2001; Lakha 2002).

12 These tensions reflected the shift in the class composition of the BJP in the 1990s. The party moved to a wider electoral base in geographical and social terms and as the party membership has expanded through an influx of new supporters from the middle class, particularly in urban areas and among former supporters of the Indian National Congress Party. Hindu nationalist organisations are traditionally most closely associated with the small-scale sector and the petty trading community. This shift and the party's increased proximity to power and various political and big business lobbies led to an internal critique of a general loss of ideological and organisational cohesion.

13 In contrast to international examples of 'social movement unionism', the BMS is aligned with an authoritarian and exclusionary ethno nationalist politics. It is an integral component of a network, which has been characterised as neo-fascist in its ideological and organisational form. For a critique of the association of the Sangh Parivar with fascism see Vanaik (2001).

14 In Andhra Pradesh and Tamil Nadu, regional parties aligned with the BJP-NDA were defeated while in Kerala and Karnataka pro-reform Congress-led governments were removed from office. Suri (2004) surveyed that the post election debate represented an unambiguous rejection of liberalisation policies.

15 Anti-incumbency, however, was not a uniform trend throughout India. On this point and on the complex nature of the 2004 election results see Yadav (2004).

References

AITUC (2002) *Views of national trade union centres [AITUC, CITU, HMS, TUCC, AICCTU and UTUC] on certain important matters covered by 2nd National Labour Commission*, New Delhi.

Anderson, W. and Damle, S. (1987) *The brotherhood in saffron: the Rashtriya Sayamsevak Sangh and Hindu revivalism*, New Delhi.

Bajpai, N. (2002) 'India's unfinished reform agenda-II', *The Hindu*, 18 April.

Bhattacherjee, D. (1999) *Organized labour and economic liberalization in India: past, present and future*, Labour and Society Programme, International Labour Organization. Discussion Paper, DP/105/1999), Geneva.

Bhattacherjee, D. (2001) 'The evolution of Indian industrial relations: A comparative perspective', *Industrial Relations Journal*, 32:3.

Breman, J. (1999) 'The study of industrial labour in post-colonial India. The formal sector: an introductory review', in Parry, J., Breman, J. and Kapadia, K. (eds), *The worlds of Indian industrial labour*, New Delhi.

—— (2001) 'An informalised labour system: end of labour market dualism', *Economic and Political Weekly*, 36: 52, 29 December.

Candland, C. (2001) 'The cost of incorporation: labor institutions, industrial restructuring, and new trade union strategies in India and Pakistan', in Candland, C. and Sil, R. (eds), *The politics of labor in a global age: continuity and change in late-industrializing and post-socialist economies*, Oxford.

Chandrasekhar, C. P. (2004) 'The verdict and the way ahead', *Frontline*, 21:12, 18 June.

Gillan, M. (2001) 'Swadeshi politics in a left dominated state: economic liberalisation and the BJP in West Bengal', *South Asia*, 24:1.

—— (2002) 'Assessing the "national" expansion of Hindu nationalism: the BJP in Southern and Eastern India, 1996–2001', *South Asia*, 25:3.

Hensman, R. (2001) *The impact of globalisation on employment in India and responses from the formal and informal sectors*, IIAS/IISG CLARA Working Paper, No. 15, Amsterdam.

Jaffrelot, C. (1996) *The Hindu nationalist movement in India, 1925 to the 1990s. Strategies of identity-building, implantation and mobilisation (with special reference to Central India)*, New Delhi.

Jenkins, R. (1999) *Democratic politics and economic reform in India*, Cambridge.

Lakha, S. (2002) 'From *Swadeshi* to globalisation: the Bharatiya Janata party's shifting economic agenda', *South Asia*, 25:3.

Mayer, P. (2002) 'The Hindu rate of reform: privatisation under the BJP – still waiting for that "Bada Kadam"', *South Asia*, 25:3.

McGuire, J. (2002) 'The BJP and governance in India: an overview', *South Asia*, 25:3.

Muralidharan, S. (2003) 'Labour and liberalization', *Frontline*, 20:18, 12 September.

Rajalakshmi, T. J. (2002a) 'Loaded against labour', *Frontline*, 19:16, 3 August.

—— (2002b) 'Conflicting class interests', *Frontline*, 19:21, 12 October.

Rangarajan, M. (1999) 'Federal pressures', *Seminar*, 480.

Roychowdhury, S. (2003) 'Public sector restructuring and democracy: the state, labour and trade unions in India', *The Journal of Development Studies*, 39:3.

Rudolph, L. I. and Rudolph, S. H. (2001) 'Iconisation of Chandrababu: sharing sovereignty in India's Federal Market Economy', *Economic and Political Weekly*, 36:18, 5–11 May.

Saxena, K. (1993) 'The Hindu trade union movement in India: The Bharatiya Mazdoor Sangh', *Asian Survey*, 33:7.

Second National Commission on Labour (2002a) *Second National Commission on Labour. Volume 1 Main Report*, New Delhi.

—— (2002b) *Second National Commission on Labour. Volume 2 Conclusions and Recommendations*, New Delhi.

'Second NCL Report Submitted: PM to meet TU leaders' (2002) *Labour file*. www.labourfile.org/labourfile/News%20Update2/News3.htm.

Sen Gupta, A. K. and Sett, P. K. (2000) 'Industrial relations law, employment security and collective bargaining in India: myths, realities and hopes', *Industrial Relations Journal*, 31:2.

Suri, K. C. (2004) 'Democracy, economic reforms and election results in India', *Economic and Political Weekly*, 18 December.

'There is a move to dilute labour laws, Interview with Gurudas Das Gupta, general secretary, AITUC', (2003) *Frontline*, 20:18, 12 September.

Tripathi, P. S. (2004) 'A performance deficit', *Frontline*, 21:20, 25 September.

Vanaik, A. (2001) 'The new Indian right', *New Left Review*, 9.
—— (2004) 'Rendezvous at Mumbai', *New Left Review*, 26.
Venkata Ratnam, C. S. (1995) 'Economic liberalization and the transformation of industrial relations policies in India', in Verma, A., Kochan, T. A. and Lansbury, R. (eds), *Employment relations in the growing Asian economies*, London.
Venkatesan, V. (2003) 'The judicial response', *Frontline*, 20:18, 30 August.
Yadav, Y. (1999) 'The third electoral system', *Seminar*, 480.
—— (2004) 'The elusive mandate of 2004', *Economic and Political Weekly*, 18 December.

Part III
Patterns of resistance across the globe

9
Problems of social movement unionism

Bill Dunn

Introduction

Social movement unionism (SMU) has been proposed as a new strategy for labour. More inclusive and internationalist than established workers' organisations and orientations, it offers the hope of effective resistance even against a highly globalised and postmodern capitalist system.

I recognise the widespread experience of union decline and welcome the examples of broadening struggles and co-operation beyond workplace trade unionism, of cross-border links and moves towards greater union democracy and participation. However, SMU is usually more than a description and general endorsement of such mobilisation. It constitutes a set of proposals about why the new directions are needed and how they can be established. It is these I want to question. In particular, I think labour supporters should be wary of mainstream characterisations of capitalism and more catastrophist depictions of restructuring. These leave few grounds for effective pro-labour strategies. A more careful interpretation of change would also leave room for engagement with lessons from labour's historical experience and with questions of organisation, which tend to be excluded by SMU and theories of radical social transformation.

In the first section I do this in general terms, suggesting that silences on questions of labour action in mainstream theories are not mere oversight but follow from the way they conceive society. Labour supporters should therefore at least reflect critically on these characterisations before taking them as the basis for new orientations. A re-emphasis on subjectivity provides a welcome contrast with descriptions of workers simply as passive victims or bearers of social processes. However, in several influential descriptions this is predicated on a radical change in the nature of society and leads to an outright denial of 'objective' interests – of exploitation and of class. Even without necessarily explicitly repeating these conclusions, some theories of SMU confirm the fundamental novelty of contemporary society and the independence of subjects, which then means avoiding the awkward but still essential questions of how structure and agency are articulated.

In the second and third sections I try to develop this critique more concretely. At the core of SMU is the need for more outward looking agenda to address labour's increasing spatial and social dispersal. The reorientation may be desirable but I argue against notions of 'globalisation' and of an objectively more heterogeneous working class as useful descriptions from which to build labour strategies. They tend to exaggerate local and sectional weaknesses but also the problems of overcoming them. Finally, precisely because labour's situation cannot be understood simply as determined by objective economic change, I argue that we should reflect more critically on questions of its own institutions and ideas and consider how new orientations can be won.

One recurring problem is that SMU means different things to different people. Initially referring to practices in the 'South', of trade unions in South Africa, Brazil and South Korea for example, the concept of SMU became 'broader and vaguer' in moving northwards (Robinson 2000). For some, it is a reform agenda incorporating more activist 'organising models'. For others, these retain too much of the 'old' and a more radical reorientation is required. Some writers emphasise the global, others predominantly national developments. Some writers seek to stabilise capitalism, others to overthrow it. Many scholars would probably repudiate much of the interpretation presented here. However, while apologising for any specific misrepresentation, if I provoke some clarification of what exactly is being proposed and why, this chapter will not have been entirely in vain.

Positioning labour in the postmodern political economy

Many theorists describe how restructuring, the transformation into a 'speeded-up, globalised, postmodern world' (Munck 2002: xi) either promotes, or perhaps more typically requires, social movement unionism as an effective response. Its attractions seem clear, contrasted with conservative business unionism, which forlornly clings to past practices while for ever being undermined by the changeability of contemporary capitalism.

However, assumptions of paradigmatic socio-economic change as the basis for labour's reorientation are potentially problematic. There are huge controversies about 'globalisation' and a whole range of 'post-isms', postmodernism, post-Fordism, post-industrialism, post-Marxism and so on, which cannot be reviewed here. However, for those who see the world as radically transformed, one recurring theme is that the workers' movement is something of a spent force. Labour is more fragmented across space, more socially heterogeneous and ever less motivated by notions of common material interest. Should workers somehow contrive to act on their own behalf, they are unlikely to succeed against an increasingly powerful, flexible capitalism.

For such accounts, neo-liberalism is not simply a project that seeks to remove obstacles to the operation of the market. Such barriers have fallen. The world has become more liberal. There is no alternative, resistance is futile. There is a danger that this sort of message succeeds as ideology, even as it exceeds the material foundations it purports to describe. Such (mis-)use of theory against labour has been well documented. Of course, any misapplication does not disprove a social theory but it might signal caution. I have attempted to outline my own largely 'sceptical' position elsewhere (Dunn 2004a, 2004b). Here, I will concentrate on identifying some tensions between SMU and contemporary social movement theory based on notions of postmodernism and post-industrial society.

An extensive literature contrasts old social movements, principally the workers' movement, with new social movements (NSM). The latter are understood to be based on networks (more appropriate than formal institutions in the age of disorganised capitalism) constituted by diverse and fragmented actors and orientations. They are motivated less by possibilities of material gain than by the realisation of identities and of transformed cultures and lifestyles. Rather than being based around narrow class divisions they are characteristically seen as inclusive and integrative. Strategies are likely to take place in the realm of 'civil society', insisting on autonomy from, rather than attempting to win power within, the state or market. Any crude economic determinism of the sort exemplified by 'orthodox Marxism' is not (or is no longer) valid.

However, empirical studies have noted the enduringly working class nature of some significant contemporary struggles (Mathers 2003; Moody 1997; Nissen 2003). The implication, for Evans (2003), is that discussion of both social movements and pro-labour practices would be enriched by their integration. In doing this we might begin to overcome the dichotomy involved in reading social movements as either narrowly economistic or as based on entirely plastic and subjective identities. People may simultaneously identify themselves both as workers and as new social subjects (Waterman 1997).

Yet the manoeuvre to constitute SMU by assimilating labour within discourses of NSM is perhaps rather more awkward than this might imply. For many writers the shift is predicated on something essentially more 'primary' involved in the subjective identities of religion, ethnicity, territoriality and nationality (Castells 2000), more 'fundamental' about peace, ecology and human rights (Waterman 1999) or on a paradigmatic shift away from class based, material politics (Touraine 1982). Indeed, the theoretical work on NSMs has rather uniformly argued that class cannot (or can no longer) provide the basis for social action. Information has supposedly replaced material production as the source of wealth and opposition in post-industrial society focuses instead around questions of knowledge (Touraine 1982) or is based around subjective, post-material identities and symbolic rather than instrumental challenges (Melucci 1989).

Many advocates of SMU, of course, shy away from the more thoroughgoing readings of economic change and labour's irrelevance. Yet, while professing all due caution, vital elements of the NSM account often seem to be retained and to inform the proposed strategies. The analyses of contemporary capitalism of Castells and Touraine, for example, which reject this very possibility, are nevertheless explicitly taken as the starting point for several theories of labour action (Hyman 2001; Munck 1998, 2002; Waterman and Wills 2001). Capitalism is 'simultaneously omnipotent and intangible' (Waterman 1997: 3). A society based on information does 'undermine organised labour and facilitate the development of disorganised capitalism' (Munck 2002: 115). Labour 'organisation' should indeed be superseded by the 'network' (Waterman 1997).

This appears to leave a number of awkward tensions at the core of SMU in particular in terms of how a movement is conceived and built in relation to a society's structure and ideas. Flagged up by my parenthetical 'no longer', earlier paragraphs have alluded to a familiar but recurring ambiguity. Crude determinism is either newly invalidated or was always wrong. If the latter, this acknowledgement provides a necessary corrective to any facile 'orthodox' Marxism – should anybody feel they require it. Labour's own institutions and orientations were never simply determined by the structures of capitalism. The past too, was less than rigidly determined. In this vein, some accounts recall past movements such as the Industrial Workers of the World (IWW) and the Congress of Industrial Organisations (CIO), or earlier traditions of syndicalism and socialism, which appear to have many of the required features of SMU (Robinson 2000). Such continuities, however, leave one wondering about the significance of all the chatter of transformation. It seems unclear what we learn from the *theories*, as opposed to the *experiences*, of new social movements or postmodernism.

Alternatively, we are asked to believe that crude determinism was, but is no longer, right. We are asked to rewrite our labour strategies on a determinist caricature of previous social practices, of the labour movement growing automatically from capitalist structure. As if material concerns were once the sole basis of social and political mobilisation and questions of labour organisation, of forging internal community and alliances, simply did not arise, being economically determined by objective class interests. The era of indeterminacy is new; albeit one that critics see as itself determined by techno-economic change (Bromley 1999; Rosenberg 2000). More consistent with the claim that the world has changed, several theorist of SMU seem to subscribe to something closer to this second interpretation. Waterman, for example, while in principle recognising both continuity and transformation, describes how base '*no longer*' determines superstructure (1999: 249). For Munck, it is specifically the 'postmodern globalised world' which 'cannot be reduced to a simple opposition between capital and labour' (2002: 57).

Theories of NSM, and advocates of SMU who echo them, thus have the great merit of now insisting on the 'subjective'. We are not simply victims but can fight to transform the world. However, it is not simply a pedantic quibble to suggest they misinterpret the past. Such a perspective does imply that there is little if anything to learn from labour's historical experience. Moreover, the insistence on subjectivity often goes further, identifying a post-material world beyond structures and flipping into an assertion that we are *only* subjects, in no sense victims with anything to fight about. Stated most strongly, such theories question the very concept of labour, providing rather dubious foundations for its strategies. It does often appear that we are being invited to resist exploitation on the basis of theories which leave considerable doubt whether exploitation exists and to organise in a world which is essentially disorganised. While social life seems to become ever more commodified and politicised we are invited to struggle on a new terrain of 'civil society' 'outside, or independent of, capital and the state' (Waterman 1999: 251). The very disciplinary convergence on the need for more 'hybrid, open, fluid and multipolar solutions' (Munck 1998: 4) might itself suggest caution.

Posing the basis of SMU this starkly will doubtless provoke objections that this is too crude and literal an interpretation of the suggested transformation. It ignores the many words of caution and qualification most theorists are careful to interject. 'Independence' is simply the opposite of dependence. And 'indeterminate' is a suitable corrective to crass determinism. It is 'never all or nothing' but, perhaps contemporary global change has shifted the relative weight of structure and agency, making the world more, but not absolutely, indeterminate.

'Postmodernism' perhaps lets us choose whatever meaning we desire. But numerous critiques and perspectives are more or less explicitly anti-labour, insisting struggle becomes purely mental and immaterial. If their interpretation is substantially different, the onus is surely on supporters of labour to explain their meaning, where they depart from such perspectives and why they so readily defer to such texts and adopt the same language. Such is the chasm between outlooks and repertoires of action that for labour internationalism to sit 'somewhere between' them seems at least a little uncomfortable (Munck 2002: 163–4). The next sections will discuss how even stated more prosaically, some of the more concrete claims for transformation, of post-Fordism and globalisation, offer little clear basis for any strategic reorientation.

Labour, globalisation and the state

'Globalisation', of course, is a much contested term. Perhaps it is possible to identify a common theme in terms of temporal and spatial change or what Scholte (2000) has described as 'deterritorialisation'. In particular, social relations can no longer be contained within national boundaries and states must simply obey the imperatives of the global economy. Thus workers cannot rely on support from ever weakening 'democratic government' (Burnham 1997). Globalisation, read as the retreat of the state, means the national level becomes increasingly irrelevant for labour strategies. While some writers have looked to various global institutions to redeem this democratic deficit, SMU usually places more emphasis on an alternative, 'grass roots' or 'bottom up', internationalism.

Certainly, there are tensions between capitalism and democracy, out of which labour previously won significant gains, for example in terms of welfare and union rights, which have been attacked. Nevertheless, there are dangers of overstating past state capacities and the extent to which they were ever free from international constraints or likely to be exercised on labour's behalf. Social relations have never been essentially national and territorial (Harvey 1973; Radice 2000). However important, and however effectively reforms have sometimes been institutionalised, they were never absolute and inviolable. They continued to be contested. The State was never simply labour's ally. Many achievements have themselves been contradictory. For example, the turn towards labourite politics and peak-level bargaining may have undermined active shop-floor membership and left unions particularly weak when state support was withdrawn (Fairbrother and Yates 2003).

Similarly, the problems of associating with national states and national capital, perhaps most obvious in American Federation of Labor (AFL)/CIO support for US foreign policy, the failures of 'genuine' internationalism in the workers' movement and its deleterious impact on domestic organisation, have been well documented (Brecher and Costello 1998; Munck 2002; Rupert 1995).

Conversely, for all its problems, labour in most rich countries continues to enjoy diverse protections and advantages compared, say, with the situation at the beginning of the twentieth century or with that in many parts of today's world. The very existence of substantial national differences suggests that struggles within borders continue to matter. This is not to insist they are wholly adequate but to resist ceding the national arena to labour's opponents. In practice most struggles still begin locally and are often oriented towards the State, for example opposing attacks on welfare, pensions or legal systems of industrial relations (Wood 2002). If we see the State reduced to a mere transmission belt from the global to the local, an entirely appropriate identification of limits to purely national action slips into joining the chorus sounding their futility, rather than encouraging their (limited) success and attempting to extend this beyond borders.

If attitudes towards the State present problems, globalisation is also, and perhaps to some extent alternatively, understood as a more direct transformation of the relations between capital and labour. The increasingly immaterial and migratory nature of capital, especially relative to immobile workers, increases its options and its power. If, in extremis, we perceive globalisation as something already achieved, the completion of the process of capital internationalism (Waterman 1999), labour internationalism, or anti-nationalism, and strategies at the same scale as global capital again become necessary for effective action. Labour must invent new ways of working, for example utilising the potential of new media (Hyman 1999b; Lee 1999; Waterman 1997). Capital can simply bypass local resistance.

However, it has always been in capital's nature to move, and workers have often perceived the need to spread action within and across borders. Nineteenth century Britain provides significant examples from the 'turnouts' of the 1842 general strike to the 1889 dock workers' reliance on financial support from Australia. The International Trade Secretariats were formed in the decades before World War I, the International Confederation of Free Trade Unions (ICFTU) shortly after the second. Meanwhile capital continues to be at least relatively immobilised, amongst other things, by its continual need for particular concentrations of labour (Holloway 1995).

Perhaps we are experiencing new dimensions of old problems as capital organises an unprecedented and ever-changing international division of labour, adeptly playing off groups of workers against each other. This may increase the need for labour solidarity at a distance. However, this changes rather than severs the relationship between different possible scales of action. Indeed, local struggles may have international consequences as never before, exemplified by the UPS strike in the US and car workers' strikes in Europe. The lesson to be learned, writes Herod, might be that 'organising locally can, in fact, be an effective strategy for use against social actors (e.g., corporations) who are organised at the global and other extended scales' (2001: 12). Positing international solidarity and local action as alternatives might excuse, or contribute towards, the failure of the latter. Tellingly, perhaps, the real world models, the Southern examples of SMU, were largely 'national' in their orientation. COSATU president Willie Mashida insists 'local struggles are as important as international struggles. In fact they are a precondition to international battles because we cannot win on the international terrain what we failed to achieve at a national level' (cited in Akca 2001: 13).

Labour inaction can reflect exaggerated (and sometimes carefully cultivated) perceptions of local powerlessness. Here the State, too, reappears as an active contributor – anti-union laws prohibiting national and local solidarity and requiring overseas assistance. At worst, apparently radical accounts reinforce this, as Herod (1991, 2001) suggests, appearing to echo neo-liberalism that workers cannot fight unless or until they can match the reach of global capital. Furthermore, while supporters of SMU are usually keen to stress rank and file internationalism, the need to act globally can also increase the dependence on actors at the top of hierarchical structures. Western or Northern leaderships are most likely to have access to, and control of, the necessary transport or communications. None of which is intended to decry international solidarity. To the extent that capital becomes more globalised, labour may need to direct greater energies to the international arena but this should not mean rejecting the potential significance of other levels (Sutcliffe and Glyn 1999). If we understand internationalisation to be an ongoing, ambiguous and contested process there is likely to remain an interdependence of scales and important roles for local and national action out of which – and in realising the limits of which – a more thoroughgoing internationalism might develop.

New strategies for the new workers

The difficulties which SMU seeks to overcome are not only those of globalisation. Indeed, as mentioned above, some writers see SMU as primarily a national phenomenon (Akca 2001; Bezuidenhout 2000; Nissen 2003; Robinson 2000), confronting less labour's spatial than its social dispersal. Sometimes described in terms of 'post-Fordism' or 'flexible specialisation'; this involves a transformation of work and of relations between and within firms. Often closely associated with geographical transformations and the advent of a globally networked or disorganised capitalism, the processes may at least be distinguished analytically.

According to such scenarios, political and economic power becomes diffuse. The more dramatic characterisations of reorganisation and labour's demise include depictions of smaller, more flexible and less hierarchical firms and a marketisation of relations in and between production processes (Lash and Urry 1987; Vilrokx 1999). This again shades off into the postmodern account of the end of class: 'capital fragments into a thousand splinters of production capacity blurring the distinction between ownership of working capital and labour' (Hoogvelt, cited in Colas 2002: 203). Less emphatically, intra-firm relations change and workplace size declines while a polarising transformation of work means that workers behave more individualistically (Jacobi 2000). The former core constituency of skilled and semi-skilled male workers dwindles as labour becomes 'increasingly polyglot, feminized and internally differentiated' (Laffey and Dean 2002: 94).

As one prominent advocate of the new social unionism argues, flexible, networked capitalism 'makes the employer/enemy increasingly difficult to identify' (Waterman 1997: 3). Consequently 'the overwhelming majority of the [world's] poor, powerless, marginalised and alienated are not unionisable' (Waterman 1999: 248). Less drastically, technological change is understood to have polarising consequences, increasing the proportions of those least susceptible to traditional union agendas, the unskilled and highly skilled. That is it increases the periphery and core and the distance between them. Strategies of resistance become accordingly more difficult (Hyman 1999a; Vilrokx 1999), requiring 'new strategic imaginations' in a move beyond industrial age priorities such as wages and conditions (Hyman 1999b). At the very least unions must catch up with the information age with a transformed agenda and a broader appeal (Munck 2002).

Neither highly skilled computer scientists nor low paid clerks readily conjure up images of militant trade unionism. Yet directly attributing labour's prospects to the changing nature and skill bases of work seems to tread a treacherous path between technological determinism and circularity. I do not wish to dismiss important debates about labour processes and their influences on workers' consciousness and propensity to organise (Braverman 1974; Burawoy 1985; Watson 1995). There may be significant tendential differences between groups of workers. However, there do appear to be problems with the assertion that material, or technical differences lie at the root of contemporary processes of polarisation and with the assumption that a shift in strategy is required because of a core/periphery distinction inscribed by capitalist restructuring.

Assessing skill is notoriously problematic. Liberal economics starts with pay, assumes this reflects human capital, and so maintains that pay differentials reflect skill divergence. However, the empirical evidence for any association between skill and pay is more ambiguous. Labour supporters might be inclined to see organisation rather than skill as the most significant independent variable and workers as low paid because they are unorganised rather than poorly organised because low paid and low skilled.

The extension of the designation 'periphery' to women and to non-white workers (with its concomitant assumptions of distance from union organisation) highlights the dangers of circularity or, worse, risks slipping into sexist and racist assumptions about the nature of their work and capacity to organise. Women and ethnic minority workers undoubtedly often face labour market and workplace discrimination and social obstacles to their inclusion within labour organisation. However, they do organise and evidence suggests are at least as likely to have positive attitudes towards, and to gain as much from, unionisation and traditional concerns like pay and conditions as white men (Fairbrother and Yates 2003; Levi 2003). Of course, many specific experiences of oppression but also exclusionary practices within the labour movement need to be fought. 'New workers' may indeed be more responsive to a more inclusive unionism (Robinson 2000).

However, there are reasons to suppose that what is required is neither entirely novel, nor simply a question of imagination.

Intra-class differentiation is familiar. As Panitch (2001) remarks, without heterogeneity notions of 'solidarity' would be meaningless. Even 'Fordist' capitalism never begat trade unionism in any immediate way and workers were always marginal until they organised. It took thirty-eight years to unionise Ford. Both the historical record and contemporary surveys show that all sorts of skilled and unskilled workers organise successfully. Dock work and building labour in the early part of the twentieth century were also both thoroughly casualised, and apart from their gender and colour had many of the characteristics of twenty-first century's 'periphery', until they were successfully unionised.

The post-Fordist argument also suggests that the giant industrial firms, once labour's strongholds, have been replaced by much more complex inter-firm networks. There are both historical and practical reasons for believing it easier to organise big workplaces than small. And despite much exaggeration and counter trends of mergers, acquisitions and industrial concentration, there is evidence of inter-firm fragmentation, whether in terms of subcontracting or in the breaking up of large public utilities. However, the relationship between firm size and labour organisation is rather weak. Some sectors such as mining and construction were long characterised by relatively modest workplace sizes and strong union traditions while contemporary practices come nowhere close to recreating the genuinely small scale, familial or artisan production of the sort that preceded industrial capitalism and might plausibly in the future preclude labour organisation. Amidst any general decline – of unions and of firm and workplace size – there are numerous examples of concentration, from auto component manufacture to call centres, which did not nurture union organisation in any obvious way.

Moreover, extended production networks can have more positive implications for labour. There is some evidence, for example in the motor industry, of workers in parts suppliers having the ability to stop downstream operations and therefore exercise effective power regardless of formal inter-firm organisation. Contemporary Just-in-Time production systems can also increase rather than decrease capital's vulnerability (Herod 2000; Thelen and Kume 1999). Capitalism continually changes and undermines existing forms of labour organisation, and it is surely right for SMU to emphasise questions of labour strategy but problematic if we begin with an assumption that labour's heterogeneity makes organisation newly difficult.

SMU challenges many conservative practices and determinists reading of workers' potential. It advocates more effective coalitions and community alliances, which I agree would strengthen labour. However, why SMU should be predicated, as it so often appears, on the decline of the industrial workers (Moody 1997) or new-found weakness and subordinate position is less than clear. Even rather 'orthodox' Marxists have long recognised the need to forge alliances both within and beyond classes. The radical counterposition of old and new, structure and agency and different forms and arenas of action, tends to suggest these are exclusionary alternatives and to affirm the perspective of labour's opponents, underestimating the potential of local scales of action, sectional strengths and the significance of labour's historical experience. Instead these might remain important bases for action; for a practice upon which theorists of labour might still be able to base more inclusive and internationalist orientations. Perhaps unions indeed once 'tended to reflect and replicate' the standardisation of Fordism, excluding the marginal (Hyman 1999b) and that as the marginal became the norm, this accentuated labour's weakness. But this suggests we look at labour's institutional failings rather than seeing these as simply determined by capitalism's changed structures.

Winning the social movement unionism agenda

The previous sections suggested SMU may pose the need for more inclusive and internationalist agenda somewhat one-sidedly, being too ready to attribute the need for these to transformations in the nature of capitalism. This section describes how this is reflected in difficulties conceptualising how such objectives might be attained. Our understanding of society is, again, likely to have implications for how we believe change is likely to be affected. In much of the literature of postmodernism, subjectivity tends to oust questions of political action and organisation (Eagleton 1996). I will argue that this is echoed in the more hyperbolic versions of SMU. Even when posed more carefully as a reform strategy, perhaps as an agenda around which different 'progressive' currents might unite, its silences on questions of organisation show a commonality with more radical interpretations of change and fail to articulate how any such programme might be achieved. Minimally, if there is an enduring interaction between structure and agency neither is effective labour organisation necessarily precluded by the objective nature of capitalism but nor can it be achieved, wished into being, independently of existing institutions and structures. This may seem obvious but the path between determinism and idealism can be treacherous.

SMU is occasionally presented as an evolutionary process. Conservative, business unionism becomes increasingly outdated – unable to meet even its own modest ends of servicing existing memberships – and either adapts or is replaced through a competitive struggle by more appropriate organisations. Evidence from the US offers some support for such a thesis (Robinson 2000) and perhaps the success of more militant leadership slates elsewhere, in Britain for example, might be interpreted in the same way. However, amongst other things, there is the empirical difficulty that any change in leadership and direction would appear to be a rather hesitant and faltering process, at least compared with the sheer radicality of the break in material conditions which are usually understood to produce it.

Alternatively, and perhaps more typically, the emphasis is on agency. Accordingly, some theories of SMU appeal generally towards the unions or even simply labour as a whole. There is no privileged target audience. There are no vanguards and rearguards, no labour aristocrats or wretched of the earth more likely to respond, nor do institutional structures constitute much of an obstacle to innovation. The specificities of social location cannot form the basis of strategy nor explain any reluctance to embrace change. Thus, rather than dismissing labour's existing institutions as hopelessly anachronistic, along with the limited struggles upon which they were built, we often find a perhaps surprisingly positive attitude towards them. Even historically conservative organisations are seen as potentially important contributors towards SMU. Several accounts devote considerable space and seriousness to efforts within the institutions of established labour internationalism such as the ILO (International Labour Organisation) and ICFTU to build more inclusive organisation and to extend labour's global links. Individuals and organisations can recognise their failings and overcome them. Waterman (2001) insists criticism of internal social or ideological differentiations within its existing unions is 'out of place, or out of date'. We find, as Piore describes in one US union, 'its diverse membership and its staff have a single identity and share a sense of common purpose and mission. The source of that identity is not their industry or occupation, but it is a moral vision' (cited in Robinson 2000: 123).

Elsewhere, advocates of SMU do seek to describe an interrelation between structure and agency. This allows (or at least cannot be dismissed by postmodernist fiat) some 'material' basis to account for the tenacity of 'bad' policies, an institutional 'drag' explaining resistance to radical reorientations. Trade Unions remain contradictory institutions that continue to negotiate against but within capitalism. Leaderships and union staff may have much in common with rank and file members but also enjoy different conditions and prospects (von Holdt 2002). Conversely, even while unions may have failed to provide fully adequate strategies to defend their members or to even maintain their numbers the evidence on pay and employment conditions suggests they still made a significant difference. Institutionalisation and routinisation need not then simply be read as a 'mistake' but interpreted in terms of relatively successful, if contradictory, social practices.

To overcome union conservatism several theorists of SMU re-emphasise workers' own struggles; struggles to strengthen unions through more militant and inclusive approaches including a greater engagement with non-workplace based issues, struggles for more activist 'organising models' against the 'top down' servicing approach and struggles for internal transformations towards greater union participation and democracy (Moody 1997; Waterman 1999). It may be necessary to institutionalise SMU, as a 'social movement *within* the trade unions' (Waterman 1997: 7).

The retreat from more catastrophist readings of discontinuity may be extended, leaving small-scale workplace action and existing practices as an important basis for more inclusive practices. Unions need not then face an either/or choice; the services they provide might themselves be valued and provide important grounds for recruitment and grass roots activism. Effective trade unionism, even as it mobilises both internally and externally, may usefully offer members all sorts of institutional support (Danford *et al.* 2003). Other studies have suggested that it is where traditional trade unionism has been strongest that more outward looking agenda have been most successfully established (Frege and Kelly 2003). Such interpretations encourage a process of change involving struggle, which seeks to develop moves towards greater internationalism and universalism but without rejecting other bases of action. SMU thus develops out of processes within but also beyond existing institutions of labour. 'Struggle' can now fill the middle ground between structure and agency.

This is clearly a substantially different perspective to that of many advocates of SMU discussed above. However, in common with 'harder' versions, labour's tasks often continue to be seen in very general terms. Although they may need to be 'articulated' with other political or other social forces, this remains a project *for* the unions, tending to blur internal differentiations, to conflate 'unions' and 'labour', and to underestimate the social and political differentiation of both.

Politics or 'the party', it is usually agreed, should be subordinate to the social movement (Lambert 2002; Waterman 1999). This may be particularly appropriate as a reaction to the conservatism of former social democrats, the disastrous imposition of party lines on union movements, and the isolation and sectarianism of leftist currents. However, without addition or qualification this demotion of politics, along with the emphasis on struggle and inclusiveness, recalls antecedent anarchist and syndicalist traditions. My stress on continuity as well as change should indicate that I think their antiquity is insufficient grounds for dismissing them. In common with much of the literature on NSM, this syndicalism nevertheless offers few answers to the important questions it raises of relations with existing institutions but also of inclusiveness and exclusivity, of leadership and led and of hierarchy and accountability. The disavowal of politics also rests somewhat awkwardly with elements of the SMU perspective and what often seems to be an avowedly programmatic endeavour. For example, Levi sees social movement unionism as one 'in which unions fight for better conditions for all' (2003: 45), and Waterman recommends 'the unionist who is simultaneously and equally a feminist, an ecologist, an anti-militarist, a radical-democrat, or an internationalist' (1997:7). Both he and Moody at times re-admit the word 'socialism' while Munck explicitly emphasises the need to reintroduce 'union politics' (2002: 191). The proposals, however, often appear rather more developed than the struggles upon which they are supposedly subordinate. SMU draws on many impressive but largely isolated examples. It often seems to be a strategy of revival, needed precisely because of the low level of struggle.

It is therefore tempting to see 'subordination' as aimed towards alternative or rival institutions. The retreat even from social democracy and the weakness of more radical currents makes their omission, at least from 'Anglo-American' academic discourses, readily comprehensible. Yet numerous struggles do appear to have been informed by various pre-existing conceptions of transformative politics. In some of the earlier experiences invoked by theorists of SMU, political organisation clearly mattered. An adequate account of the rise and decline of the US unions, for example, could hardly ignore the role, for good or ill, of the Communist Party. It is perhaps not surprising that the Left's contemporary absence is perhaps less marked, as is any perceived move towards SMU, in some countries of continental Europe (Frege and Kelly 2003), while von Holdt (2002) argues that the South African experience again shows the priority of politics, informing and directing union practice. But even elsewhere, the refusal to acknowledge long-standing traditions within the labour movement, advocating apparently similar universalist agendas (albeit perhaps using somewhat different vocabularies) seems to repeat any sectarianism and obstruct potentially useful dialogue.

So we have some awkward tension, a political project that insists on its subordination to struggle whose very weakness is in a sense its *raison d'être*. Similarly, ideas are more autonomous than ever, yet Waterman, for example, insists 'it is *no longer* a matter of intellectuals bringing the necessary consciousness to the workers' (1999: 257, emphasis added). The role of theory is diminished. Of course, these are familiar difficulties, albeit in a new guise. The path between idealism and determinism, or between vanguardism and economism, is one the Left has had trouble negotiating throughout the twentieth century. And far from stumbling unknowingly into such contradictions, many theorists of SMU are attempting to grapple with these problems to provide more appropriate solutions for our new circumstances. These are difficulties that can perhaps be ridden, ideas and institutions transformed in struggle. However, it is less clear to what extent SMU offers any novel solution.

There is a tension within trade unions between the pursuit of the general and the particular. It is possible, as SMU asserts, that the need for greater emphasis on the general has grown as the world economy becomes more global, as capitalism divides workers from each other in ever new ways. However, the desire to subsume the particular, the local and sectional battles, the strategy and tactics of institution and alliance building, into general prescriptions often seems to leave us with a rather abstract universalism. Even posed more cautiously, the acceptance of globalisation and a new economy does tend to suggest that we need pay little attention to questions of labour's exploitation or strategic potential and have little to learn from the past. SMU emphasises the importance of ideas and ideological struggles in establishing effective pro-labour practice but these too often seem to be posed abstractly rather than related concretely to the specific circumstances of labour or its institutions. If it is to contribute to building more inclusive and internationalist labour practices, more attention might be given to the relationships within established unions and with other radical organisations and currents.

Conclusions

Much of the agenda of SMU is very attractive. It advocates a universalism against the narrow defence of local and sectional interests. It emphasises movement and activism against a staid institutionalism. It describes many practices and experiences which have pushed the boundaries of conventional trade unionism but out of which unions have been able to grow and resist neo-liberal restructuring more effectively. For many writers the encouragement and attempt to learn from such struggles seems to be what constitutes SMU.

However, it is usually also something rather more than that. In its most radical guise, SMU accepts much of the neo-liberal argument. Change appears to be required by the new omnipotence of global capital. Labour's former social power evaporates into the ether of an immaterial economy. Only new ideas can overcome its weakness. We seem to approach not just the perspectives of labour's opponents but also some rather old idealism.

The world continually changes and it is quite appropriate to suggest that strategies must adjust accordingly. Most accounts refrain from explicitly endorsing the more dramatic conclusions of labour's disempowerment. However, important elements of these analyses of restructuring and their negative implications for labour are often retained. The need for radical reorientation and more general and inclusive action seems to be posited on an overstatement of specific weaknesses, which helps to naturalise labour's differences and divisions. Only seldom do we find attempts to evaluate critically the social changes and their impact on labour's strategic potential, to discuss how specific strengths might provide the basis for moves beyond narrow sectional and local action or of what should be kept from the armoury of the past and what should be jettisoned.

There are also ambiguous attitudes towards labour's established organisations. Downplaying local and specific strengths might suggest that something quite novel is required but more usually, we find a relatively enthusiastic embrace of the existing unions as vehicles for change, and SMU posed as a strategy for union renewal. Here the emphasis on discontinuity appears to underestimate the embedded nature of established social practices, the tenacity of opposition and the need for allies winning more universalist agenda. It remains unclear how any reorientation is to be achieved.

References

Akca I. (2001) '"Globalization", state and labor: towards a social movement unionism', paper prepared for the International Studies Association, Chicago, 21–24 February.

Bezuidenhot, A. (2000) 'Towards global social movement unionism? Trade union responses to globalization in South Africa', ILO International Institute of Labour Studies Discussion papers, DP/115/2000.

Braverman, H. (1974) *Labour and monopoly capital*, New York.

Brecher, J. and Costello, T. (1998) 'A "new labor movement" in the shell of the old', in Mantsios, G. (ed.), *A new labor movement for the new century*, New York.

Bromley, S. (1999) 'The space of flows and timeless time: Manuel Castells's information age', *Radical Philosophy*, 97.

Burawoy, M. (1985) *The Politics of Production*, London.

Burnham, P. (1997) 'Globalisation: states, markets and class relations', *Historical Materialism*, 1.

Castells, M. (2000) *The rise of the network society*, 2nd ed., Oxford.

Colas, A. (2002) 'The class politics of globalisation', in Rupert, M. and Smith, H. (eds), *Historical materialism and globalization*, London.

Danford, A., Richardson, M. and Upchurch, M. (2003) *New unions, new workplaces: a study of union resilience in the restructured workplace*, London.

Dunn, B. (2004a) 'Capital movements and the embeddedness of labour', *Global Society*, 18.

—— (2004b) *Global restructuring and the power of labour*, Basingstoke.

Eagleton, T. (1996) *The illusions of postmodernism*, Oxford.

Evans, P. (2003) 'Labor as a global social movement: notes toward bringing labor into the theorizing of transnational social movements', available at www.yale.edu/ccr/evans/rtf (accessed on 13 May 2004).

Fairbrother, P. and Yates, C. A. B. (2003) 'Unions in crisis, unions in renewal', in Fairbrother, P. and Yates, C. A. B. (eds), *Trade unions in renewal: a comparative study*, London.

Frege, C. M. and Kelly, J. (2003) 'Union revitalization strategies in comparative perspective', *European Journal of Industrial Relations*, 9.

Harvey, D. (1973) *Social justice and the city*, London.

Herod, A. (1991) 'Local political practice in response to a manufacturing plant closure: how geography complicates class analysis', *Antipode*, 23.

—— (1995) 'The practice of international labor solidarity and the geography of the global economy', *Economic Geography*, 71.

—— (2000) 'Implications of just-in-time production for union strategy: lessons from the 1998 General Motors – United Auto Workers dispute', *Annals of the Association of American Geographers*, 90.

—— (2001) *Labor geographies: workers and the landscapes of capitalism*, New York.

Holloway, J. (1995) 'Capital moves', *Capital and Class*, 57.

Hyman, R. (1999a) 'An emerging agenda for trade unions', Labour and Society Programme, available at www.ilo.org/public/english/bureau/inst/papers/1999/dp98/index.htm (accessed on 9 April 2001).

—— (1999b) 'Imagined solidarities: can trade unions resist globalization?', in Leisink, P. (ed.), *Globalization and labour relations*, Cheltenham.

—— (2001) 'European integration and industrial relations: a case of variable geometry?', *Antipode*, 33.

Jacobi, O. (2000) 'Transnational trade union cooperation at global level and European level – opportunities and obstacles', *Transfer*, 6.

Laffey, M. and Dean K. (2002) 'A flexible Marxism for flexible times', in Rupert, M. and Smith, H. (eds), *Historical materialism and globalization*, London.

Lambert, R. (2002) 'Labor movement renewal in the era of globalization: union responses in the south', in Harrod, J. and O'Brien, R. (eds), *Global unions? Theory and strategies of organized labour in the global political economy*, London.

Lash, S. and Urry, J. (1987) *The end of organized capitalism*, Cambridge.

Lee, E. (1999) 'Trade unions, computer communications and the new world order', in Waterman, P. and Munck, R. (eds), *Labour worldwide in the era of globalisation: alternative models in the new world order*, New York.

Levi, M. (2003) 'Organizing power: The prospects for an American labor movement', *Perspectives in Politics*, 1.

Mathers, A. (2003) 'The European marches network against unemployment, job insecurity and social exclusion: collective action beyond class?', unpublished Ph.D. manuscript, University of the West of England.

Melucci, A. (1989) *Nomads of the present*, Philadelphia.

Moody, K. (1997) *Workers in a lean world*, London.

Munck, R. (1998) 'Labour in the global: discourses and practices' available at www. amtenna.nl/~waterman/munck2.html (accessed on 9 April 2001).

—— (2002) *Globalisation and labour: the new 'great transformation'*, London.

Nissen, B. (2003) 'Alternative strategic directions for the U.S. labor movement: recent scholarship', *Labour Studies Journal*, 28.

Panitch, L. (2001) 'Class and inequality: strategy for labour in the era of globalization', paper to the International Studies Association, Chicago, 23 February.

Radice, H. (2000) 'Responses to globalisation: a critique of progressive nationalism', *New Political Economy*, 5.

Robinson, I. (2000) 'Neoliberal restructuring and U.S. unions: toward social movement unionism', *Critical Sociology*, 26.

Rosenberg, J. (2000) *The follies of globalisation theory*, London.

Rupert, M. (1995) *Producing hegemony: the politics of mass production and American global power*, Cambridge.

Scholte, J. A. (2000) *Globalization: a critical introduction*, Basingstoke.

Sutcliffe, B. and Glyn, A. (1999) 'Still underwhelmed: indicators of globalization and their misinterpretation', *Review of Radical Political Economics*, 31.

Thelen, K. and Kume, I. (1999) 'The effects of globalization on labor revisited: lessons from Germany and Japan', *Politics Society*, 27.

Touraine, A. (1982) *The voice and the eye*, Cambridge.

Vilrokx, J. (1999) 'Towards the denaturing of class relations? The political economy of the firm in global capitalism', in Leisink, P. (ed.), *Globalization and labour relations*, Cheltenham.

von Holdt, K. (2002) 'Social movement unionism: the case of South Africa', *Work, Employment and Society*, 16.

Waterman, P. (1997) 'Conceiving an "international social-movement unionism" requires a 21st, not a 19th century, vocabulary' available at www.labournet.org.uk/oct97/waterman/html (accessed on 2 June 2004).

—— (1999) 'The new social unionism: a new union model for a new world order', in Waterman, P. and Munck, R. (eds), *Labour worldwide in the era of globalisation: alternative models in the new world order*, New York.

—— (2001) 'Trade unionism in the age of Seattle', *Antipode*, 33.

—— and Wills, J. (2001) 'Space, place and the new labour internationalisms: beyond the fragments?', *Antipode*, 33.

Watson, T. J. (1995) *Sociology, work and industry*, 3rd edition, London.

Wood, E. M. (2002) 'Global capital, national states', in Rupert, M. and Smith, H. (eds), *Historical materialism and globalization*, London.

10

Self-regulating markets, restructuring and the new labour internationalism

Rob Lambert

> Those who define, create. 'Democratic' politics, that is, modern mass politics, is a battlefield in which the most important move is that which decides what the battle is about, what the issue is. To be able to define the contending parties, name them and thus establish where the barricades should go up, or where the trenches should be dug, gives one a powerful and at times decisive advantage. This is what all the major movements for social change have had to do. (Sassoon 1996: 7)

Introduction

Restructuring should be defined as the twenty-first century's overriding workplace issue for market driven change has adversely affected the lives of citizens, except for elites who benefit from the new work regime. Whilst this experience is one of social dislocation and material hardship, market discourse presents these events as an inexorable force that cannot be resisted. Can unions forge the capacity to assert social control over this force, thereby challenging the logic of neo-liberal restructuring? Despite the countermovement's relatively underdeveloped, fragile existence, the emergence of a new labour internationalism (NLI) in the south provides some indication of a possible pathway towards this goal. Whilst there are other instances of a shift towards a NLI, this chapter focuses on the emergence of The Southern Initiative on Globalisation and Trade Union Rights (SIGTUR), which southern unions established in May 1991 (Sandbrook 2003; Taylor 2004; Waterman and Wills 2001). We begin this analysis of SIGTUR's contribution to the revitalisation of civil society by identifying the union predicament.

Restructuring and trade union decline

Restructuring asserts a corporate perspective on the necessity of 'reform' in four synchronized spheres: mergers and acquisitions; the changing geography of production; privatisation; and the transformed world of work. Economic and financial deregulation that characterise neo-liberal globalisation has accelerated corporate mergers and acquisitions within nations and across these boundaries.

Such a rationalisation process spawns factory closures that decimate the trade union base. The geographic shift from relatively high waged, unionised zones of the global economy to non-union, cheap labour havens further erodes unionism. Privatisation is accompanied by substantial job loss and a decline of public sector unionism. Finally, the changing world of work accelerates the demise as significant segments of the workforce are casualised. With only a few notable exceptions, unions are seemingly frozen in their base of full-time workers and traditional bargaining strategies. For the most part, union leadership has been outmanoeuvred and left bereft of effective alternatives.

These impacts are reflected in union density statistics, which reveal a remarkable decline during the phase of restructuring. Union density in Australia has collapsed from a high of 63 per cent in 1953 to 23.1 per cent in August 2002. The decline accelerated during the restructuring of the 1990s when the movement lost 50 per cent of its base with density declining from 40.5 per cent in 1990 to the meager 23.1 per cent in 2002 (Bamber *et al.* 2004: 127; Peetz 1998). This trend is similar in other nations. In the United States for example, union density fell from a peak of 35 per cent in the early 1950s, to 20 per cent in 1983, and to 13.5 per cent in 2000 (Bamber *et al.* 2004: 67). In France, there was a collapse from 23 per cent in the mid-1970s to a mere 10 per cent by the mid-1990s; in Italy membership dropped from 50.8 per cent in the 1950s to 28.5 per cent by the 1990s (Bamber *et al.* 2004: 157, 178).

Membership collapse, largely as a consequence of restructuring, is further exacerbated by the generally confused response of union leadership to the restructuring discourse. Global corporations and states seeking to attract investment, present the four complementary forms of restructuring as a 'reform' process; a move towards 'higher productivity', which will 'reinvigorate the economy'; a change which will render individual corporations and the economy as a whole more 'efficient' and more 'competitive', thereby generating a dynamic national economy to the benefit of all citizens. For example, this is the language of the 2004 OECD (Organisation for Economic Cooperation and Development) economic survey of Australia, which asserts that further labour market deregulation (union marginalisation) is essential to 'reinvigorate economic reform and sustain productivity growth' (*The Australian*, 3 February 2005; OECD 2004). Instead of challenging this discourse with an alternative perspective, a range of unions in the developed economies have sought to demonstrate that far from being an efficiency barrier, they are ideally positioned to realise these goals. Such an orientation has led to various forms of 'strategic', 'best practice' or 'business' unionism (Ogden 1992: 11).

Degrees of union seduction into this discourse have spawned a legitimacy crisis, which has exacerbated the decline. The crisis stems from the disjuncture between the union leadership's positive advocacy of restructuring, and workers' bitter experience of social dislocation and material hardship. Most significantly, adoption of this discourse has eroded unionism's commitment to class interests over individualism, and co-operative over competitive relations, thus imprisoning unions within liberal economic values. This has profound implications because discourse is a moment of communication and persuasion regarding lines of action and belief (Harvey 1996: 83). Failure to present an alternative discourse confirms neo-liberalism's success. Organised labour's historically forged beliefs and values are mocked in the corporate controlled media, as reflecting those of a bygone era. They are deemed barriers to progress, which undermine the economy.

When unions adopt these beliefs and values and when they assume the role of market agents, class consciousness is eroded. This orientation has reinforced the notion of market necessity, and in so doing has asserted that the foundational values of trade unionism are now market values: individualism, competition, efficiency, profit, shareholder enrichment. This model's social vision is of a society of individual opportunity and upward mobility, producing a politics that stimulates individual aspirations, assuaging the desire to scale the social ladder. Such a value shift is radical, corroding the essential driving power of unionism – the culture of solidarity.

Touraine highlighted the implications of this value shift. He noted, 'Beliefs and convictions have been lost, with the result that militant workers lack certainty and sometimes even feel that they no longer know what their action means . . . it is impossible not to notice how much weaker ideas of a desirable future have become'. A worker explained: 'We are at the end of our tether because there is no prospect of a more just, amicable society' (1987: 115). Others observed that 'the trade union movement is less and less ethically identified . . . trade unionism must rediscover these values in order to give meaning to its activities' (Touraine 1987: 112–18).

Undermined in this way, unions need to imagine a new restructuring discourse and in so doing make a vital choice: jettison their role as agents of restructuring and rediscover a history where their core identity was forged by their justice role. Such a choice is the distinguishing characteristic of democratic unions in the south as they strive to construct a NLI. Creating this discourse is a first step in building a more effective resistance.

Transforming market discourse

The discursive moment is 'a form of power, it is a mode of formation of ideas and beliefs' (Harvey 1996: 83). Corporations articulate a singular world view of self-regulating markets. This perspective is advanced so forcefully and comprehensively because it is advocated by global, regional and national institutions, each harmonising these free market views, thereby advocating an identical position on key issues.[1] Continuous restructuring is prioritised and exists at the core of the free market project. The corporate capture of significant sections of the media further consolidates this perspective. Thus unions, workers and citizens are saturated with a singular perspective on restructuring, namely, that these 'reforms' are a sign of economic vitality and the only route to economic well-being and security.

Restructuring is the event through which workers experience markets directly. When factories are closed, when work is intensified, when insecurity and casualisation are extended, workers experience 'reform' as life changing (Lambert 2005). They experience the power inequality that markets embody, for they soon realise that they have no voice in the change process. Voiceless, they experience themselves as inanimate objects, assuming a commodity-like existence. This is no abstraction.

It takes concrete and specific meaning from lived experience, from the attack on a way of life, security and material conditions. In this process workers become conscious of the credibility gap between market discourse and their lived experience. However, in the absence of an alternative discourse, workers are isolated in their individual anger and frustration, which in many instances leads to depression and consequent inaction.[2]

Polanyi (1944) captures this contradiction and in so doing provides a theoretical basis for an alternative restructuring discourse. In the course of the nineteenth century (and in the late twentieth century) markets became 'disembedded', that is, freed from social, political and moral regulation. In this transformation labour is described as a commodity, functioning in the market like any other commodity. This 'commodity fiction' became 'a vital organizing principle in regard to the whole of society affecting almost all its institutions in the most varied way, namely, the principle according to which no arrangement or behavior should be allowed to exist that might prevent the actual functioning of the market mechanism on the lines of the commodity fiction' (Polanyi 1944: 73). In the south, the commodity status of labour in the Asian 'miracle' economies is acute, setting competitive benchmarks that reverberate around the globe. Working hours are extreme, wages minimal, health and safety standards non-existent (Lambert 1997: 2003).

An alternative discourse challenges the commodity description of labour. Such an intervention should aims to expose the 'crude fiction' for as Polanyi (1944: 72–3) argues:

> Labor is only another name for human activity which goes with life itself, which in its turn is not produced for sale but for entirely different reasons, nor can that activity be detached from the rest of life . . . to allow the market mechanism to be the sole director of the fate of human beings . . . would result in the demolition of society . . . For the alleged commodity 'labor power' cannot be shoved about, used indiscriminately, or even left unused, without affecting also the human individual who happens to be the bearer of this peculiar commodity. In disposing of a man's labor power the system would, incidentally, dispose of the physical, psychological, and moral entity 'man' attached to that tag.

Thus self-regulating markets 'could not exist for any length of time without annihilating the human and natural substance of society', and if not controlled 'would have physically destroyed man and his surroundings into a wilderness (Polanyi 1957: 3; Munck 2002: 2). Free markets create 'a dislocation which attacks the very fabric of society' (Munck 2002: 2; Polanyi 1957: 130).

In advocating this discourse, the Polanyi argument should embrace both production and reproduction. His intervention led to a focus on welfare interventions by the state as the key to restricting the commodity fiction. Whilst this is an element in de-commodifying labour, the role of corporations should not be neglected. Market discourse reifies the corporation, asserting that closures, geographic relocations and changes in work organisation are the outcome of the market mechanism, thereby obscuring the role of corporate leadership in choosing social dislocation (Bakan 2004: 22). Market ideology aims at hiding the processes of profit driven corporations, which appear unshackled from social responsibility.

An alternative discourse exposes this class basis of restructuring, which enhances shareholder value through attacking the physical, psychological and moral being of those being restructured.

In Polanyi's view, historically these changes led to a 'double movement'. The commodity status of labour gave rise to 'a deep-seated movement' which 'sprang into being to resist the pernicious effects of a market controlled economy. Society protected itself against the perils inherent in a self-regulating market system.' (1944: 76) Munck argues, 'counter-movements cannot be seen as spontaneous, practically automatic responses; they are rather constructed and then they impact back on the definition and resolution of the crisis itself' (2004: 7).

This chapter analyses SIGTUR's construction as a nascent global social movement of southern workers, and speculates on the movement's capacity to contribute to a global effort to define and resolve the restructuring crisis. This sketch of labour's predicament highlights the barriers to a countermovement project, for as Sartre has argued 'collision with barriers is an indubitable fact of human reality. The existential question is, how do we account for the barriers we meet and how do we deal with them?' (Meszaros 1979: 139) At this juncture in history restructuring advocates are united, whilst the opposition is weak. Yet the road to freedom begins with choice, commitment, the notion that you ought to, therefore you can. SIGTUR grew out of this moral choice; a desire for justice within a global order constructed on the negation of all values, except those consistent with the measures of the market.

Creating a movement against restructuring

The impetus to create a southern movement against restructuring derived from Australia. Prior to the radical market reforms of the 1980s, Australian society reflected the classic features of Polanyi's first Great Transformation. The social regulation of markets (corporate power) was the central tenet of the reform process early in the twentieth century. Deakin, a founding father of the Australian federal state, argued that these changes would establish Australia as a model social democracy, a 'social lighthouse to the world', where the state would protect the individual against the vagaries of the market. In his view the state should not be considered, 'as an object of hostility to the labourer, it should now become identified with an interest in his works, and in all workers, extending to them its sympathy and protection, and watching over their welfare and prosperity' (Pusey 1991: 1). Contradicting the world of self-regulating markets, the architects of Australian social democracy contended that this distinctive state role required union recognition. A legally binding industrial relations system was central to the achievement of the political objective of a more egalitarian society. A centralised judicial determination of wages, and the conscious protection of industry and jobs, secured the highest standards of living of any nation on earth (Pusey 1991: 1).

Ironically, the first steps in the dismantlement of this system were initiated by a Labor government in the 1980s. The Hawke government embraced the market, declaring class interest politics redundant. Henceforward Labor would realise the national interest through promoting corporate interests. This was the only way to secure Australia's place in the global economy as a mature trading nation (Lambert 1996: 226). Ceaseless restructuring then followed. As the impacts of these changes became apparent, left union leaders (metals, construction, maritime and the public sector) decided that the new context demanded a new global union response. Asia's exploited workforce represented a threat and an opportunity (Lambert 1998: 271; Lambert 1999: 72).

After considerable debate, Australian labor adopted the outward-looking strategy consistent with their rich tradition of international solidarity. Building enduring relationships with democratic unions in the Asian region became a priority. Individuals who were part of a political generation of committed activists in Asia and South Africa were identified, and encouraged to become part of this venture. The Philippines, Malaysia and Indonesia were visited, leading to the discovery that these organisations faced circumstances similar to the South African and Brazilian unions' recognition struggles of the 1970s and 1980s (Lambert 1990: 258; Lambert 1997; Seidman 1994). Social movement unionism resonated with the vision of the NLI that SIGTUR's founders articulated. Indeed, it was felt that given the scale of the challenge unions faced in market society a global social movement model was the only pathway to empowerment. Problems surrounding the realisation of this model have preoccupied SIGTUR's leadership since the 1990s. Tentative steps towards realising this vision were taken in May 1991 when a small meeting of democratic unions from the region was organised in Perth. Importantly, COSATU participated in this founding meeting. South African unions had traversed a social movement as a form of empowerment against the exclusionary and repressive apartheid state (Adler and Webster 2000). It was felt they could provide valuable lessons on how to organise and mobilise workers in the repressive Asian environment.

As SIGTUR's founding document reveals, challenging the logic of neo-liberalism's self-regulating markets was the essential goal:

> The experience of workers in Johannesburg factories, in the scarred shack lands of Manila, in the vast ship yards of South Korea and in the dense cities of India, will be shared on a continuous basis.... The response of Australian workers has been positive because they recognise that global issues do connect with their everyday experience in the factories, the mines, the construction sites and the waterfront.
>
> Within Australia we are all too aware of the decisive character of the present decade of global restructuring. How are the Australian unions to compete in a region based on ultra-cheap labor power, secured through severe trade union repression? We can restructure until the cows come home, but we will never hold our ground on existing conditions, while levels of exploitation in the region are so high. This is the point of convergence between the current agenda of Australian trade unions, and the unions in the region. There is an objective basis to the merging of our interests with their interests (SIGTUR 1998: 2).

SIGTUR's genesis provides insight into the difficult process of building a countermovement, which is always a profoundly political affair. Munck is correct in his assessment that this is not a spontaneous or automatic process (2004: 7). The internationalist choice was contested within the politically factionalised Australian union movement. The Right immediately attacked the 1991 meeting.

The initiative for the conference came from the far left of the trade union movement in Western Australia, and appeared to have a distinct World Federation of Trade Unions (WFTU) flavour about it. The Soviet backed WFTU has been anxious to build regional initiatives between unions allied or favourable to it and unions associated with the International Confederation of Free Trade Unions (ICFTU). The meeting was criticised as 'unrepresentative'. 'The delegates did not necessarily represent recognised trade unions in their respective countries' (Social Action 1991: 11). Martin Ferguson, The President of the Australian Council of Trade Unions (ACTU), who was from the left faction, and who was committed to the Labor government's restructuring agenda, backed the right wing. He attacked the Asian delegates for being unrepresentative, and was in turn attacked by certain Asian delegates for being, in their view, condescending and racist.[3] Ferguson's intervention was serious, given his power position within the ACTU and ICFTU. The ICFTU leadership attacked the new venture as politically inspired, with no place in the structures of international trade unionism. Certain International Trade Secretariats (ITS) also went onto the offensive, arguing that this was nothing more than an ultra-left venture.

The fact that this fragile initiative survived these attacks provides insight into the cardinal challenge unions face in the market era, namely, that the values, beliefs, vision and organising skills of leadership are vital to the countermovement's emergence. Sassoon in his impressive history of socialism argues that leadership is critical to this process. In the late nineteenth century a socialist leadership gave 'ideological cohesion and an organizational unity' to a highly fragmented working class (1996: 8):

> Class consciousness was constructed by political activists, just as nationalism was constructed by nationalists. . . . This process does not, of course, depend solely on activism. For the activists to be successful, they must build on real foundations, not on thin air. The appeal must be recognized and interiorized. As Machiavelli explained, the Prince, to be successful, must rely not only on his own skills, his *virtu*, but also on objective circumstances, on his *fortuna*.

Fortuna resided in the presence of left ACTU leaders, who recognised that the fight against market forces required a global movement response grounded in identifying with democratic unions in the south. Most significantly, this leadership bravely asserted that is was essential to move beyond ICFTU unions in the south, because these organisations were largely ineffectual company-styled or state-run entities, often under the control of corrupt leaderships. From the outset SIGTUR made the strategic choice to work solely with democratic unions that had arisen outside this official framework. What then evolved was an organic relationship between national leaderships from differing cultural and historical backgrounds, who were nevertheless united in their commitment and vision. They were persons marked by a lifetime of struggle, unconcerned with personal status and material reward, whose sense of self had been moulded by suffering and conflict. Their style was anti-bureaucratic; they were movement builders; they lived on the edge, with no personal expectations only a commitment to the marginalised, to those whom market forces had reduced to a commodity like existence. As a consequence, the connection across national boundaries proved deep and enduring, with the core SIGTUR leadership remaining stable since 1990. Despite setbacks, SIGTUR is gradually establishing itself as a force against restructuring because of this *virtu*, and because self-regulating markets are creating the foundations conducive to movement building.

The initiative grew steadily through the organisation of regional Congresses. The first three Congresses were held in Western Australia in 1990, 1992 and 1994. The year 1995 marked a turning point when the recently-elected Conservative government in Western Australia introduced anti-union laws. This radicalised the West Australian union movement, generating strong resistance to the proposed changes. Pressures on the government, including a threat by the Indian and South African members of SIGTUR to initiate a shipping and trade boycott, led to a withdrawal of the legislation. Points of vulnerability had been discovered.

The fourth SIGTUR congress, held in Calcutta, India, in 1997, was organised by the Centre of Indian Trade Unions (CITU). At this first meeting outside Australia, the dynamic, style and procedures were shaped by the Indian leadership. Banners and posters lined Calcutta's crowded streets and more than 20,000 workers participated in the opening events. CITU organised factory and community visits that revealed the union federation's social base in West Bengal's working class. The success of the Indian meeting consolidated the vision of a southern, rather than a geographically-bound network of democratic unions. The Calcutta meeting highlighted the impact of market ideology on workers through downsizing, outsourcing, casualisation and the privatisation of state assets. Further congresses have been held in South Africa, Korea and Thailand.

Four organisational traditions can be distinguished within SIGTUR that reflect distinctive histories and strategic approaches. Firstly, three key constituents – Brazil's Central Unica dos Trabalhadores (United Workers Central) (CUT), Congress of South African Trade Unions (COSATU) and the Korean Confederation of Trade Unions (KCTU) – have been at the cutting edge of developing social movement unionism (Lambert and Webster 1988; Seidman 1994; Webster 1988). Seidman contends that in the case of South Africa and Brazil, similar patterns of rapid labour process transformation, despotic systems of labour control, lack of social infrastructure in the community, and restricted access to political power under authoritarian rule, were objective conditions creating a social movement response. Her account of the rise of social movement unionism during the 1970s and 1980s stresses the key role of leadership in forging links between the new unions and emerging movements in the community (Seidman 1994: 202). The KCTU followed a similar strategy.

The second organisational tradition relates to the emergent democratic unions in South-East Asia, a region where United States-inspired systems of labour control are most evident. Faced with hostile states, new social movement-oriented democratic unions have emerged in the Philippines, Indonesia, Thailand, Sri Lanka and Pakistan. Many unionists have spent long periods in prison for their endeavours. The left of the Indian trade union movement, CITU and the All India Trade Union Congress (AITUC) represent a third tradition. These unions have taken the lead in the anti-globalisation movement on the sub-continent, organising mass campaigns and general strikes embracing a range of organisations in civil society. The fourth tendency is the ACTU in Australia. In periods of conflict such as the 1998 maritime dispute, the latter evidenced social movement characteristics, which have not been sustained.

This brief narrative reveals that Munck is right when he argues that counter-movement construction is not a spontaneous reaction to self-regulating markets. Crucially, movements grow out of conflict, and struggle against the status quo within the institutional labour movement. This is over and above having to contend with hostile corporations and authoritarian states. Inevitably established party and industrial structures react defensively. This process embodies a clash of ideas between the old and the new, thus the struggle for political hegemony is at the heart of countermovement construction. Self-regulating markets are socially destructive, and it is this objective circumstance that provides fertile soil for the idea of a new movement. With the exception of Australia, SIGTUR participants never experienced Polanyi's first Great Transformation. A democratic welfare state was not constructed; full union rights and social citizenship were never secured. The tenuous situation of the working class in these countries was further exacerbated by the second Great Transformation. This historical trajectory has established the objective conditions for a Polanyi countermovement in the south. In the following section the character of this movement is detailed.

The NLI and the struggle to de-commodify labour

Table 10.1 captures the characteristics of SIGTUR's NLI. These are choices made to construct a particular kind of countermovement, one that is democratic, participatory and action orientated.

Table 10.1 Characteristics of SIGTUR's NLI

Old Labour internationalism	New Labour internationalism
Career bureaucrats	Political generation of committed activists
Hierarchy and large bureaucracy	Network
Centralisation	Decentralisation
Restricted debate	Open debate
Diplomatic orientation	Mobilisation and campaign orientation
Focus on workplace and trade unions only	Focus on coalition building with new social movements and non-governmental organisations
Predominantly established northern male white workers	Predominantly struggling southern Afro, Asian and Latino workers

These features of the NLI create the potential for a psychological transformation vital to the movement building project. In this regard, the psychological impact of commodity status is central. Mead's analysis on how the self concept emerges provides a basis for exploring this dynamic (1934). Persons achieve the feelings and the idea of a self through seeing themselves through the eyes of the other. Cooley conveyed this process through 'the looking glass self' metaphor (1956). Self-image is formed in this process of social interaction where persons take on the mind of the other. The relevance of these insights for commodity status is obvious. When treated as a commodity, feelings of negative self worth dominate mind and emotion. This status is materialised in poor physical conditions (low wages; long hours; poor health and safety conditions) and in subordination to authoritarian work relations. Being treated in this way drains life of meaning and value. Fromm (1947: 72) observed, 'If the vicissitudes of the market are the judges of one's value, the sense of dignity and pride is destroyed'.

The fundamental aim of the NLI is to transform this sense of worthlessness. A decade of qualitative interviews has led to the following insights into the psychology of movements. Movement building creates a sense of purpose, and gives meaning to existence because individuals integrated into movement drive change. Movements create a space to reinterpret experience, for it is here that the alternative discourse emerges, clarifying how market ideology produces negative self worth. Each of the features of the NLI listed in Table 10.1 generates a positive sense of self, through creating the space for the realisation of each person's creative capacity, consequently market personality is transformed into productive personality (Fromm 1947: 67, 82). This psychological transformation is a first vital step in the de-commodification of labour. Persons experience human liberation *within the movement* and can thereby distance themselves from the insidious influence of market ideology. As individuals rediscover their essential worth, their dignity and their inherent value, their sense of anger at the injustice of commodity status is magnified. Such anger is the motor of collective action.

The distinctive southern experience

Freedom is choice, a response to an existential predicament. Exploring the roads to freedom is also an encounter with the manifold obstacles to freedom (Meszaros 1979: 16). Choosing to fight for the negation of commodity status is a question of leadership, and in this regard the historical experience of southern workers has provided a fertile ground for the emergence of a leadership consonant with the democratic character of the countermovement project.

Commodity status is cardinal to the historical experience of southern workers whose identity is marked by colonialism and racism in which 'coercion – direct and persistent – was an essential element in organizing a labor force' (Munck 1988: 27). Munck (1988: 30) notes: 'Today, the descendents of Indian and Chinese forced labourers are a sizeable portion of the working population of Southeast Asia, Africa and parts of the Americas'. This southern experience was further conditioned by political independence struggles, and the disillusionments of the post-colonial era. Our leadership interviews capture this distinctive southern identity.[4]

These political changes occurred at a time of profound transformation in the world economy, as the old colonial division of labour gave way to a new international division of labour and the emergence of a substantial manufacturing sector in parts of Asia. The relocation of production from the developed northern economies to these newly industrialising societies was the paramount feature of this new economic map, a shift which was driven by self-regulating markets. The new industrialisation created a new working class in Asia, youthful and desirous of transcending grinding rural poverty. However, their aspirations were soon eroded by the harsh conditions of the new factories, and they became open to the new democratic unionism that was being advanced in the region (Lambert 1997, 1999). These are the unions that SIGTUR engaged.

The experience of disenfranchisement and exploitation that characterises this southern identity has been exacerbated by the second Great Transformation. As our research since the mid 1990s at SIGTUR congresses in India, South Africa, Korea and Thailand has shown, the consciousness of southern workers is marked by the negative impact of neo-liberal globalisation.[5] The surveys highlighted a common experience of work restructuring in the new era, where insecurity overwhelmed workers as a result of downsizing, casualisation and privatisation. For those who managed to retain employment, conditions changed with restructuring as they experienced work intensification, a deterioration in the quality of jobs, working and living conditions, reduced real wages and the erosion of culture. The surveys' bleak picture of restructuring was reinforced by the view that privatisation is leading to a crisis in the reproduction of labour itself.

Significantly, this harsh reality underpinned the delegates' perspective that there is no solution to their predicament through reliance on traditional modes of organising, hence the stress on the need to build social movements committed to challenging rent evictions, electricity cut-offs, lack of access to public health and poor transportation. Evidence of concerted collective action in the workplace, and in the community, led delegates to conclude that the most vigorous and determined resistance to neo-liberal restructuring had indeed come from the south. Having never experienced the reformist capitalism of the first Great Transformation, there is a sense of continuity between the forced labour regimes of colonialism and the restructuring that they now confront. For this reason southern workers evidence a more overt and determined resistance to restructuring than northern workers. This is why a NLI is being driven from the south rather than the north, where workers may still cling to the hope of the welfare state protecting their interests to some degree. In the south, movement leadership is under no such illusions, choosing instead to build a social movement response. Commitment is central to such an endeavour.

Commitment

Market ideology narrows commitment to individual advancement. Sennet observes that orientation leads to the 'acid erosion of those qualities of character, like loyalty, commitment, purpose, and resolution, which are long term in nature' (1998: 30). Self-regulating markets on a global scale has produced, 'chameleon values' jettisoned as swiftly as a change of clothing, as long-term social commitment dissolves before short-term private opportunity. This 'corrosion of character' is the antithesis of social commitment and vision so critical to the countermovement project.

When SIGTUR was formed the search was for activists with these values, not the time-serving union bureaucrats from company and state-sponsored unions. This choice led to the discovery of a generation of labour leaders who had fought to win democratic union rights in the south, often at a high personal cost. Many in the SIGTUR leadership have endured prison terms, torture and other methods of victimisation.[6]

These persons had formed identities centred on justice and the empowerment of working people. Interviews reveal how these identities are grounded in value choices – service to the community rather than individual careerism and personal material reward; collective solidarity in place of upward mobility; freedom, democracy and participation over hierarchy and control; social, economic and political equality against elitism; and social control over market logic. This southern movement has arisen because of the value choices of its leadership. For example, Dita Sari, a leader of democratic unions in Indonesia, chose not to accept the Reebok human rights award and an accompanying check of US$50,000 in March 2002. The award was to be presented by Robert Redford, Desmond Tutu and other international celebrities at a glittering ceremony planned to coincide with the Winter Olympics at Salt Lake City. In a letter to the Reebok CEO, she stated (Dwyer 2002):

> We know how you treat your workers in the Third World. I know because I helped organize them and carried out actions with them. We know you paid your workers less than a dollar a day when your sneakers were selling for a hundred and that you rented the police to destroy us. Understanding this, we feel that it isn't appropriate for you to put the lid on the wrongs you've committed toward workers by giving this kind of award.

Such values generate the organisational characteristics listed in Table 10.1. A feature of this leadership is a lifelong commitment to worker struggle. Malaysian union leader Arokia Dass's personal identity is inseparable from the colonial past, and its impact on his father as an indentured labourer. This sense of his own personal history is a factor in his lifelong commitment. This long-term leadership commitment is critical to the growth and survival of SIGTUR as the movement has achieved a notable degree of stability since the 1990s through being able to maintain a core leadership group.

Interviews with SIGTUR leaders reveal a distinct political generation who were shaped by their experiences of oppression in their formative years. Many are in their late fifties. The way in which Arokia Dass's political commitment was formed typifies this political generation (Dass, interview, 2001):

> One day I was walking along the road and there was this person staggering and walking in front of me. Suddenly, he dropped dead. Someone told me he died of hunger. I turned around and saw that there was so much food. Why should this person die of hunger? Then I realized that religion had no answer to this question. I wanted the eradication of poverty. I started reading Marx. I became a socialist.

What is also distinctive about this age cohort is that they became active in a variety of 'social justice' movements in their youth in a similar way to union activists in Southern California (Voss and Sherman 2000). They then carried their vision and organisational experiences into the labour movement. Importantly, they brought to the trade union movement a broader conception of labour that mobilises workers in the totality of their lives.

Rubina Jamil, President of the All Pakistan Federation of Trade Unions and leader of the Working Women's Organisation, illustrates this process. She stressed that it was not possible to recruit women workers into the union movement without a close relationship with the family. Furthermore, she said (Jamil, interview, 2001):

> If there's any problem inside the factory, we try our best to resolve the family problems, too. If the father of the girl needs a job, we try our best with the help of our male colleagues to find him a job. If the father or the mother are suffering from any disease we help them to go to the hospital and we assist them, so we are very much in touch with the family members of the women workers and we organize family counseling programs because we think it is really important for the family members to know why trade unions are important.

At the centre of the leadership style of these activists is a commitment to union democracy and accountable leadership. A struggle against bureaucratic and corrupt leadership has been at the heart of trade union struggles in Asia in the post-war period. Again, this is captured in the interview with Dass (Interview, 2001):

> When we took over leadership we posed the question, what is the difference between us and those we kicked out of the union? We did participatory action research. Three to four thousand workers were interviewed. They all said that decision making must be left to the members; the union must be democratic and independent; it should not be affiliated to political parties.

Giving workers a direct voice in organisational decision-making builds a positive sense of self, and psychologically transforms feelings of worthlessness. Our leadership interviews revealed that the *process* of building democratic unions de-commodified labour. Friendship networks lay at the core of the project. Activists establish enduring friendships with workers in the factory. Friendship is about the recognition of uniqueness, and the union network is essentially a friendship network, undermining the anonymous, instrumental relationships of factory culture. As the friendship networks consolidate a sense of community emerges. These shifts are reinforced by the decentralised network character of the NLI, which has the potential to empower new forms of global action.

Networking and the geography of power

The intersecting nodes of SIGTUR's cyberspace communications are shown in Figure 10.1. Networking may contribute to the transformation of commodity status, because the process has the potential to create a new power dynamic from below. The new labour geography, most notably the work of Harvey (2000) and Herod (2001a, 2001b) has provided insights in this regard.

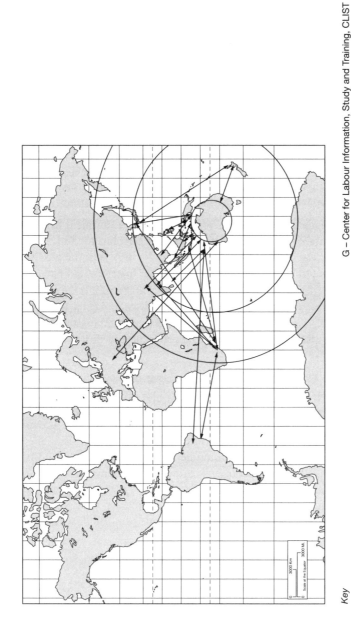

Key

A – CUT Brazil
B – Congress of South African Trade Unions, COSATU
C – Center of Indian Trade Unions, CITU; All India Trade Union Center, AITUC
D – Transport and General Workers Union, Sri Lanka
E – All Pakistan Federation of Trade Unions, APFTU
F – Center for Indonesian Workers Struggle, FNPBI

G – Center for Labour Information, Study and Training, CLIST
H – Malaysian Congress of Trade Unions, MTUC, certain unions
I – Korean Confederation of Trade Unions, KCTU
J – KMU Philippines
K – New Zealand Council of Trade Unions

Figure 10.1 Mercator projection of the world

Networking lies at the heart of the NLI. Castells (1996: 470) has argued that a new stage in the development of capitalism has ushered in the network society, which creates open, innovative structures. However, he contends that this change will result in labour becoming localised, disaggregated, fragmented, diversified and divided in its collective identity (1996: 475). He concludes, 'Under the conditions of the network society capital is globally coordinated, labour is individualized' (1996: 476). Consequently (1997: 360):

> The labor movement seems to be historically superceded ... Labor unions are influential political actors in many countries . . . yet the labor movement does not seem fit to generate by itself and from itself a project identity able to reconstruct social control and to rebuild social institutions in the Information Age. Labor militants will undoubted be part of new transformative social dynamics. I am less sure that labor unions will.

The NLI demonstrates quite the opposite. Cyberspace networking offers the possibility to reconfigure national unions into a networked, movement-orientated global unionism. Far from being historically superseded, global networking that follows the geographic contours of global corporations is a countermovement innovation. Herod and Wright's (2002) edited collection, *Geographies of power: placing scale*, captures debates central to such an endeavour. At one level, the issue seems self evident: if corporations have increased their power immeasurably through globalising the scale of their operations, so too should unions. Scale is central to such an initiative, and as Herod (2003: 237) has argued: 'how we conceptualize the ways in which the world is scaled will shape how we engage with that world'. Scale as hierarchy is challenged by labour geographers (Gibson-Graham 2002; Herod 2003; Herod and Wright 2002; Latham 2002; Sadler and Fagan 2004). In contrast to hierarchical notions of scale, NLI networking conceives of the world of places not as bounded spaces, but as intertwined, networked together, connected in a single whole, 'simultaneously global and local (and regional and national) without being wholly one or the other' (Herod and Wright 2002: 8). It is not by chance that experiments in the NLI have adopted a network style of organising locally and connecting globally. The non-hierarchical, flat, open form of a networked NLI maximises grass roots participation that transforms the commodity experience of workers.

Networking global action

In striving for social emancipation, SIGTUR has uncovered how globalisation represents an opportunity for place to place networking grounded in local actions that are coordinated and integrated into a global scale. This occurs within the geographic contours of corporations, and the communities impacted by restructuring. In a speech to the 7th Congress of SIGTUR in Bangkok in June 2005, the Vice President of the KCTU argued that the union movement needs to embrace a phase of bold experimentation. 'We need to fundamentally transform ourselves. We cannot rely on traditional methods of organising and struggle. If unions fail in this we have no future. The mission is to develop a new type of labour movement. This project is both urgent and deadly serious' (SIGTUR October 2005).

SIGTUR is at an early stage of experimenting with networked global action against global corporations and against repressive states. Much has been learnt from the movement's involvement in campaigns against Rio Tinto and the imprisonment of union leaders in Korea and Malaysia. Rio Tinto is one of the world's largest private mining corporations, with sixty operations in forty nations, mining aluminium, copper, coal, uranium, gold, industrial minerals and iron ore. John Maitland, President of the Australian Construction, Forestry, Mining and Energy Workers Union (CFMEU) and also President of International Chemical, Energy and Mining, ICEM, which is a global union federation, played a key role in evolving a networked response to the company's attack on union rights and working conditions. The Rio Global Union Network (RGUN) was formed by the ICEM and was coordinated from California. Cyberspace was used to promote the campaign, to instantaneously communicate union actions, and to keep track of the corporation's responses. ICEM's demands included a commitment to core ILO (International Labour Organisation) Conventions that protect worker rights, the negotiation of a global agreement with effective monitoring mechanisms to give effect to these principles, and the resolution of disputes in the light of these principles. A key innovation of the campaign was the formation of a capital committee that coordinated action at Rio's shareholder meetings. SIGTUR integrated its network into the campaign, leading to protest action across the south. A similar process of networked action took place soon after the SIGTUR Congress in Korea in November 2001. Here the focus was the imprisonment of union leaders in Korea and Malaysia. Local country actions, centred on mass protest action at the relevant embassies, were linked through cyberspace networking. The actions may well have contributed to the release of the prisoners.

Following the 7th Congress in Bangkok, networked action will again be put to the test. Congress resolved to initiate a long term campaign against repressive labour law in the south. Despite many Asian countries establishing parliamentary democracies, their industrial relations systems have become ever more repressive, with governments believing that such regimes are essential to maintaining comparative advantage in global markets, through low wages, extreme hours and poor working conditions. An innovation in Korea has been the introduction of amendments that allow the state to impose extreme financial penalties on workers who take industrial action outside the strict constraints of the industrial relations system (KCTU 2005). Fines of KRW 110 billion have been imposed on workers and their families, leading to the closure of bank accounts and the confiscation of apartments, rendering families destitute. Amendments also allow for the banning of wages of union organisers. In India opposition to labour law amendments has led to workers 'finding themselves in jail, severely beaten by police and facing dismissals' (CITU 2005). In Australia, once the bastion of union rights and social democracy, the Conservative government is introducing amendments that will replace unions and collective bargaining with a system of individual contracts.

These changes are justified in terms of the need to create and maintain a globally competitive and flexible economy. The SIGTUR Congress challenged this logic by reasserting a democratic discourse on labour law (SIGTUR 2005). 'A Universal Declaration on Labour Law and Labour Rights in the Economic South' was adopted. The document asserts, 'The history of the trade union movement in the economic south is intertwined with the struggle for freedom and democracy. Across the south, the union movement made a critical contribution to the transition from repressive, authoritarian regimes to parliamentary democracy. It is therefore ironic that in the light of this history, unions in the south now find themselves under an extreme attack as these "democratic" regimes "reform" labour law in the name of global competitiveness and flexibility. In our struggles against these "reforms" we have to again return to our roots in the south and rediscover what drove the freedom struggle. We need to attack the ideology of the market and assert a Universal Declaration of Labour Rights, which is based on freedom and justice in the workplace and in society.'

The declaration then lists key democratic rights in the workplace that SIGTUR will fight for in the coming decades:

- Freedom of Association and the right to join a union of our own choice, without interference from corporations and governments.
- The right of collective bargaining that recognises the *essential* role of unions in the bargaining process.
- The right to bargain collectively on workplace issues *and* broader social and political concerns.
- Collective bargaining must include the right to bargain and negotiate corporate restructuring in all its dimensions.
- Right of entry with no restrictions so that the union can strengthen itself.
- The right to democratically elect union delegates (shop stewards) in every section of the organisation.
- The right of this workplace based leadership to have time off work to freely and openly conduct union business without fear of victimisation. This includes the right to call work meetings in the workplace to discuss union issues.
- The right to strike and take industrial action without any threat to life or the threat of legal or financial sanctions against union members and their unions.
- The right of all workers and including public sector workers, who are often excluded in Asia, to these democratic labour rights.
- The right of all workers to job security and social security.
- The right of all women to equal wages, security of tenure and respect for their trade union rights.

The document concludes:

This is a significant element of the freedom struggle. This is a struggle against corporate greed and repression. This is a struggle against governments who use labour law to weaken our movement.

We, the workers who produce the wealth of nations have an inalienable right to share in that wealth. We have the right to a democratic voice in the issues that affect our lives.

We will not rest until the democratic freedoms listed in this declaration are fully achieved in every nation.

The SIGTUR Congress committed to struggle for these democratic rights through a globally-coordinated mass mobilisation for the democratisation of labour law. This will take the form of an International Day of Action on Labour Law in each country. This commitment is another facet of a ceaseless struggle against labour's commodity status, for democratic labour law is indeed a crucial state intervention contradicting market logic. This is why dismantling democratic labour law is a primary focus of the neo-liberal project. When unions are severely constrained and when collective bargaining is marginalised, workers face corporate power isolated and alone, and as Marx (1976: 280) portrayed so vividly, workers enter this situation 'timidly and holding back, like someone who has brought his own hide to the market and now has nothing else to expect but – a tanning'.

The historic transformation of trade unionism

The transformation of work under capitalism is a contradictory process that closes down options and opens new opportunities. The destruction of craft work by machine-based production undermined craft unionism. In the 1930s this led to dire predictions that organised labour would disappear in the United States. These predictions were, as Cobble (2001) reminds us, issued literally on the eve of the dramatic upsurge of labour organising that began in 1933. Instead of labour disappearing, a new form of worker organisation – industrial unionism – emerged, and grew in strength through much of the twentieth century.

The globalisation of capitalism has now created a similar crisis for industrial unionism, as the global restructuring of work threatens traditional union organisation. Across the South, this climate of insecurity is further exacerbated by the direct attack on basic organising rights. Yet the crisis has produced a Polanyi type countermovement, formed and driven by a committed leadership, making full use of the potential of cyberspace to transform the geographic scale of unionism linking, coordinating and transforming local action into a potentially powerful global force.

SIGTUR will never succeed in realising this historic transition in isolation. This southern movement needs to synchronise with other initiatives that are serious about the construction of a global resistance movement. Here the new direction of the Service Employees International Union in the United States is pertinent. It has taken the lead in tracking global corporations and organising global unionism as a response. John Maitland organised a joint meeting of maritime, mining and construction unions in Los Angeles in May 2005 as a step towards the formation of global unionism. The old international trade secretariats have created a new identity, calling themselves global union federations (GUFs). Given their base in industrial sectors, the GUFs have a crucial role to play in the transition. However, this presupposes a political shift away from the Eurocentric politics of social partnership to the politics of social movements, and active resistance against corporate power and the restructuring agenda (Gallin 2004; Wahl 2004). Here the barrier to change seems substantial, leaving a wide gulf between the politics of north and south.

However, leaders of existing internationals are likely to experience intense pressures from below to change their style of internationalism, from diplomacy with the captains of industry to movement based resistance. In May 2004 the author shared a panel with union delegates at the inaugural meeting of the World Social Forum held in Brussels. They were shopfloor workers from Arcelor Steel, a large factory in Liege, Northern Belgium. They faced the prospect of closure following the buyout by an American multinational corporation (MNC). A leader stated:

> When the MNC decided to close down the factory in Liege, we knew that 10,000 jobs would be lost. We refused to accept this logic. They plan to close the plant in 2005 and shift production to Brazil, China and Poland where the workforce can be exploited. They told us that this decision was final and was not subject to negotiation or discussion at local level. The decision had been taken by the Board and there would be no change. There is a strong global economic logic to this. The MNC sees itself as building history and becoming so powerful that its power extends beyond regions and continents. They see themselves as the real masters – masters of countries, police forces, citizens.
>
> They have only one aim – to become a leading global steel corporation. To achieve this they are willing to break any laws, conventions and rights on their way to building their power base. They don't take account of human beings and communities. They don't discuss or negotiate. They only present a monologue. They are out to dismantle an entire industry in a region. This is worse than a war, much worse than death – this is the dismantling of the solidarity of the working class. this war, this is death we are suffering.
>
> In the face of this, we have to set up a global trade union movement that has to discover how to act in the face of this power. We have to give a global answer. You can't give a local answer to a global question. We have to establish a new kind of dialogue with workers across the globe. We have to discover how we can react more effectively.

This concluding quote captures the will to resist that knows no north/south divide. The NLI of SIGTUR will seek to play a constructive role in this global struggle that is shaping a new kind of labour movement.

Notes

1   The level of coordination is remarkable. Following its election victory in 2004, the conservative Coalition government in Australia is preparing for a fresh attack on trade union rights. They have been supported in this by the OECD, the governor of the Australian Reserve Bank and various employer associations. Each articulate the same perspective.
2   As part of the Australian Research Council research project on white goods manufacturing, contact with workers from the Chef cooker plant in Melbourne Australia has been maintained and interviews conducted. This factory was closed after it was acquired by the Swedish multinational corporation Electrolux. The social and psychological impact of restructuring is never assessed, confirming the commodity like status of the victims. No longer useful, they are assigned to the margins of society where they are again the objects of new rounds of welfare cuts and restructuring.
3   The conflictual exchange is significant in that it reveals much about the difficulties of constructing a new countermovement. Ferguson is undoubtedly no racist. However, his assertions were interpreted as racist because delegates felt he ridiculed their efforts.
4   Certain Southeast Asian leaders are conscious of their family's experience as indentured laborers on plantations. All evidenced a sense of political betrayal as the exploitative

conditions of workers remained largely unchanged while post-colonial states consolidated new elites. Part of this sense of history is shaped by the leaders' view of the United States as a dominant and politically-manipulative power in the region, playing a key role in the repression of democratic unionism and the construction of pliant workplace organisation.

5   This assessment is based on the survey and the interviews. The impact is 'searing' in that the restructuring completely alters conditions of existence, without reference to workers' needs to provide for families. This leads to intense anger and emotional distress. Since our focus is southern workers, we analyse this impact on southern identity. In fact, the literature reveals that northern workers in the advanced industrialised nations are experiencing similar consequences of the change.

6   We are engaged in in-depth interviews with key activists associated with SIGTUR. For example, Malaysian union leader Arokia Dass, who has played a key role in the development of SIGTUR, was detained under Malaysia's Internal Security Act between 1987 and 1989. He was psychologically tortured, blindfolded and moved to different prisons up to three times a week. Dita Sari, a leader of the independent unions in Indonesia, was imprisoned for three years under Suharto. She campaigned against prison conditions, organising other prisoners, and, not surprisingly, found herself placed in isolation. As of 2006, eight Korean unionists were serving long prison terms.

References

Adler, G. and Webster, E. (eds) (2000) *Trade unions and democratization in South Africa, 1985–97,* Johannesburg.

Bakan, J. (2004) *The corporation: the pathological pursuit of profit and power,* London.

Bamber, G., Lansbury, R. and Wailes, N. (2004) *International and comparative employment relations: globalisation and the developed market economies,* Sydney.

Batliwala, S. (2002) 'Grassroots movement as transnational actors: implications for global civil society', *Voluntas* 13:4.

Breakwell, G. (1986) *Coping with Threatened Identities,* London.

Buhlungu, S. (2002) *Comrades, entrepreneurs and career unionists: organisational modernisation and the new cleavages among full-time union officials in South Africa,* Friedrich Ebert Stiftung Occasional Paper No. 17, Johannesburg.

Burawoy, M. (2002) 'Types of sociology', Paper presented at the colloquium on the *Southern African in transition program,* Department of Sociology, University of the Witwatersrand.

Calland, C. and Sil, R. (eds) (2001) *The politics of labour in a global age: continuity and change in late-industrialising and post-socialist economies,* Oxford.

Castells, M. (1996) *The information age: economy, society and culture: volume 1, the rise of the network society,* Oxford.

—— (1997) *The power of identity, volume 2, the rise of the network society,* Oxford.

Centre of Indian Trade Unions (CITU) (2003) *United struggles and the organizational consolidation of the trade union movement,* Calcutta.

—— (2005) 'The attack on labour rights in India', paper presented to the 7th Congress of SIGTUR, Bangkok, June 2005.

Cobble, D. (2001) 'Lost ways of unionism: historical perspectives on reinventing the labor movement', in Turner, L., Katz, H. and Hurd, R. (eds), *Rekindling the movement: labor's quest for relevance in the 21st century,* Ithaca.

Collinson, C. (2001) 'Southern unions link up on globalisation', *Western Teacher,* 7 December.

Cooley, C. H. (1956) *Human nature and the social order*, Glencoe, Illinois.

—— (1998) *On self and social organization*, Chicago.

Deyo, F. C. (ed.) (1987) *The political economy of the new asian industrialism*, Ithaca.

Dwyer, L. (2002) 'Reprimand for Reebok', Correspondence with the author, 25 March 2002.

Erikson, E. (1968) *Identity: youth and crisis*, New York.

Fromm, E. (1947) *Man for himself*, New York.

Gallin, D. (2001) 'Propositions on trade unions and informal employment in times of globalisation', in Waterman, P. and Wills, J. (eds), *Place, space and the new labour internationalism*, Oxford.

—— (2004) 'Political education and globalisation', paper presented to the International Federation of Worker Education Associations seminar, Eastbourne, 9 October, 2004.

Gibson-Graham, J. K. (2002) 'Beyond global vs local: economic politics outside the binary frame', in Herod, A. and Wright, M. (eds), *Geographies of power: placing scale*, Oxford.

Gruen, F. H. 'How bad is Australia's economic performance and why?', Discussion Paper No. 127. Center for Economic Policy Research, Australian National University.

Harris, N. (2002) *What's new in the new labor internationalism: SIGTUR as a global network*. Unpublished Honours Dissertation, Department of Organizational and Labor Studies, University of Western Australia.

Harvey, D. (1996) *Justice, nature and the geography of difference*, Oxford.

—— (2000) *Spaces of hope*, Edinburgh.

Hathaway, D. (2000) 'Allies across the border: Mexico's "Authentic Labor Front" and global solidarity', Cambridge, Massachusetts.

Haworth, N. and Ramsay, H. (1986) 'Workers of the world untied: a critical analysis of the labor response to the internationalisation of capital', *International Journal of the Sociology of Law and Social Policy*, 6:2.

Herod, A. (2001a) *Labor geographies*, New York.

—— (2001b) 'Labor internationalism and the contradictions of globalisation: or, why the local is sometimes still important in a global economy', in Waterman, P. and Wills, J. (eds), *Place, space and the new labour internationalism*, Oxford.

—— (2003) 'The geographies of labor internationalism', *Social Science History*, 27:4.

—— and Wright, M. (2002) *Geographies of power: placing scale*, Oxford.

Kelly, P. (1992) *The end of certainty: the story of the 1980s*, Sydney.

KCTU (Korean Confederation of Trade Unions) (2005) *KCTU report on the recent situation of labour law and industrial relations*, paper presented to the 7th Congress of SIGTUR, Bangkok, June 2005.

Johnston, P. (2001) 'Organize for what? The resurgence of labor as a citizenship movement', in L. Turner, C. Katz and W. Hurd (eds), *Rekindling the movement: labor's quest for relevance in the 21st century*, Ithaca.

Lambert, R. (1990) 'Kilusang Mayo Uno and the rise of social movement unionism in the Philippines', *Labor & Industry*, 2:3.

—— (1996) 'Asian trade and Australian labour market restructuring', in Robison, R. (ed.), *Pathways to Asia*, Sydney.

—— (1997) *State and labor in new order Indonesia*, Perth.

—— (1998) 'Asian Labour Markets and International Competitiveness: Australian transformations', *International Review of Comparative Public Policy*, 10, Special edition.

—— (1999) 'Australia's historic industrial relations transition', in Leisink, P. (ed.), *Globalisation and labour relations*.

—— (2003) 'Transnational union strategies: civilizing labour standards', in Sandbrook, R. (ed.), *Civilizing globalisation: a survival guide*, New York.

—— (2005) 'Death of a factory: an ethnography of market rationalism's hidden abode in inner-city Melbourne', *Anthropological Forum*, 14.

—— and Webster, E. (1988) 'The re-emergence of political unionism in contemporary South Africa', in Cobbet, W., Cohen, R. and Trenton, R. (eds), *Popular struggles in South Africa*, NJ: Africa World Press.

Latham, A. (2002) 'Retheorizing the scale of globalization: topologies, actor networks, and cosmopolitanism', in Herod, A. and Wright, M. (eds), *Geographies of power: placing scale*, Oxford.

Lee, E. (1997) *The labor movement and the internet: the new internationalism*, London.

Lund, F. and Skinner, C. (1999) 'Promoting the interests of women in the informal economy: an analysis of street trader organizations in South Africa', Research Report No. 19. School of Development Studies, University of Natal, Durban.

Maher, T. (2000) Speech by Tony Maher, President of CFMEU Mining Division, to Rio Shareholders Meeting, 10 May. An ICEM communiqué, circulated through RGUN.

Marx, K. (1976) *Capital: volume 1*, London.

Mead, G. (1934) *Mind, self and society from the standpoint of a social behaviourist*, Chicago.

Meszaros, I. (1979) *The work of Sartre: the search for freedom*, Brighton.

Moody, K. (1997) *Workers in a Lean world: unions in the international economy*, London.

Munck, R. (1988) *The new international labor studies: an introduction*, Oxford.

—— (2002) *Globalisation and labor: the new 'Great Transformation'*, London.

—— (2004) 'Introduction: globalisation and labour transnationalism', in Munck, R. (ed.), *Labour and Globalisation*, Liverpool.

Nayak, N. (2001) '"No women, no fish": a feminist perspective on fisheries in developing countries', *Labor Movements Research Committee Newsletter*, October 2001.

O'Brien, R. (2000) 'Workers and world order: the tentative transformation of the international union movement', *Review of International Studies*, 26.

OECD (2004) *OECD economic surveys: Australia*, Paris.

Ogden, M. (1992) *The future of unionism in Australia*, Australian Council of Trade Unions (ACTU), unpublished manuscript.

Olle, W. and Schoeller, W. (1977) 'World market competition and restrictions on international trade union policies', *Capital and Class*, 2.

Peetz, D. (1998) *Unions in a contrary world: the future of the Australian trade union movement*, Cambridge.

Polanyi, K. (1944) *The Great Transformation: the political and economic origins of our time*, Boston.

—— Arensberg, C. M. and Pearson, H. W. (1957) *Trade and Market in the Early Empires: Economies in History and Theory*, Glencoe, Illinois.

Press, P. (1989) 'A critique of trade union internationalism', in Press, M. and Thomson, D. (eds), *Solidarity for survival: the Don Thomson reader*, Nottingham.

Pusey, M. (1991) *Economic Rationalism in Canberra*, Cambridge.

Ramsay, H. (1999) 'In search of international union theory', in Waddington, J. (ed.), *Globalisation patterns of labor resistance*, New York.

—— and Bair, J. (1999) 'Working on the chain gang: global production networks and their implications for organized labor', paper presented to the European Sociological Association, Congress *Will Europe Work?* 18–21 August 1999.

Rickard, J. (1984) *H B Higgins: a rebel judge*, Sydney.

Rio Tinto Global Union Network (RGUN) (2000) *Rio Tinto global campaign factsheet*. Available from tconrow@igc.org.

Ross, A. (ed.) (1997) *No sweat: fashion, free trade and the rights of garment workers*, London.

Sable, C., O'Rourke, D. and Fung, A. (2000) 'Ratcheting labor standards: regulation for continuous improvement in the global workplace', paper presented to *Congress on Citizenship in a Global Economy*, University of Wisconsin, Madison.

Sadler, D. and Fagan, B. (2004) Australian trade unions and the politics of scale reconstructing the spatiality of industrial relations, *Economic Geography* 80:1.

Sandbrook, R. (ed.) (2003) *Civilizing globalisation: a survival guide*, New York.

Sassoon, D. (1996) *One hundred years of socialism: the West European left in the twentieth century*, London.

Scipes, K. (2000) 'It's time to come clean: open the AFL-CIO archives on international labor operations', *Labor Studies Journal* 25:2.

Seidman, G. (1994) *Manufacturing militancy: workers' movements in Brazil and South Africa, 1970–1985*, Berkeley.

—— (2002) 'Deflated citizenship: labor rights in a global order', paper presented at the Annual Congress of the American Sociological Association, August 2002, Washington.

Sennet, R. (1998) *Corrosion of character: the personal consequences of work in the new capitalism*, New York.

Silver, B. (2003) *Forces of labor: workers movements and globalization since 1870*, Cambridge.

—— and Arrighi, G. (2001) 'Workers North and South', *Socialist Register 2001*.

Social Action (1991).

Southern Initiative on Globalization and Trade Union Rights (SIGTUR) (1990) Report on the evolution of the Indian Ocean region secretariat concept: towards a new network of solidarity, 24 September 1990. Perth, Western Australia. SIGTUR Archive, Department of Organizational and Labor Studies, University of Western Australia.

—— (1998) *Founding Document*, unpublished manuscript, author's personal archive.

—— (1999) *Principles for participation in SIGTUR*, unpublished manuscript, author's personal archive.

—— (2005) *The 7th Congress of SIGTUR, Bangkok, June 2005*, Sydney.

Taylor, R. (2004) *Creating a better world: interpreting global civil society*, Bloomfield.

Touraine, A. (1983) *Solidarity: the analysis of a social movement, Poland, 1980–1981*, Cambridge.

—— (1987) *Workers' Movement*, Cambridge.

Turner, L. and Hurd, R. (2001) 'Building social movement unionism: the transformation of the American labor movement', in Turner, L., Katz, H. and Hurd, R. (eds), *Rekindling the movement: labor's quest for relevance in the 21st century*, Ithaca.

—— Katz, H. and Hurd, R. (eds) (2001) *Rekindling the movement: labor's quest for relevance in the 21st century*, Ithaca.

von Holdt, K. (2002) 'Social movement unionism: the South African case', *Work, Employment and Society*, 16:2.

Voss, K. and Sherman, R. (2000) 'Breaking the iron law of oligarchy: union revitalization in the American labor movement', *American Journal of Sociology*, 106:2.

Wahl, A. (2004) 'European labour: the ideological legacy of the social pact', *Monthly Review*.

Waterman, P. (1984) *For a new labor internationalism*, The Hague.

—— (1998) *Globaliszation and social movements and the new internationalisms*, London.

—— and Wills, J. (eds) (2001) *Place, space and the new labor internationalis*, Oxford.

Webster, E. (1988) 'The rise of social movement unionism: the two faces of the black trade union movement in South Africa', in Frankel, P., Pines, N. and Swilling, M. (eds), *State, resistance and change in South Africa*, North Ryde.

—— and Adler, G. (1999) 'Towards a class compromise in South Africa's double transition', *Politics and Society*, 27:2.

11

Recasting the story of David and Goliath in the global electronics industry

Anibel Ferus-Comelo

Introduction

The nature of contemporary capitalism, our modern-day 'Goliath', puts immense pressures on workers and prevailing forms of trade union organisation. Globalisation, with the enhanced mobility of capital, desegregation of production and subsequent divisions of labour, challenges the ability of existing unions to expand their membership and extend their protection to workers at the same pace that workers are integrated into the global labour market. There is growing evidence that unions, our 'David', are also largely constrained by their own structures, ideology and priorities, which make them ill-equipped to redress the pernicious aspects of network capitalism. A critical assessment of the state of labour therefore needs to be based on both an understanding of corporate restructuring strategies and the inadequate, fragmented response of labour movements in particular places. Drawing upon research on electronics production and its implications for workers and labour organisations in two different parts of the world, this chapter aims to contribute three key arguments to the debate regarding globalisation and labour.[1]

First, a careful analysis of the implications of forms of production for labour organising reveals challenges but also some opportunities for coordinated and strategically aimed collective action in order to place workers' demands on the corporate agenda. Second, the extent to which these opportunities can be exploited on behalf of workers is hindered by the remarkably limited and weak trade union presence in the industry. Third, the emergence of a variety of community-based organisations to fill the gap in trade union representation challenges the prevalent assumption that trade unions are the primary agents of a working-class movement.

Accordingly, this chapter is organised into three sections. The first outlines the supply chain strategy deployed by electronics producers in the two sites of study with a view to highlight working conditions and problems for labour organising that arise from the political and organisational characteristics of electronics manufacturing. The second section explores the potential space for strategies to reassert workers' collective voice. The third examines a few reasons for the low level of collective representation of workers, and documents existing forms of support for workers locally. Finally, the concluding section draws together some theoretical conclusions about labour organisation under conditions of globalisation.

Electronics production in this chapter refers specifically to hardware manufacturing in the computer and peripherals segment, which includes mainframes, personal computers, laptops, hand-held computers as well as related items such as disk drives and printers. This study was conducted in the city of Bangalore, capital of the state of Karnataka in south India and in Silicon Valley in California (US). These places are not only important nodes in global production networks but they are also strongly linked to each other through flows of capital and labour. In both places, interviews were conducted with corporate managers, workers and labour activists, as well as other important industry players such as government officials and representatives of industrial associations.

The challenges of electronics production

The high technology industry is growing at a phenomenal pace in both financial and geographical terms. Computer manufacturing companies are some of the biggest and most profitable companies in the world. Competition among high technology transnational corporations (TNCs) is based upon their capacity to reinvent existing products to make them faster, more attractive and easier to handle. As the performance capabilities of chips double about every eighteen months, according to 'Moore's Law', product life cycles are short and older models become hard to sell. While technology has been advancing swiftly, the price of computers and electronic components has fallen dramatically since the mid 1980s (Berndt *et al.* 2000). Electronics manufacturers have had to compensate for this trend in dropping prices amidst rapid product turnover by inventing new business models and developing various strategies to reduce production costs and accelerate technological innovation.

Global production networks

Production methods in the computer and peripherals industry are defining a paradigmatic shift in global manufacturing with the decentralised and spatially desegregated production of PCs through the 'network enterprise' (Castells 1996). Computers are no longer built 'in-house' by name-brand companies such as Hewlett-Packard (HP) and IBM, also known as original equipment manufacturers (OEMs), but are assembled from components such as motherboards, disk drives and monitors that are produced in different places by contract manufacturers (CMs) and several tiers of suppliers. A unique feature of electronics production is the increasing power of CMs such as Solectron and Flextronics, which do not have name-recognition among consumers but must be seen in the same light as OEMs.

Subcontracting has taken root in the industry to such an extent that it is the central principle behind the organisation of electronics production. An American OEM based in Silicon Valley, for example, subcontracts its production to two contract manufacturers in different countries (Malaysia and Mexico). These contract manufacturers handle virtually all manufacturing services, including network coordination and logistics to the point of distribution. In comparison, the subsidiary of an American TNC in Bangalore coordinates its own production network doing its own 'back-end' production while relying on numerical flexibility of its workforce. Although both the companies outlined above are American MNCs (multinational corporations), their supply chains take different forms because of the different market orientations and production opportunities of the companies. The first produces hand-held computers for an international market whereas the second imports components to assemble PCs in its Bangalore plant for an Indian market. However, in both places, production is orchestrated along complex supply chain networks which cross national and organisational boundaries involving several tiers of subcontractors, and sometimes even home-based workers during peaks in the production cycle. This practice has a tangible impact on workers and labour organising.

Working conditions
Despite some differences in working conditions, workers in both places generally face limited earning capacity, job discrimination, high insecurity due to tenuous employment relations and health risks in the workplace. In Bangalore, the reported starting salary of shop-floor production workers ranged from Rs.1,000 to Rs.7,000 (US$20–140) per month, depending on whether they are employed by large foreign or Indian MNCs or small, local contractors, as well as on their qualifications. Assembly workers in Silicon Valley are part of the growing population of the 'working poor' (not the unemployed or welfare-dependent) (Joint Venture 1998). An exposé of the extent of homeworking in Silicon Valley reported that workers were paid sub-minimum wages at piece rate (Ewell and Oanh Ha 1999). The salaries of factory-based assemblers start at the statutory minimum wage, which in the State of California is $6.15, to a maximum reported scale of $15 per hour. This range corresponds to the qualifications and experience of workers, as well as their job tasks. For example, lead soldering, which is injurious to human health, is often paid at a higher scale. There has been almost no pay rise for assemblers in the valley in recent years. Between 1995 and 2000, entry-level wages for electronics assemblers increased only $0.79, from $5.86 to $6.65, whereas salaries of skilled occupations in the industry such as computer programmers are high and steadily rising.

This wide disparity in income within the industry has a racial and gender dimension. Based on 1990 US Census data, Asians and Latinos were over-represented in the lower-wage 'machine operator' category while Whites comprised 76 per cent of executives and managers in the country. Such 'occupational hierarchy' by race is getting more entrenched in the industry with a significant rise of the percentage of Asians and Latinos in the low-wage blue-collar workforce (which includes assemblers, operators and inspectors), from 75.6 per cent to 86.8 per cent between 1990 and 1999. Moreover, the 1998 US Department of Labour statistics show that non-white, immigrant women are disproportionately represented in low-wage, insecure employment in the electronics industry. Upward mobility is rare, particularly for the largely immigrant and non-white workforce. According to some workers interviewed, managers found ways to circumvent the anti-discrimination laws to retain workers in low-paid positions.

While discrimination against immigrants and women in Silicon Valley is apparent in labour market segmentation and job promotion, in Bangalore, it was manifested at the level of worker recruitment and retention. Most firms employed as many or more men than women in production due to the legal exemption of women from a third shift after 10pm. As the demand for production fluctuates based on orders at any given time, overtime shifts are a necessary part of operations in the sector. Employers prefer to have on hand trained employees who can work overtime, if necessary to complete an order on time, thereby limiting the number of women employed in electronics production.

In both places, in order to maintain their flexibility, electronics companies were increasingly relying on contract labour, part-time and temporary workers, rather than hiring production staff as direct, full-time, 'regular' employees. According to an executive manager of the largest temporary employment agency in Silicon Valley, 10–35 per cent of a workforce of 6,000 that they place in various jobs on a weekly basis is placed in electronics firms and a majority of these do assembly work. Generally, the erosion of direct employment not only negatively affects workers' wages but also reduces their ability to access non-salary benefits such as affordable health care, seniority privileges, paid vacation and sick leave.

In Bangalore, contract labourers were paid a fraction of the salaries that regular, permanent employees receive. According to a union leader, about 44 per cent of the staff in a large public sector electronics firm was hired on a casual basis as contract labour. They received a daily wage of Rs.75 (US$1.50) and were forced to take a day off each month so that they did not have continuous six-month employment, which would legally qualify them for permanent status and associated benefits. To avoid paying workers statutory wages and the full range of benefits, employers in Bangalore used the 1961 Apprenticeship Act in India, which requires that factories accept a certain ratio of apprentices on their payroll, in order to retain workers in a prolonged state of tenuous employment. Employers also worsened working conditions by stretching work hours for example, to force workers to resign voluntarily within five years of continuous employment as this makes a worker ineligible for seniority benefits. Women workers are most adversely affected by this practice as the conditions they are subjected to at work are compounded by the immense family pressure they face at home to quit their jobs after marriage. In Silicon Valley, contractors insist that homeworkers, who assemble components in their homes, are 'independent contractors' rather than employees. Along with other contingent workers who are not legally recognised as 'employees' they have no recourse to the legal system in case of work-related injuries or chronic health problems such as migraines and deteriorating eyesight, which are common in the industry.

Contrary to the stereotypical image of manufacturing factories as 'grime-spewing smoke stacks', the high-tech industry is considered to be a clean industry with pleasant campus-style facilities, 'clean rooms', where chips are manufactured in tightly controlled environments, and workers sporting white lab coats and 'bunny suits' or protective clothing worn over street clothes (Byster and Smith 1999). In reality, electronics production is 'one of the most chemical-intensive industries ever conceived' (LaDou and Rohm 1998: 1). The use of literally thousands of chemicals and other hazardous materials makes electronics manufacturing an extremely dangerous industry, exposing workers and communities around production facilities to severe health risks. Working or living near the industry is known to cause various types of cancers, reproductive ailments, including miscarriages and even death.

Workers and labour activists in both Bangalore and Silicon Valley reported that companies often violate statutory requirements such as the provision of health and safety measures. The situation is far worse in Bangalore than in Silicon Valley. Activists in Silicon Valley have used a number of systematic studies conducted on health effects of the industry to campaign for positive legislation relating to the use, storage and disposal of toxic materials. In India, the combination of a relatively nascent electronics manufacturing industry and blind faith in it as a route to national economic development has meant that production workers in Bangalore are exposed to high occupational health risks. For example, workers in a small, domestic workshop were observed to carry out tasks such as lead soldering and cleaning of printed-circuit boards (PCBs) with alcohol by hand without any masks against fumes, anti-static gloves, slippers, coats or wrist straps to ground electrical currents.

Obstacles to unionisation

In addition to the negative implications for individual workers, industry-specific factors in Silicon Valley and Bangalore also drastically affect workers' ability to collectively negotiate their employment terms and conditions. One of the biggest problems for unions is the restructuring of capital from large manufacturing sites to multiple medium- and small-scale units that are geographically scattered either locally or around the world. This implies a need to adjust organising strategies from the traditional method of targeting workers at large factories.

Corporate reliance on subcontracting and contingent employment creates major divisions among workers which inhibit the development of a collective class consciousness, a prerequisite for any opposition to exploitation. Products are assembled in different places around the world by workers who are employed by different companies. Although they may be (indirectly) producing for a company like HP, they are neither aware of their peers in the other places nor would they necessarily consider sharing interests in common with them. In some cases, the workforce may include home-based workers who are even further isolated from the rest, as they do their assigned tasks in their own homes without any contact with other workers or knowledge of their place in the global production chain.

Besides being separated across space and company-boundaries through the desegregation of production, electronics workers *in* the two places are divided on the basis of local corporate geography, employee demographics and hierarchies of occupation and employment status. In Bangalore, it is common practice among electronics company management to recruit workers from areas of the city that are far from the facility and to provide special charter buses (paid for by workers) to transport workers to and from work. For example, workers employed in Electronics City were bussed from specially designated bus stops, past the heavily guarded main entrance to the enclave, right to the gates of the individual firm at which they worked. This practice severely restricts union access to workers and prevents a sense of geographical community among workers that may otherwise pervade the workplace.

Moreover, workers' ethnic and national origins also play a potentially divisive role. According to the executive manager of a temporary agency in Silicon Valley, the electronics manufacturing workforce reflects the 'United Nations [with] at least twenty to thirty different countries represented'. In Bangalore, electronics workers are migrants from different southern states in India drawn to the city by the heavy inward investment in high technology and a myriad of vocational institutes which provide job training required to work in the industry. They bring with them different configurations of ethnic, religious and caste affiliations. Finally, workers in any given production unit are divided by their employee status as either 'permanent' or part-time, temporary and contract workers. Hence, they do not share the same employer of record and are not usually considered part of the same collective bargaining unit. Such divisions stemming from workers' place in the production process, geographical location, social demographics and employment status complicate the process of fostering unity among workers for collective action.

One of the most difficult issues to overcome in the pursuit of legal recognition for workers' rights is pinpointing ultimate corporate responsibility for employment along the production chain. By outsourcing production and employment, OEMs and major CMs are able to deflect their responsibilities as (indirect) employers even though they control the conditions under which subcontractors work. In most cases, working conditions at small, local supplier firms are not controlled by the direct employer but influenced by downward pressure from large, powerful corporations that demand quality, efficiency, low cost and quick delivery from their subcontractors. Corporate managers in Silicon Valley and Bangalore reported using multiple suppliers for specific parts, which raises the possibility of contract termination or shift of production from one contractor to another to mitigate the effects of potential industrial action.

In sum, the current ways in which production is organised poses tremendous challenges to workers and labour organisation. An examination of industrial relationships and corporate hiring practices in two different places highlights striking similarities in workers' limited earning capacity, job insecurity, discrimination and health and safety problems. Labour organisation in the electronics industry is also complicated by the spatial and corporate desegregation of production, local workforce demographics and hybrid forms of employment.

Potential opportunities for collective action

Despite these challenges, it would be an error to ignore possible sites for labour intervention to improve working conditions. Examples of tactics and strategies used in other industries such as garments and car production are useful to identify corresponding campaign targets, allies and sources of leverage for workers in electronics manufacturing.

Corporate accountability

Corporate accountability for labour conditions is elusive when production is carried out for OEMs and CMs in units that do not belong to them by workers who are not their direct employees. However, the garments and car industries provide valuable lessons for the electronics industry in this regard. In a careful study of industrial dynamics and power relationships in the garments sector, labour activists concluded that justice campaigns needed to target fashion retailers and name-brand 'manufacturers' such as Liz Claiborne and Gap which 'sweat' the subcontractors and indirectly, the seamstresses through several tiers of the production network in a cut-throat industrial environment (Louie 2001). Hence, the garment workers' union sought to inform and mobilise fashion consumers, most notably middle-class women and university students, to develop a broad-based anti-sweatshop movement. A parallel approach based on the politics of consumption in the high-tech industry may imply targeting large institutional buyers such as schools, universities, hospitals and governmental branches.

There have also been successful attempts to extend union protection to workers at suppliers of firms where unions are already recognised in the car and garments industries. Jobbers' agreements or joint liability, which holds the manufacturer responsible for conditions in its contracting shops, originated in the experiences of the garment workers' union in New York (Bonacich 2001). In a similar style, the Canadian Auto Workers (CAW) developed new collective bargaining concepts of 'work ownership' and 'satellite bargaining' to challenge the artificial organisational boundaries that restrict the terms and conditions outlined in union contracts to the corporation's direct employees. At the international scale, international framework agreements (IFAs) are a form of corporate codes of conduct that global union federations such as the ICEM (International Chemical, Energy and Mining) and IUF (International Union of Food, Agriculture, Hotel, Restaurant, Catering, Tobacco and Allied Workers' Associations) are negotiating with large corporations (Wills 2002). Although this approach is not easy to achieve or problem-free at the implementation stage, as Bonacich (2001) and Wills (2002) admit, it points to directions in which labour organisation needs to move to redefine the traditional collective bargaining unit in accordance with predominant contracting systems.

Another tool to demand corporate accountability is through the attachment of decent standards of employment as conditions for state subsidies. Governmental officials and industrial representatives in both Silicon Valley and Bangalore revealed that there is a great deal of public investment in the high-tech industry, specifically for job creation and economic development. While industrial lobbyists are placing many demands on the government (lower taxes and excise duties exemption), the labour movement is silent on questions of job quality and social burdens (e.g. low return for investment, pollution) imposed by the industry. Social spending and job training schemes to promote economic development provide the space for the labour movement to exercise its influence to benefit working-class communities.

The Living Wage campaigns in the US, which have linked public subsidies to labour rights, particularly the right to organise in a neutral environment, demonstrate that the participation and intervention of workers' representatives in debates about the use and impact of public funds can complement union organising campaigns.

The weakest link

Highly decentralised networks of production deployed by interdependent corporations, while consolidating corporate power also allow labour to assert its demands. As Moody notes, TNCs 'have deep pockets to resist strikes or other forms of action, but they are also vulnerable at many points of their cross-border production chains' (1997: 280). This vulnerability to local activism is apparent in the transnational production arrangements in the electronics industry.

Managers in both Silicon Valley and Bangalore agreed that shortening the time absorbed in transporting goods from one point to another and eliminating storage is vital in this industry due to the high obsolescence rate of electronic products. Just-in-time systems, described by a company manager in Bangalore as 'the right materials at the right place and at the right time', in this climate are indispensable. Rather than being stored for long periods of time in warehouses, materials and components are pulled directly into production lines and into the final products within just hours of their delivery. Several tiers of suppliers are linked to each other under similar high-pressure settings on the basis of a strict forecasting schedule from OEMs or CMs, making punctuality and right quantity of delivery essential.

As Herod (2000) has argued using the case of the UAW's (United Auto Workers) 1998 strike at two GM (General Motors) plants in Flint, Michigan, a well-calculated work-stoppage or slowdown at key points in the arteries of global production networks could raise the financial stakes of union resistance. Similarly, Beukema and Coenen (1999) maintain that companies which provide logistics services, or 'the planning, execution, and control of the flow of goods from purchase up to and including distribution to end-users', can also be important sites of resistance (Beukema and Coenen 1999: 142). Using the case of a Dutch distribution company, they demonstrate that, due to their contact with and knowledge about important clients of their employer-firm, logistics workers (e.g. transport workers) can play a significant role in providing leverage to workers at the weaker links in global production networks. High union density in the transport industry and active networks of organised labour that exist in this sector internationally open up some space for worker action and solidarity across industries.

Cross-movement alliances

Given the environmental degradation and health risks that the electronics industry poses to workers and communities, environmental activists in many high-tech hot spots around the world such as Taiwan, Thailand, Silicon Valley and Scotland, have proven to be workers' allies for corporate social and economic responsibility. A number of high-profile, landmark lawsuits have been filed against TNCs such as IBM, RCA (now Thompson Multimedia) and Seagate Corporation on behalf of workers and their descendants, whose health has been permanently damaged due to their exposure to a 'witch's brew' of chemicals and hazardous materials in the workplace.

The Silicon Valley Toxics Coalition (SVTC) is an environmental justice organisation which grew out of interrelated concerns about environmental degradation, public health and workers' issues. Since the 1980s, SVTC has been conducting research, public education and advocacy centred on the environmental impact of the electronics industry starting with ground water contamination in the 1970s resulting in ground-breaking environmental policies in the US. SVTC's demands for environmental accountability of the industry has had significant implications not only within the region or the country but beyond the US through the formation of the International Campaign for Responsible Technology (ICRT), an online network of public health specialists, labour activists and environmental advocates in the 1980s. The Rio Tinto campaign, which brought together a similar cross-border coalition of indigenous people's organisations, unions and environmental groups, is an example of how the ICRT could serve as a platform upon which local labour campaigns can be linked to global issues of business practice, corporate governance, shareholder value and social responsibility (Sadler 2004).

Transnational linkages

The potential for the geographical relocation of electronics jobs makes it evident that a purely localised organising strategy is no longer adequate in the contemporary phase of capitalism. As workers are divided by the geographies of production, unifying workers across national boundaries must be a central component of organising in the electronics industry.

During the summer of 2002, a delegation of workers formerly employed by the multinational electronics firm RCA in the northern county of Taoyuan, Taiwan toured the US to seek solidarity from American labour and environmental organisations in their struggle for just compensation. The US tour was organised by the Self-Help Association of Former RCA Employees, which was founded in 1998 to support hundreds of RCA workers who have died or are suffering from cancer developed from exposure to toxic substances in their workplace. Workers' representatives visited five major US cities, including Silicon Valley, to present their story to American electronics workers and allies. Their aim was to build support for a public hearing and lawsuit to hold their former employer accountable for serious environmental pollution and a huge cancer cluster. In the process, they were able to share information and develop personal ties directly with workers in other places. In Silicon Valley, the RCA workers were struck by the ethnic diversity of workers and their stories of unfair treatment in the industry. Thus, a cross-border worker exchange can not only result in practical campaign support but also creates a realistic image of working conditions in places around the world through personal contact.

Global union federations (GUFs) such as the International Metalworkers Federation, which recognises that labour organising in the information and communications technology (ICT) sector 'requires special trade union efforts', can play a vital role in internationalising labour campaigns in the industry (IMF 2002: 8).

Such international union structures can lend institutional pressure in labour disputes, conduct corporate research, lobby governments, raise public awareness in several countries, and mobilise union members for coordinated days of action through their national affiliates. As several well-known cases have shown (e.g. 1997 UPS-Teamsters strike), international solidarity mobilised through these organisations can make a huge difference in contract negotiations and struggles for union recognition.

In sum, obstacles to the protection of labour rights in the high-tech industry are not insurmountable. Unions in other similarly organised industries have developed pioneering tools such as joint liability and framework agreements that can be applied to electronics manufacturing. Existing union structures such as GUFs and corporate vulnerabilities can be used in labour campaigns to gain leverage for workers.

Labour response

Despite the need for labour organisation and potential opportunities that exist for it, research in the two sites exposes a fundamental dilemma. Not only is the electronics industry globally marked by a very low degree of unionisation but trade unions in Bangalore and Silicon Valley have not yet been successful in establishing an institutional presence in the industry. In Bangalore, unionisation is limited to the traditional public sector electronics companies set up just after India's independence leaving the relatively newer private sector unorganised. In Silicon Valley, the industry remains a union-free zone despite a couple of notable attempts to organise workers in the 1980s and mid-1990s. In both places, unions, in large part, are not responding to the growing power of the IT sector and the associated challenges of its working conditions. While the political and economic context of these two locations create external conditions that are not conducive to organising high-tech workers, the internal politics of the union movement are also responsible for the lack of collective bargaining rights for electronics manufacturing workers.

Unions: missing in action

The most common reason given by labour activists in Bangalore for union lapse in the IT sector is the defensive battles in which unions in Bangalore, as in the rest of India, are engaged against privatisation and plant closures and the subsequent retrenchment of workers in traditional industries. They also face an extremely hostile environment in the context of deregulation and an intensification of interstate rivalry to attract the inward investment of domestic and foreign capital. Electronics, telecommunication and informatics feature as the top three 'key projects' of the State for the period 2001 to 2006 (DIC 2001: 25). Due to the high priority placed on the IT industry in the State of Karnataka's industrial development policy, the government 'is committed to simplify all the [state and central government labour] enactments for the IT sector' leading the State Labour Department to 'streamline' these as it is 'aware of the industry's concerns' (DIT 2000: 17). As a result, the IT industry is exempted from several acts of protective labour legislation and remains a daunting challenge to unions.

However, the low union density and a lull in organising efforts generally, even in the public sector electronics firms where unions were established at the very start, is equally attributed to union complacency as unions, described by a labour leader, have been 'sedated' by past victories. A structural feature of the Indian labour movement that complicates matters further is the operation of unions at the plant, rather than industry level. This form of 'enterprise unionism' means that workers in a particular job classification at a given firm can be represented by different unions, and subsidiaries of the firm in different places are likely to have different unions representing its employees. Moreover, as there are twelve central union federations at the national level, each being the labour arm of a different political party, enterprise unions embody competing political ideologies. This has resulted in an extremely disjointed labour movement incapable of mobilising a large amount of resources to tackle a formidable opponent that the high-tech industry has proven to be.

The 1998–99 unionisation drive at BPL, a $1 billion Indian multinational consumer electronics company, is an exceptional example of union attempts to organise high-tech workers. The goal of the union, BPL Group of Companies Karmikara Sangha, was to bring together more than 6,300 workers, most of whom were women, employed at fourteen units of BPL in and around Bangalore under one collective bargaining agreement. The company, however, successfully challenged this strategy in court by denying the existence of a legal entity called the BPL Group. Instead, it claimed that the various manufacturing units that employed these workers were separate entities. Corporate opposition to the workers' union was implicitly and explicitly reinforced by the State, through the unrestricted violence meted out by the police and by the State of Karnataka's Labour Commissioner, who judged the registration of a multi-site company union null and void. The public defeat of this isolated union struggle may well have had a chilling effect on the prospects for further efforts to organise high-tech workers.

In Silicon Valley, the decrease in manufacturing employment is widely held to be the main reason that unions have turned their attention away from the electronics industry since the 1990s. Labour activists in the valley admitted that organising in an industry in which most of the workers are concentrated in small-scale enterprises is extremely difficult because, as one industry observer stated, 'companies go in and out of business.' Organising efforts in the late 1980s and early 1990s were quickly crushed when companies shifted their operations to other states or overseas. However, some long-time activists claim that, rather than industry-specific challenges, the inadequacy of institutional protection for electronics assemblers is due to the union movement's own lack of ideological vision due to the 'de-politicisation of American labour and the impact of the purge of the left in the 50's', according to a former union organiser. Changing demographics and the hidden nature of subcontracted electronics assembly demand considerable investment of resources that unions are generally reluctant to make. Unions have been criticised for their tendency 'to go after hot shops, for short-term gains of a quick membership', in the words of an industry observer and social activist. This approach, which seeks 'targets of opportunity' instead of investing time, effort and most importantly, resources where workers need collective strength, would be impossible to implement in the electronics industry due to the challenges discussed earlier.

A multi-union effort called the Campaign for Justice to organise workers across the industry, instead of individual plants, in the mid-1990s was short-lived because unions 'can't get along' as one labour leader remarked. According to the former organising director of the lead union involved in this campaign, despite the highly innovative and dynamic methods of organising deployed in this effort, its demise 'was not due to anything negative on the ground but due to the lack of will of unions'. Since this Campaign for Justice, there has been no other substantive union attempt to enforce corporate responsibility toward workers and the community.

A different face of labour
Despite this glaring lacuna in union representation of electronics assemblers in both places, except at public sector companies in Bangalore, a number of community-based efforts have emerged in Silicon Valley to support workers and community residents whose lives are affected by the industry. These initiatives, spearheaded by non-profit organisations, are oriented toward the multi-ethnic, young and female population that makes up the majority of the workforce on the bottom rungs of the electronics industry.

Two are popular education projects conceived to lay the foundations for organising women workers in the electronics industry. The first is WE LeaP!, the Working Women's Leadership Development project, a training programme of the Santa Clara Centre for Occupational Safety and Health (SCCOSH), which focuses on the issue of health and safety in the workplace. A central component of the teaching framework used in this project is that it draws upon workers' ethnic cultural backgrounds while integrating political discussions about gender and family issues with workplace issues. This heightens the participants' awareness of how their race, gender, class and immigration experience place them in a particularly precarious position within the industry, and enables them to develop cross-cultural relationships with other women workers. The latter is particularly significant in an ethnically divisive working environment.

The second is the Asian Immigrant Women Advocates (AIWA), which provides English and citizenship classes as well as workplace literacy workshops to electronics assemblers in Silicon Valley. Interviews with workers and employment agency representatives in the region reveal that there is a close link between knowledge of English and workers' earnings. The ability to speak English allows workers better access to jobs at a higher rate of pay and conversely, poor language skills act as a barrier to the broader labour market. AIWA's classes, which are bilingually and biculturally taught by trained peer educators, are a combination of 'survival' English and political education with an emphasis on the development and assertion of workers' collective voice. Such hands-on workshops on employment rights have proven to be critical to labour organising as they have led to a high-profile Garment Workers Justice campaign undertaken among local garment workers (Louie 2001).

AIWA has also formed an active Membership Association for Korean assemblers, who are all women.

The other two are new initiatives that were launched by activists who recognised the need for more organisational support for young, immigrant workers in the Valley. The first is called the High Tech Collaborative. This is a partnership between AIWA, the Services, Immigrant Rights and Education Network (SIREN) and the Equal Rights Advocates (ERA), a public-interest law firm, to address the need to organise low-wage electronics workers in Silicon Valley. The Collaborative plans to advance its work in the areas of policy advocacy, litigation and community organising among the different immigrant communities that are represented in the industrial workforce in phases starting with the Vietnamese and Korean populations, followed by Latinos and other workers. The second is Silicon Valley De-Bug which is a bi-monthly youth magazine designed by and for the young people of colour who work in Silicon Valley's low-wage, temporary jobs packaging printers, testing computer chips and assembling modems. Through bilingual (English and Spanish) poetry, art, personal essays and stories the contributors highlight issues such as low pay, poor working conditions, disrespect and the absence of opportunities for upward mobility that they or others like them face in the high technology industry.

In addition to these, the South Bay Labour Council (SBLC), a regional branch of the American Federation of Labor-Congress of Industrial Organisations (AFL-CIO), runs a temporary staffing services agency which offers training and development as well as portable, affordable employment benefits to workers. This agency essentially serves as an employment registry for those who are not members of any union and are further marginalised by their precarious employment situation. Following the foundation of a Membership Association for temporary workers in Silicon Valley, the SBLC is also lobbying major employers to adopt and implement a Bill of Rights that includes affordable health care, time off, holiday pay and so on for temporary workers. Both of these initiatives seem to be overwhelmingly utilised by white-collar, clerical workers.

The notable absence of union representation in the industry in both places (and low union density in the industry globally) casts doubt about the potential of a union movement being able to tackle the challenges of globalisation. However, the ongoing work of community-based organisations among electronics workers in Silicon Valley points to some innovative ways in which a foundation for organising can be laid among workers with varied ethnic, occupational and employment status. The issues they tackle – immigrant rights, environmental pollution, health and safety, employment insecurity – serve as a lens through which workers can begin to recognise their collective interests both in the workplace as well as in the community. These initiatives, albeit encouraging, are still at an early stage and their evolution conditional upon further funding. An additional drawback is that there is limited collaboration among them. Nonetheless, their 'bottom-up' approach of worker outreach and base-building activities prepare the ground for workers to collectively challenge corporate power in the field of employment. Most importantly, the crucial intervention of these organisations indicates that the structure and composition of the labour movement itself is undergoing a transformation, and that such community-based organisations are proving themselves indispensable to the struggle for workers' rights in a global economy.

Conclusion

This comparative study of electronics manufacturing presents an alternative version of the story of David and Goliath, one that must be fully understood if workers' cause is to be advanced under contemporary capitalism. Goliath, under the guise of large high-tech companies, remains an unruly menace to workers and communities which are negatively affected by subcontracting on a global scale, outsourcing of labour, environmental pollution and economic insecurity. Reining the power of these transnational corporations is extremely difficult given the fragmentation of the production processes among different units and across national boundaries. Traditional methods of organising are clearly not sufficient in this context and the international labour movement needs to explore more imaginative ways of organising and representing a divided workforce. Just as David had analysed his strengths in relation to Goliath's weakness and subsequently, rejected the standard armour for a simple sling, so must the labour movement take stock of its own potential sources of power.

Indeed, contrary to pessimistic readings of globalisation for labour, there are some significant openings for collective action. While corporations have been consolidating their power and increasing their profitability through globally extended production networks, they are also vulnerable to well-placed and creatively choreographed forms of worker action that use corporate geography to redefine targets, collective bargaining units, pressure points and political allies. Whether or not these openings will lead to expected outcomes is contingent upon particular circumstances and political characteristics of place. Yet research in Silicon Valley and Bangalore shows that unions have been slow to grasp the opportunities that present themselves in the industry's operation. Rather than gathering stones for the sling like David, it is evident that organising the high-tech industry, a growth sector, is not a high priority for the union movement in these two locations. Apart from the two (failed) union-led attempts to organise electronics workers, the lack of response from unions can be understood in terms of the defensive position they are forced into as well as their tendency toward short-term gains as a survival mechanism. In contrast, the ongoing work of community-based organisations which are mobilising workers' non-work related identities and non-wage issues as an entry point for collective action illustrates new forms of labour organisation that need to be adopted in order to rebuild a workers' movement in the twenty-first century. An important lesson from this story is that unions have political allies among alternative labour formations which are courageously and creatively confronting the high-tech Goliath, and workers would benefit enormously from better institutional links within such a heterogeneous labour movement.

Notes

1   The research for this paper is part of a larger doctoral research project on the restructuring of the global electronics industry and its impact on labour. For financial support of this project, I am grateful to the Geography Department of Queen Mary, University of London; *Antipode: A Radical Journal of Geography*; the Developing Areas Research Group of The Royal Geographical Society; and the University of London Central Research Fund.

References

Berndt, E., Dulberger, E. and Rappaport, N. (2000) *Price and quality of desktop and mobile personal computers: a quarter century of history*, submitted to the Summer Institute of the National Bureau of Economic Research, 17 July. www.nber.org/~confer/2000/si2000/berndt.pdf (accessed 15 December 2003).

Beukema, L. and Coenen, H. (1999) 'Global logistic chains: the increasing importance of local labour relations', in Leisink, Peter (ed.), *Globalisation and labour relations*, Cheltenham.

Bonacich, E. (2001) 'The challenge of organising in a globalised/flexible industry: the case of the apparel industry in Los Angeles', in Baldoz, C., Koeber, C. and Kraft, P. (eds), *The critical study of work: labour, technology and global production*, Philadelphia.

Byster, B. and Smith, T. (1999) 'High tech and toxic', *FORUM for Applied Research and Public Policy*, Spring.

Castells, M. (1996) *The rise of the network society*, Oxford.

Department of Industries & Commerce, Government of Karnataka (2001) *New Industrial Policy, 2001–2006*, Bangalore.

Department of Information Technology, Government of Karnataka (2000) *IT for the Common Man: The millenium IT policy*, Bangalore.

Eisenscher, M. (1993) 'Silicon fist in a velvet glove', revised version of a paper published in German as 'Gewerkschaftliche Organisierung in der Computerindustrie: Die Erfahrungen des UE Electronics Organizing Committee in "Silicon Valley"' in Lüthje, B. and Scherrer, C. (eds), *Jenseits Des Sozialpaktes – Neue Unternehmensstrategien, Gewerkschaften und Arbeitskämpfe in den USA*, Münster.

Ewell, M. and Oanh Ha, K. (1999) 'Why piecework won't go away: the practice helped fuel growth at Solectron, and others imitated it', *Mercury News*, 28 June.

Herod, A. (2000) 'Implications of just-in-time production for union strategy: lessons from the 1998 General Motors-United AutoWorkers Dispute', *Annals of the Association of American Geographers*, 90:3.

International Metalworkers Federation (2002) 'IMF Action Programme, 2002–2005: dealing with global challenges', Geneva.

Joint Venture (1998) *Silicon Valley 2010: A regional framework for growing together*, San José, California.

LaDou, J. and Rohm, T. (1998) 'The international electronics industry', *International Journal of Occupational and Environmental Health*, 4:1.

Louie, M. C. (2001) *Sweatshop warriors: immigrant women workers take on the global factory*, Cambridge, Massachusetts.

Moody, K. (1997) *Workers in a lean world: unions in the international economy*, London.

Sadler, D. (2004) 'Trade unions, coalitions and communities: Australia's Construction, Forestry, Mining and Energy union and the international stakeholder campaign against Rio Tinto', *Geoforum*, 35.

Wills, J. (2002) 'Bargaining for the space to organise in the global economy: a review of the Accor-IUF trade union rights agreement', *Review of International Political Economy*, 9.

12

Sintraemcali and social movement unionism: trade union resistance to neo-liberal globalisation in Colombia

Mario Novelli

Introduction[1]

Colombia is the most dangerous country in the world to be a trade unionist. Trade union leaders and activists suffer from a systematic policy of assassination; intimidation and persecution carried out by paramilitary death squads closely linked to the Colombian state. Over 4,000 trade unionists have been assassinated since 1986. In the midst of this repression the Colombian trade union movement continues to resist the imposition of neo-liberal globalisation. Sintraemcali (Municipal Workers Union of EMCALI) has fought off several attempts to privatise EMCALI, the state provider of electricity, water and telecommunications in Colombia's second city of Cali. This chapter explains how this was achieved. A reorientation occurred within the union in the mid-1990s that led to the emergence of four central strategies. First, an economic strategy that produced an alternative blueprint for the management of public services. Second, a trade union and community alliance in Cali in defence of public services. Third, a mobilisation strategy which included a series of militant occupations of public buildings, the most important being a 36 day occupation of the Central Administration building of the headquarters of EMCALI that began on 25 December 2001. Fourth, a human rights strategy accessing local, national and international legal and advocacy mechanisms that facilitated the union's ability to 'globalise' its struggle against privatisation.

Two developmental processes modified the context within which Sintraemcali operates: transborderisation and horizontalisation. The former challenges the view that labour organisations can be successful only when operating at the local scale. The latter highlights the benefits of a rearticulation of union objectives towards an ethic of citizenship and citizen rights. This allows for the development of reciprocal alliances between social movements and marginalised communities from the local to the global. These twin processes are linked to contemporary literature on 'social movement unionism' and 'new internationalism' (Moody 1997; Munck 2002; Waterman 2001) and the possibilities and limitations for union renewal under neo-liberal globalisation.

Counter-hegemonic globalisation movements and organised labour

Since the mid-1990s an upsurge in resistance to neo-liberal globalisation has occurred, not least in Latin America. From the Zapatistas to the World Social Forum (WSF), observers argue that we are now witnessing a re-emergence of struggle and a body of critical literature has emerged seeking to analyse these processes.

Some studies have focussed on the activities and strategies of the transnational anti-globalisation and anti-capitalist movements (Callinicos 2003; Escobar 2000; Sen *et al.* 2004). Others examine social movements challenging the imperatives of hegemonic globalisation, such as the Zapatistas in Mexico (Holloway and Peláez 1998; Morton 2002), the Landless Workers Movement in Brazil (Branford and Rocha 2002) and the anti-water privatisation movement in Bolivia (Olivera and Lewis 2003).

Labour studies have charted the re-emergence of trade union struggles across the world (Herod 1998, 2001 and 2003; Moody 1997; Munck 2002; Waterman 2001) and have sought to theorise this within the context of neo-liberal globalisation. The literature documents two major interrelated processes in the international union movement: 'New Internationalism' and 'Social Movement Unionism'. The first relates to union responses to the globalisation of capital and shows how unions and international trade secretariats are finding new geographical terrains and spaces to protest and advance the interests of their members (Herod 1998, 2001 and 2003; Waterman and Wills 2001). There is some doubt whether 'internationalism' is the appropriate conceptual tool for exploring the new and complex geographical territories of contestation and solidarity that are emerging under conditions of neo-liberal globalisation. Herod's *Labor geographies* (2001) provides a fruitful approach, exploring the nature of global restructuring as a process involving reconfiguration and contestation on a range of scales from the local to the regional, national and supranational. Hence, rather than 'internationalism' this chapter utilises the concept 'transborderisation' be they local, national or international. This approach overcomes the binary understanding of contemporary labour strategy, which reifies the global scale and suggests that workers can only be successful if they operate at the global level.

While many authors recognise that 'new scales' of activity are important, they also assert that the question of union renewal is not only about geography. Revival also relates to the internal reorganisation of unions into 'social movement unionism'. This research focuses on the 'horizontalisation' of union structures (Moody 1997; Waterman 2001) and argues for a more 'politicised' rank and file democratic unionism that can interact and ally with other social groups and movements that have been marginalised by neo-liberal globalisation. The 'old' social movements are not the only historical subject, but that there are a plurality of resisting subjects: environmentalists, community activists, indigenous organisations, women's movements, non-unionised labour, and that trade union renewal takes the form of articulating union struggles in alliance with these different 'resisting subjects'

These two linked bodies of literature challenge Castell's (1997: 354) thesis that the labour movement will 'fade away' under neo-liberal globalisation. Instead they argue that 'just like capitalism, trade unions as a social movement are capable of mutation, transformation and regeneration' (Munck 2002: 190). How do these unions transform their activity? What were the specific processes through which trade unions became aware of the need to change tactics? How did they develop these new strategies? The chapter explores Sintraemcali's transformation in the 1990s from a corporate trade union fighting locally for its members' interests to a social movement union leading a transnational struggle in defence of public services in Cali.

Background to Colombia

Colombia is the pariah nation of the international trade union movement. Since 1986 over 4,000 union leaders and activists have been murdered by death squads linked to the Colombian state (Human Rights Watch 1996, 2000, 2001). On average there are between 6,000 and 8,000 political assassinations per year and over 2.9 million people are internally displaced out of a population of 45 million (CUT 2004).

These statistics can be understood, at least in part, as a low-level civil war between Marxist guerrillas and state and parastate forces for several decades. Colombia has received extensive military support and training in 'counterinsurgency' from the US and this has led to the conscious blurring of the line between combatant and civilian. Trade unions and social movements have been systematically targeted by both state and parastate forces in a 'dirty war' (McClintock 1985). In the post cold war era the 'communist' threat has been refashioned into the 'narcotics' threat and Colombia's now infamous role as cocaine producer has provided the justification for increased US intervention. The language has changed, but the targets and tactics of counterinsurgency continue (Stokes 2004).

The reason for the severity of the conflict in Colombia, outlined above, lies in the fact that underpinning the military conflict is a deeply rooted social conflict being fought over the distribution of the benefits of Colombia's rich natural, agricultural and human resources. The country has vast deposits of coal, emeralds, oil, ferronickel, gold and water; a fertile agricultural terrain which makes Colombia a leading producer of coffee, flowers and bananas, and a vast pool of skilled and unskilled labour available at a fraction of the cost of workers in the industrialised north (Fernandez 2003). Geopolitically and geostrategically it is located at the crossroads both by land and by sea to a range of crucial transnational communication links (Petras 2001). Topographically it is also a highly mountainous country, making state territorial control a difficult task, and this, coupled with its fertility, helps to explain why it has become one of the world's major producers of illegal narcotics, particularly cocaine and opium.

This conflict has been intensified since the beginning of the imposition of a neoliberal economic model in the country in the early 1990s. The shift in economic model has led *campesinos*, indigenous communities, black communities, social organisations and trade unionists to engage in struggles to retain their land, resources and rights. They have also sought to defend national wealth and independence as the government attempts to privatise, develop mega-projects, create tax free export zones, reform labour laws and cutback on state and social benefits (Higginbottom 2004; Hylton 2003).

Opening up the agricultural sector to external competition has meant that large sectors of agriculture have all but collapsed, with over a million hectares of arable land abandoned (Ahumada 2000: 36). Likewise industrial production saw a year on year fall during the 1990s, affecting particularly, though not exclusively, small and medium producers (Ahumada, 2000: 40). Unemployment has risen from 10.5 per cent in 1990 to its highest levels in the twenty-first century and in 2001 reached 20.4 per cent. The informal labour sector increased from 52.7 per cent in 1996 to 60.3 per cent in 2000 (ENS 2003). While in the 1980s GNP grew on average 4 per cent, in the 1990s it grew only 2.6 per cent. In 1998 there was zero growth, and in 1999 it was −5 per cent. Meanwhile, despite claims that austerity measures would reduce the public debt this has multiplied since the 1990s (Ahumada 2000; Castillo 2000; Sarmiento 2001). Not surprisingly, this skewed development model has left, according to the World Bank's own figures, 64 per cent of the population living below the poverty line (World Bank 2002).

Throughout the 1990s there was a marked upsurge in foreign direct investment. Multinational corporations from the US, Japan and Europe profited from new laws allowing increased foreign involvement in natural resource extraction, the privatisation of public services and state companies, and the liberalisation of the financial sector, and thus now control large sectors of the Colombian economy. There has also been a notable strengthening of the national elite. In 1990 the ratio of income between the poorest and richest 10 per cent was 1: 40, at the end of the decade that rested at 1: 80 (Palacio 2001: 89). This polarisation of extreme wealth and poverty coexisting has produced what Santos (2002) calls 'societal fascism', whereby the rich live in luxury gated communities while the poor reside in ghettos excluded from basic human rights, and subject to highly repressive policing. It is in this context that the conflict between Sintraemcali and the State took place.

From corporate to social movement union

The impulse to begin a process of transformation within Sintraemcali resulted from recognition that the way the union had operated up to 1991, was no longer appropriate for the successful defence of public services under conditions of neo-liberal globalisation (Interview with Alexander Lopez 2002). In the early 1990s the union was, for the first time, faced with the threat of privatisation. Prior to that, according to Alexander Lopez (who would lead the transformation of the union), Sintraemcali 'was just a calm, normal union working on normal grievances' (En Camino 2003) but the new environment forced the organisation to rethink its strategic direction. Yet there was nothing automatic or deterministic about the new more 'movement' direction that the union would take. In many countries neo-liberal globalisation has ushered in 'business unionism' that attempts to accommodate capital's drive to cut costs and improve productivity at the expense of its members' terms and conditions (Moody 1997). This may well have been the course for Sintraemcali had it not been for a radical break in leadership that occurred in the second half of the 1990s.

The new leadership emerged from a rank and file committee that was born in the sewerage section of the company. The initial challenge to the union leadership was related to the 'deplorable working conditions' in the sewerage section and the lack of disinfectants, protective clothing and hygiene facilities. As workers began to organise and mobilise, these conditions improved, and as a result a group of around 250 workers began to develop a political direction within the union itself, meeting twice a week in the plant to discuss the situation of the company and the country. The group became known as the 'Comité de Base' (Rank and File Committee). From the early improvements in working conditions they began to push for political representation in the Executive Committee (EC) of the union. Alexander Lopez was chosen as the candidate, and eventually entered Sintraemcali's EC in 1994. Inside the union's leadership there was deep suspicion about the intentions of this group, and Alexander Lopez was immediately marginalised. However, after sustained pressure from the Comité de Base he was eventually given the position of treasurer.

The position of treasurer allowed him to investigate the finances of the union and during this period he discovered irregularities in the handling of money by some of the union leadership. He denounced the irregularities at the workers' assemblies and became a 'stone in the shoe' (Interview with Alexander Lopez 2002) of the union leadership, whilst simultaneously gaining credibility amongst the workers and strengthening his position within the union. From modest beginnings the 'Comité de Base', would begin to develop in other directions and lay the foundations for the later transformation of the union.

In the first half of the 1990s the process of privatisation in Colombia was set in motion. During this period a consensus developed amongst trade unionists nationally on questions of national sovereignty and citizenship rights:

> We were clear that behind a privatisation, behind the sale of a public service, in the case of water, or electricity we were handing over national territory and if we look at the scenario of telecommunications and electricity we were handing over the aerial space, the electromagnetic spectre and all our resources in these areas, and when we refer to water companies we are handing over a source of natural resources represented in the rich virgin forests that we have in our country. (Interview with Alexander Lopez 2002)

In Cali, the union developed a range of activities against the planned privatisation of EMCALI by the then mayor of Cali, Mauricio Guzmán. This included a six-day occupation of the workplants in 1996, which failed to achieve its objectives, and resulted in over 600 workers being suspended from work for 60 days and the union being fined. This defeat was a bitter blow and paved the way for the continuing plans for privatisation of the company (Interview with Alexander Lopez, 2002). Defeat also led Lopez to deepen the internal educational processes taking place in the union:

> We started travelling from work plant to work plant, and brought some comrades from other unions at the national level to share their experiences with the EMCALI workers.

Each one would come and stay for a couple of weeks, even up to a month, and in that way we began regular work in each of the plants, in each of the work places to chat and discuss the real situation of the company. (Interview with Alexander Lopez 2002)

It was during these non-formal educational events that the union began to develop a cadre of committed workers that today are known as the *base fuerte* (strong base) and the *base consciente* (conscious base) of workers in the union who continue to sustain its activities. With growing support inside the union for a radical shift in direction, Lopez assumed increasing power. In 1996 he was joined by two close allies from the sewerage plant, Luis Hernandez Monroy and Robinson Masso, on the Executive Committee of Sintraemcali. From that stage onwards the union began to take on more fully the form of a social movement:

When labor surfaces as a social movement . . . it typically produces and in turn depends for its development on a very specific type of labor organization: labor as a social movement organization. Social movement organizations broadcast agendas for social change and mobilize, support and deploy networks of membership and collective action in support of those agendas. (Johnston 2000: 3)

Once support had been won for a radical challenge to privatisation then the question became one of strategy: how could the union take on a highly repressive state and its transnational allies in the complex and violent conditions of Colombia? The union from 1996 developed four interlinked strategies.

Plan PARE. Alternative development strategy

From the early union renewal in the 1990s, there had already emerged a collective understanding of the notion of public services as a question of national sovereignty. What was lacking was a negative critique of neo-liberal arguments on the inefficiency of public services, and a positive critique of how public services within EMCALI could be made more efficient. The pursuit of the answers to these questions would lead to the development of the Plan PARE for the recuperation of the company, a pedagogical process of Action Research that could be understood as an emerging form of 'workers control'. The process can be divided into three fairly clear periods.

The first period dating from around 1995 to1999 was focussed on investigation of corruption inside the company and its relationship to local and national political and economic elites. This emerged directly as a result of the trade union's need to refute the local and national government's assertions that EMCALI, as a state owned public service provider, was economically unviable. 'Anti-Corruption Teams' were set up in all the different work plants to monitor management activities, gather documents and analyse the evidence drawing on Sintraemcali's financial and legal advisers to assist. During this process it was discovered that, in the latter half of the 1990s, EMCALI's debt had increased from COP 36 billion to COP 500 billion. Much of this had been wasted on several large 'joint venture' infrastructure projects between EMCALI, local private corporations and foreign multinationals (Revista Valle 2003; Sintraemcali 2000). The revelations of corruption in EMCALI served as a powerful tool to critique World Bank, IMF (International Monetary Fund) and Colombian state's arguments that 'national industries' were necessarily inefficient. The union uncovered evidence and presented legal charges alleging that up to 1 billion COP was siphoned off in corrupt practices during the 1990s (Interview with Alexander Lopez 2002). The union argued that it was corrupt officials linked to foreign multinational private interests, not worker inefficiency, that had driven the company towards bankruptcy, and that more transparency and workers participation could remedy the situation. The union highlighted that total salary costs, including pensions represented only 28 per cent of total company income, while the debt accrued through corrupt practices amounted to 70 per cent of income. It was they argued those in charge of the company during this period and responsible for the crisis that was now pushing through plans to privatise the company and hide their corrupt practices once and for all. Nelson Sanchez, the financial adviser of Sintraemcali, noted that 'this began to widen out the critique away from merely corruption towards a broader understanding of the situation. And this led us to begin an analysis of the aggressive factors facing the company' (Interview with Nelson Sanchez 2002). These 'aggressive factors' were the debt, the PTAR (a water treatment plant), Termoemcali (a power plant), the lack of pensions and the lack of operational savings, and all of this led to the setting up of the second stage of the Action Research Project.

The second stage, from early 1999 to May 2001, saw the shift from a negative critique of the company's present and past management strategies towards the positive development of an alternative management plan based on making EMCALI a viable economic unit rooted in the interests of the community. In early 1999 an advisory team composed of lawyers, financial analysts, business administrators and experts in public service utility providers was set up by Sintraemcali, and this group worked alongside professionals inside all the company work places. The advisers ensured that the trade union would integrate within its 'social discourse' a component of efficient business management (Interview with Nelson Sanchez 2002).

The organisation was led by the union and worked with the 'anti-corruption commission' that already existed under the leadership of Robinson Masso and Luis Hernandez. It was a multidisciplinary organisation, an external team that coordinated with each of the management teams from the different sections, and with them began to develop positions for the recuperation of the company.

In August 1999 Sintraemcali called a weekend meeting for all those workers, technicians and professionals that wanted to join the union in its plan for the salvation of EMCALI. Around 120 people attended. This meeting marked the beginning of the shift from a negative to a positive critique of the company, and represents an important milestone in the union's development:

> We began with a presentation by the advisory team on the changing reality of the situation in the country for public services in a globalised world. This was crucial because the workers had to understand 'gain consciousness' about the impact of neo-liberal policies in Latin America and in Europe. This was firmly located in the changed constitution of 1991 which despite having some democratic gains, altered the hegemony

of public services as controlled solely by the state – as a social function of the state, and represented a break from Keynesian state intervention. (Interview with Nelson Sanchez 2002: 2)

By shifting the state's role from 'provider' to 'regulator' the new Constitution encouraged the entry of private capital into areas such as health, drinking water, sewerage treatment, management of the environment. All had been previously the social responsibility of the State. Sintraemcali began to question the ability of 'private interests' to deliver 'social goods' and presented the handover of national natural resources to foreign corporations as a threat to national sovereignty (Interview with Nelson Sanchez, 2002).

This discussion provided the catalyst for a comprehensive business plan subsequently known as the Plan PARE. For Sanchez, the shift from merely denouncing corruption to proposing alternatives 'allowed us to make a qualitative leap forward in the populist vision of the trade union leadership' (Interview with Nelson Sanchez 2002). For the leadership of the union the implications were clear; the future struggle for the defence of EMCALI as a state owned company was 'not a trade union theme . . . but eminently social and political' (Interview with Nelson Sanchez 2002) and thus required a broad based trade union/community alliance. For this to be achieved the union needed to reframe the problem of EMCALI away from a conflict between Sintraemcali and the State, towards a conflict between Cali citizens and the state. The problem prior to that was that the union was accused of merely defending its own members' interests. However, with a shift in discourse and focus the union could not now be so easily attacked by the government and media as it turned its focus on the social and political issues facing the city produced by the economic model being imposed from without.

Emerging out of the development plan was a clearer understanding of the financial viability of the company and the underlying reasons why the company was attracting the attention of a range of multinational corporations engaged in water, electricity and telecommunications delivery. The company provided water, electricity and telecommunications to two million users and had the capacity to expand provision greatly (Sintraemcali 2003a).

Control of EMCALI for the multinational corporations would allow them to link this rich technological platform with others running across Latin America. The task of the Plan PARE team was to develop a business plan for the company that allowed it to run both efficiently and socially. Emerging out of this was a plan that would cut wastage in the company via new work practices, reduce upper level management by giving workers increasing control over production, and renegotiate the external debt with creditors.

Plan PARE was presented in 1999 but not accepted by EMCALI management, the local council, or the Superintendent of Public Services. From that point on the union began to confront the Superintendent of Public Services, link up with other unions and provide a well-documented critique of the neo-liberal economic model that was being applied. Two crucial factors intervened to change the political situation in favour of the union's proposals (Interview with Nelson Sanchez 2002). The first was the revelation of corruption at the highest levels of government relating to private sector involvement in public service provision. In tandem with Sithe Energies, a US multinational, a web of false contracts, bribes and corruption was discovered centring on a proposed thermoelectric power plant, Thermo Rio, which began in 1997. These revelations led to the imprisonment of the Superintendent for Public Services, Enrique Ramirez Yañez, and to several high level resignations. More embarrassing still for the government was the fact that the disgraced minister was a close personal friend of the then President of Colombia Andres Pastrana (Bosshard 2002; Molinski 2002; PSI 2002).

Coupled with revelations of corruption within EMCALI, local elections for the mayor were won by an independent candidate Jon Maro Rodriguez, who stood on a platform of anti-corruption and was actively supported by the union. Jon Maro Rodriguez began his term of office on the 1 January 2001 and committed himself to implementing the Plan PARE that began in May 2001. This represented another strategic leap for the union, as they now had an ally in local government that 'officially' controlled the company as a result of decentralisation reforms brought in the mid 1990s as part of broader neo-liberal restructuring.

The third stage of the development of Plan Pare was implementation. This began in May 2001 under the leadership of the newly appointed managing director of EMCALI, Juan Manuel Pulido. This situation provided the union with the chance to put its plan into practice, and EMCALI workers began to co-manage the company. Not everyone at local or state level was happy and two narratives emerged concerning the company's future. The first, emanating from the Superintendent of Public Services and widely broadcast in the media, argued that EMCALI was financially not viable and needed external capitalisation. The second, emerging from the trade union, the local mayor and the new managing director, that EMCALI was a good business and potentially highly profitable. This generated a 'break [a] fissure of power within national government' (Interview with Nelson Sanchez 2002).

During the first months of implementing the Plan PARE there was a notable shift in the financial fortunes of the company (Mayor of Cali 2002). Sanchez noted:

> In seven months we achieved a reversal of the deficitary tendency of the company, and although the prediction for that period was that we would end with a deficit of three hundred million pesos in fact we ended in credit . . . the structure of the budget changed radically because in the recuperation plan for EMCALI we gave priority to cutting expenses and generating new sources of income, and attacking corrupt practices. Thus for the first time in 7 years the company had a viable budget, that being a balance between outgoings and expenses. (Interview with Nelson Sanchez 2002)

While the reversal of economic fortune was celebrated by all those involved in Plan Pare, there was deep anxiety in government. The concern was that EMCALI might be setting an example. Rumours surfaced that the government intended to overturn Plan Pare, which they duly attempted to do on 24 December 2001 triggering a 36-day occupation of the EMCALI headquarters, the CAM Tower (Interview with Nelson Sanchez 2002).

The worker – community alliance

Central to Plan PARE was the necessity of reframing the conflict over public services away from a trade union versus the State problem to one between the Cali community and the State. This necessitated a broad strategic alliance but the construction of this was not an easy task. EMCALI's problems could not be explained solely by corrupt management. Workers and managers were complicit in the weak performance of the company and a lack of 'service ethic' in the performance of duties carried out by the workforce. The poor service ethic legitimised government and media accusations that workers benefited from good salaries and benefits at community expense. There was a need to change the attitude of workers to the community and the attitude of the local community towards the workers. This required a sustained process of mutual education and a meeting point for workers and local communities (Interview with Alexander Lopez 2002). The question posed to Sintraemcali was how to break down these barriers and demonstrate to the poorest sections of the community that the union was fighting for those sections of the Cali community suffering from the effects of neo-liberalism.

This process of building up relations with the local community had begun in the mid-1990s. It was aimed at raising the 'political consciousness' of the local marginalised communities:

> This is the objective of our organisation, to educate the people, to generate education 'obrero-popular' [worker-popular]. That means that both the workers and the community need to learn their rights, their constitution, to develop their sense of belonging, of class consciousness, and to move closer to what it means to defend the public, to become part of the process of struggling for sovereignty. (Interview with Luis Hernandez 2002)

This community work ranged from public meetings, to workshops, joining local community demonstrations and protests, and setting up the Sintraemcali Institute, a technical school based at the union's headquarters aimed at teenagers unable to afford secondary education. A further initiative aimed at forging stronger links with the local community was the setting up of *minga comunitarios*, an indigenous phrase meaning 'to come together'. In this programme EMCALI workers would give up one weekend per month to repair infrastructure in the poorest areas of the city. These developed into popular fiesta with educational and cultural events, music, food and dancing and extended to the participation of other unions leading to the provision of free health care, hairdressing and legal advice. The economic importance of the *minga comunitarios* was substantial but they had a major symbolic value; the community and workers engaging in voluntary work together in the poorest areas in the city. For EMCALI workers this promoted solidarity with local communities; for the communities it allowed for a better understanding of the objectives and activities of the union and how these related to their own struggles. It enabled union activists to bring the problems of EMCALI to the communities, counter the arguments of the mainstream media and address the community's worries and questions. This process shifted the culture, attitude and relationship between many of the EMCALI workers and the local community members, with whom they engaged:

> There has been a closening of links with the community which has changed the mentality of the workers, so that they don't see consumers of EMCALI as clients, but see them as owners whom we are defending, as the owners of this company . . . we have tried to change the culture of the workers and this has resulted in the community seeing us in a different light, it has been important in changing the attitude towards the provision of services, to be attentive to the needs of the community, it has meant a big change on the part of the workers, but also a change in the relationship on the part of the community. (Interview with Alexander Lopez 2002)

This 'changed mentality' reflects the process of 'horizontalisation' whereby the culture and structure of the trade union flattens out and interacts more broadly and politically with the local community.

Mobilisation strategy

The third strategic trajectory of Sintraemcali recognised the conflictual nature of any alternative development plan and the necessity to construct alternative 'power' mechanisms to defend and expand the 'propositions' being developed. It recognised that the social forces intent on privatising EMCALI would not be persuaded by words alone and mass mobilisation and direct action had to be deployed.

As a result of the union's decision to challenge the attempts of the Colombian government to privatise EMCALI, the union was forced to develop a range of defensive methods of mobilisation to oppose government plans. The balance between pressurising the Colombian government and the need to build a broad base of support in Cali required the careful selection and utilisation of mobilisation strategies.

The three logics numbers, material damage and bearing witness are seen as three broad rationales behind forms of protest (Della Porta and Diani 1999: 178). Sintraemcali's tactics often reflected a combination of all these with mass, colourful demonstrations, blockades and mass meetings that would block traffic and bring the city to a standstill. The trademark of the union from 1994 became the 'occupation' of high profile buildings, a highly symbolic tool that focussed attention on an issue. Occupations raised the question of 'control' but did not inflict material damage on the company, nor cause unnecessary inconvenience to the general public. Sintraemcali's presentation to the 2003 World Social Forum at Porto Alegre highlighted a list of its 'most important actions' (Sintraemcali 2003b). One can clearly see a preference for this particular type of action:

> Peaceful Occupations: Spanish Embassy, August 1994; National Council, Bogotá, November 1994; Murillo Toro Park, Ibagué, 1995; Departmental Government, Valle, 1995; EMCALI workplants for 6 six days, 1996; EMCALI workplants, 1997; Municipal Administration, 1997; CAM Tower, EMCALI Central Administration 16 days, September, 1998; Municipal Administration, 1998, 1999; 2000; CAM Tower, EMCALI Central Administration 36 days, December, 2001. (Sintraemcali 2003b)

Occupation became the preferred mode of action. A core of several hundred union activists had been involved in the majority of the occupations since 1994. They had developed over the years a clear understanding of what to do, how to do it, and felt comfortable in the environment. They had become 'occupation experts' (Interview with G 2002).[2] The experts knew how to control and defend the space taken, they organised patrols, cleaning rotas, psychological counselling, recreational activities and, most important of all, ensured that public utilities would continue without interruption.

Occupation became the preferred tool of action for several reasons. First, strikes were counterproductive as they affected not only the government but also citizens who were potential allies. Strikes damaged union – community alliances and provide easy propaganda for the government and mass media. Second, the space of the occupation is clearly defined. In a demonstration, the immediate environment is less controllable and easily subject to 'agent provocateurs' and police and parastate attacks. Third, the occupation can be used to raise the conflict's profile and increase the 'opportunity cost ratio' for state terror (Sluka 2000). There are also other issues related to visibility. Many conflicts went unreported whereas occupations of strategic and important buildings prevented the disappearance of a conflict from the media. The psychological power of the occupation of the EMCALI buildings lay in the fact that control over production was challenged and taken over by the workers. Services were maintained and the right to govern was removed from the state, but the right to public services was not. This proved strategically important in building credibility amongst the local population. That occupations had achieved short-term objectives in the past was probably the single biggest reason for its frequent use (Interviews with Luis Hernandez 2002; Alexander Lopez 2002; Nelson Sanchez 2002).

While Sintraemcali would manage the internal workings of the occupation, it was heavily reliant on community support for the successful resolution of any conflicts. The main vehicles for the mobilisation of communities in Cali was the Municipal Strike Command created in the early 1990s to coordinate civic strikes (as opposed to national strikes which would be only for public employees) against neo-liberal reforms. This space of action included elected members of JACs (Local Action Committees), local councillors, representatives of rural constituents on the outskirts of the city, other trade unionists, students, activists and representatives of community television channels. Through these, links were created with the non-organised sectors of the community. It included other union movements in the area, with representatives of individual unions and elected members of the regional headquarters of the CUT Valle de Cauca Section.

This space of action was also a pedagogical space where workers and local communities worked out their differences and planned common action. It was a forum for political, union and community activists to meet in a non-hierarchical environment, where issues could be debated and decisions taken by consensus. There are no formal positions within the Strike Command; working groups are set up to deal with particular activities between meetings. Otoniel Ramirez, President of the CUT Valle and a leading participant in the Strike Command, refers to it as a space of 'unity of action', 'when we agree on something, a common problem, we plan action.' The Municipal Strike Command played a pivotal role in the major Sintraemcali occupations of 1998 and 2001 (Interview with Otoniel Ramirez 2002).

Sintraemcali and human rights and solidarity networks

The union's determination to mobilise to defend Emcali and its uncovering of high level corruption placed it in direct confrontation with the political and economic elite and state and parastate forces. Sixteen members of Sintraemcali have been assassinated since the mid-1990s, several wounded, kidnapped, and countless members have received death threats and were forced to leave the region and some, the country. There have been three assassination attempts on the ex-president of the Union and the entire board of directors has received death threats. The current President of Sintraemcali, Luis Hernandez, has been forced to live a semi-clandestine life, as attempts to assassinate him were uncovered. In 1996, 600 workers were arrested for involvement in the six-day occupation. In 1997, 300 workers were fined and 22 imprisoned, and 55 members of Sintraemcali have been charged with rebellion (Sintraemcali 2004). Several workers have been arrested and imprisoned under the subversion and terrorism laws, and there has been a persistent campaign aimed at undermining the union's legitimacy by alleging it is linked to the armed insurgency (Amnesty International 2000).

The increase in human rights violations after 1998 led the union closer to a range of human rights organisations active in the country. With the increased involvement of Berenice Celeyta, President of the Colombian non-governmental organisation (NGO) NOMADESC, the union embraced human rights defence and promotion as a central plank in its anti-privatisation strategy. Celeyta was central in setting up a Human Rights Department at the union's headquarters, monitoring human rights abuses across the city and beyond. It also carries out education and training work, providing local activists with practical knowledge of human rights mechanisms at their disposal. The department has become a type of community or drop-in centre for organisations and individuals facing problems in the field of human rights. The human rights focus has also injected a fresh range of practices and discourses into the activities of the union itself and diffused information to other popular organisations in the region (Interview with Berenice Celeyta 2002). The human rights discourse has provided a key mechanism through which Sintraemcali's opposition to privatisation has been re-articulated as a struggle for economic and social rights, allowing it to transcend traditional 'member' conditions and embrace citizenship rights. The actions of the Human Rights Department range from local mediation of conflicts to national and transnational advocacy, lobbying and legal work, providing new spaces within which the trade union could strengthen its ability to oppose privatisation.

At the local level, the Human Rights Department has been instrumental in training local activists in human rights norms and mechanisms for self-defence. The training provides participants with methods of intervention in conflicts, how to set up a local human rights network among social movements, and a background in the human rights legal frameworks that exist at regional and global levels. The courses typically involve both union and community leaders and activists and so provide further interaction and communication between workers and community activists. In June 2001 this process was expanded with the setting up of the National and International Human Rights Campaign Against Corruption Privatisation and the Criminalisation of Social Protest, uniting over twenty social organisations and carries out legal, political, cultural, educational and lobbying work. In all of the direct actions, human rights activists and representatives of human rights NGOs were present and were able to contact the appropriate authorities and ensure that the local police and military response was measured. Much of the power of these human rights activists derives from their ability to link up to transnational human rights networks, which are able to pressure the Colombian government to follow accepted international norms of behaviour (Keck and Sikkink 1998).

At the international level the Human Rights Department has facilitated the involvement of major human rights organisations in Sintraemcali's situation, and representatives of Amnesty International and Human Rights Watch have intervened several times. These powerful organisations engage in lobbying, the production and distribution of 'urgent actions', the compilation of reports on the human rights situation in the region and high level visits to representatives of the armed forces, the government and supranational organisations such as the United Nations Commission for Human Rights (UNCHR). The involvement of Amnesty and Human Rights Watch is understood discursively by the union's leaders as providing a cordon of protection within which they carry out their activities and a means of addressing and revealing Colombia's 'parallel state' of covert repression. These organisations have particular skills and abilities to influence governments by applying selective pressure and lobbying (Interview with Berenice Celeyta 2002).

Closely related to this network is the role of the supranational labour and human rights bodies, such as the UNCHR, and the Inter-American Commission of Human Rights (IACHR), that have the ability to sanction national governments for the failure to enforce and protect human rights. These organisations, the supranational equivalent of state labour and justice departments, have the power to sanction states rather than individuals. Sintraemcali, with the assistance of national human rights organisations, took its case of systematic persecution from state and parastate forces to the Inter-American Human Rights Court (IAHRC). On 21 June 2000 the IAHRC found the Colombian government responsible for failing to provide adequate security for the union carrying out legitimate activities. The court ordered the Colombian government to provide protection for the entire leadership of the union including bodyguards, weapons, bulletproof vehicles and communications equipment (IAHRC 2000). This protection, while not eliminating the danger, at least allowed some 'space' for activity and was a severe political defeat for the government that vigorously opposed the application and denied any responsibility. The ability, experience and success of Colombian human rights organisations to prepare cases for these processes has been a great source of concern for the Colombian government.

The Human Rights Department has also been a catalyst in building transnational links with trade union, solidarity and other activist organisations in the North. In the United Kingdom, strong international links began during the president of the union's brief period of exile in London from October to December 2000. Since that point there have been delegations, exchanges and several invitations for Sintraemcali representatives to talk at British union conferences. Sintraemcali forged strong links with the Colombia Solidarity Campaign, UK, which campaigns on human rights and political issues in Colombia, and several of its members have worked as volunteers in the Human Rights Department. Since 2000, there has been a continual process of communication and regular delegations that have forged strong bonds between Colombian and British activists. This strategy has been extended to Spain, Canada, the USA and Australia and has included links with sympathetic politicians, human rights groups, NGOs and social movements in each of these countries. The rapidly expanding Colombian exile community in these countries has strengthened the transnational links, and many are founding members and activists in solidarity organisations, as is the case in the UK.

More traditional international trade union activity has been developed alongside the Colombian CUT (the biggest of the national trade union federations) and other national trade union organisations. With the backing of the British TUC (Trades Union Congress), it has also put forward motions for 2001–3 at the annual ILO (International Labour Organisation) conference in Geneva to call for a 'Special Commission of Inquiry' into the human rights emergency of Colombian workers. The motion was defeated each time by intense lobbying by the Colombian government. The ILO's tripartite structure giving equal weight to capital, state and workers has meant that no serious sanctions have been brought against the Colombian government. Likewise the union has, on a range of occasions and often via the British TUC, managed to obtain the intervention of the ICFTU (International Confederation of Free Trade Unions) and the PSI (Public Services International).

All of these links with union, solidarity groups, and activist organisations in a range of countries have facilitated the union's ability to enter a range of transnational human rights and solidarity networks such as the anti-globalisation movement and transnational human rights networks. These have been particularly effective in relation to specific disputes and actions where human rights violations had taken place or were likely to take place. Sending out 'urgent actions' on these networks result in protest letters and pickets of Colombian embassies, which union representatives feel act as a means of protection for those workers and communities involved (Interview with Berenice Celeyta 2002). When Alexander Lopez, then President of Sintraemcali, visited the UK in 2001 a UNISON representative asked him what international solidarity meant in real terms, he replied, 'it makes it more difficult for them to kill us' (UNISON 2002).

Conclusion

Sintraemcali transformed itself from a 'quiet normal union' in the early 1990s to an organisation that was jointly administering one of the biggest companies in Colombia and had halted a privatisation process promoted by a range of powerful transnational and national forces.

What is evident is the developmental and pedagogical process that this transformation involved. There were several strands to this strategy including education for consciousness raising as well as strategy development, research, investigation and action on a range of scales from the local to the international. These processes constructed a formidable coalition of support involving local unionists, community members from the poorest neighbourhoods in the city, local professionals and non-aligned politicians and human rights and political activists beyond Colombia.

Central to understanding this are the twin processes of transborderisation and horizontalisation. Horizontalisation necessitated a shift from a corporate top-down hierarchical union mediating between management and workers, a form of regulatory trade unionism, to a social movement union with a bottom up approach that appealed to local communities. While continuing to mediate between capital and workers Sintraemcali's strategy also pointed to a far more transformatory and emancipatory role which addressed the tensions between its own workers' interests and the broader working class community. By so doing, Sintraemcali challenged the dominant neo-liberal trajectory of public service management being advocated by the Colombian government and its transnational allies. It did not only resist these processes but developed a viable alternative plan for the efficient management of public services in the city.

In doing so Sintraemcali revealed widespread corruption, losing members to the assassin's bullet, and became a major adversary of the Colombian state and its death squad. Repression and the union's broader appeal to the justice of its anti-corruption and human rights struggle facilitated the transborderisation of that struggle allowing it to operate comparable to capital and capitalists from the local to the global. These new scales of operation included transnational advocacy networks and also the new local space of decentralised government, alongside the strengthening alliance with the local poor community coordinated through the *mingas* and the Municipal Strike Command.

While the defence of public services in Cali is protracted and difficult, Sintraemcali remains committed to the route of imaginative multi-scalar coalitions and militant direct action. Beyond Colombia, the case study highlights the possibilities of the labour movement's strategic renewal and the developmental processes involved. While the story of globalisation continues to be largely written from above, alternative forms of globalisation are emerging on every continent. By globalising solidarity and resistance to corporate power and profit, Sintraemcali provides another example demonstrating that alternatives to the hegemony of neo-liberalism exist and that alternatives are built by ordinary working people collectively doing extraordinary things.

Notes

1   This chapter is based on Novelli (2005). ESRC Research Studentship R42200034313 made the research, which included ten months enthnographic fieldwork in Cali, possible.
2   Some interviewees, particularly rank and file activists who were not in the media spotlight, preferred to remain anonymous and were identified by letters for purposes of transcription.

References

Ahumada, C. (2000) 'Una década en reversa', in Ahumada C. and Caballero. A. (eds), *Que esta pasando en Colombia?*, Bogota.
Amnesty International. (2000) 'Urgent Action', 30 June. Ref: AMR 23/51/00. http://web.amnesty.org/library/index/ENGAMR230512000 (accessed December 2004).
Bosshard, P. (2002) 'Private gain–public risk? The international experience with power purchase agreements of private power projects', *International rivers network*. Available at http://www.irn.org/programs/bujagali/bujagalippa-background.pdf (accessed December 2004).
Branford, S. and Rocha, J. (2002) *Cutting the wire: the struggle of the landless movement in Brazil*, London.
Callinicos, A. (2003) *Anti-capitalist manifesto*, Oxford.
Castells, M. (1997) *The power of identity, the information age: economy, society and culture*, vol. 2, Oxford.
Castillo, R. E. J. (2000) *www.neoliberalismo.com.co: balance y perspectivas*, Bogota.
CUT (2004) *Informe sobre los derechos humanos 2004*, Bogota.
Della Porta, D. and Diani, M. (1999) *Social movements: an introduction*, Oxford.
En Camino (2003) *'Colombia's public services: an interview with Alex Lopez of Sintraemcali'* 13 April 2003. www.en-camino.org/april152003podurlopez.htm (accessed December 2004).
ENS (2003) *'Report on the violation to the human rights of the Colombian union workers'*, Escuela Nacional Sindical. www.ens.org.co/infddhhenglish/finalreport2003.htm#_ftnref6 (accessed December 2004).
Escobar, A. (2000) 'Notes on networks and anti-globalization social movements'. Paper presented at AAA Annual Meeting, San Francisco, 15–19 November. Available at www.unc.edu/depts/anthro/escobarpaper.html (accessed December 2004).
Fernández, H. V. (2003) *La política antisindical de las elites dominantes y los supuestos privilegios de los trabajadores de Ecopetrol*, Escuela Nacional Sindical. Available at www.ens.org.co/txt/costosecopetrol.doc (accessed December 2004).
Herod, A. (2001) *Labor geographies: workers and the landscapes of capitalism*, New York.
——— (ed.) (1998) *Organizing the landscape: geographical perspectives on labor unionism*, Minneapolis.
——— (2003) 'Geographies of labor internationalism', *Social Science History*, 27:4.
Higginbottom, A. (2004) 'Advancing in danger: the left in Colombia'. Paper presented at the Society of Latin American Studies Conference April 2004, Leiden, Holland.
Holloway, J. and Peláez, E. (1998) *Zapatista! Reinventing revolution in Mexico*, London.
Human Rights Watch (1996) *Colombia's killer networks: the military-paramilitary partnership and the United States*, New York.
——— (2000) *Colombia the ties that bind. Colombia and military-paramilitary links*, New York.

—— (2001) *The 'Sixth Division'. Military-paramilitary ties and U.S. policy in Colombia*, New York.

Hylton, F. (2003) 'An evil hour', *New Left Review*, 23.

Inter-American Commission of Human Rights (2000) *Medidas cautelares*. Available at www.cidh.oas.org/medidas/2000.sp.htm (accessed December 2004).

Interview with Alexander Lopez (2002).

Interview with Berenice Celeyta (2002).

Interview with G (2002).

Interview with Luis Hernandez (2002).

Interview with Nelson Sanchez (2002).

Johnston, P. (2000) 'The resurgence of labor as citizenship movement in the new labor relations environment', *Critical Sociology*, 26:1–2.

Keck, E. M. and Sikkink, K. (1998) *Activists beyond borders. Advocacy networks in international politics*, London.

Mayor of Cali (2002) Annual report of the local government of Cali. *Primeros 100 días de gestión*. Available at www.cali.gov.co/gobierno/infogobierno.htm (accessed December 2004).

McClintock, M. (1985) *The American connection. Volume I: state terror and popular resistance in El Salvador*, London.

Molinski, D. (2002) 'Colombia may lose ATPA tariff relief on TermoRio-US', *Of Dow Jones Newswires*, 7 August. Available at www.mac.doc.gov/PressMain/Aug2002/Aug7 ColombiaATPA.html (accessed December 2004).

Moody, K. (1997) *Workers in a lean world. unions in the international economy*, London.

Morton, A. D. (2002) 'La resurrección del Maíz. Globalisation, resistance and the Zapatistas', *Millennium: Journal of International Studies*, 31:1.

Munck, R. (2002) *Globalisation and labour*, London.

Novelli, M. (2005) *Trade unions, strategic pedagogy and globalisation: learning from the anti-privatisation struggles of Sintraemcali*. Unpublished Ph.D. thesis, University of Bristol.

Olivera, O. and Lewis, T. (2003) *Cochabamba. Water rebellion in Bolivia*, New York.

Palacio, E. (2001) 'El neoliberalismo: Nefasto experimento para Colombia', *Nueva Gaceta*, 2, April.

Petras, J. (2001) 'The geopolitics of Plan Colombia', *Monthly Review*, May.

PSI (2002) *Privatisation of infrastructure and public services in Colombia*, Public Services International.

Revista Valle (2003) 'Cronico de cómo quebraron a EMCALI'. Available at http://rvalle2000.tripod.com.co/denuncia.htm (accessed December 2004).

Santos, B. S. (2002) 'The processes of globalisation', *Revista crítica de liéncias sociales*. Available at www.eurozine.com/article/2002-08-22-santos-en.html (accessed December 2004).

Sarmiento, E. (2001) 'El neoliberalismo: nefasto experimento para Colombia', *Nueva Gaceta*, April, 88–97, Bogotá.

Sen, J., Anand, A., Escobar, A. and Waterman, P. (eds) (2004), *World social forum: challenging empires*, Third World Institute. Available at www.choike.org/nuevo_eng/informes/1557. html (accessed December 2004).

Sintraemcali (2000) *Plan por el salvamento de EMCALI*, Cali.

—— (2003a) *Informe anual*, Cali.

—— (2003b) Presentation prepared for the World Social Forum, Porto Alegre.

—— (2004) *Informe anual*, Cali.

Sluka, J. (ed.) (2000) *Death squad: the anthropology of state terror*, Philadelphia.

Stokes, D. (2004) *Terrorising Colombia. America's other war*, London.

UNISON (2002) *Colombia: trade unionists under siege*, London. Available at www.unison.org.uk/acrobat/B512.pdf (accessed December 2004).

Waterman, P. (2001) *Globalization, social movements and the new labour internationalisms*, London.

—— and Wills, J. (eds) (2001) *Place, space and the new labour internationalisms*, Oxford.

World Bank (2002) *Colombia poverty report*, Washington.

13

Canalising resistance: historical continuities and contrasts of 'alter-globalist' movements at the European Social Forums

Andreas Bieler and Adam David Morton

Introduction[1]

The revival of European integration since the mid-1980s, based most importantly on the Internal Market programme and Economic and Monetary Union, has been driven by neo-liberal restructuring. This has been extensively documented elsewhere (Bieler and Morton 2001; Bieling and Steinhilber 2000; Cafruny and Ryner 2003). This chapter investigates the increasing challenges to this neo-liberal order, which have come to the fore in Europe through forms of anti-capitalist resistance, or what is increasingly referred to as 'alter-globalist' resistance based on the demand for a different globalisation, within the agenda of the European Social Forum (ESF). It was at the second World Social Forum, the worldwide meeting of the 'alter-globalist' movements, in Porto Alegre in 2002 that the decision was made to also hold social forums at the regional level. The first ESF in Florence from 6 to 10 November 2002 was the European response to this call, followed by the second held in St Denis, Paris (12–15 November 2003), and the third meeting held in London (15–17 October 2004).

It is frequently assumed that such contemporary practices of resistance have either emerged *ex nihilo* as the novel expression and practice of a 'global civil society' or exhibit the structural weaknesses of organised labour. Instead, this chapter aims to pose the question of the historical continuities and contrasts of 'alter-globalist' resistance, which demands a historicist analysis able to tease out the structural linkages and conjunctural differences between resistance movements and their historical precursors. One may then say with Hobsbawm that 'it is a more interesting task of research to investigate the positive appeal of working-class operational internationalism than to demonstrate, yet again, its obvious limitations.' (1988: 9)

Our aim is to develop what we call a historical sociological approach to understanding resistance in order to examine the legacies up to and beyond the pivotal period of 1968 in the present phase of 'alter-globalist' movements. This chapter assesses the goals, strategies and achievements of labour and social movements across the three ESFs. Through this focus it will be possible to question to what extent extra-parliamentary opposition can consolidate strategies of resistance against neo-liberal restructuring, whilst also considering to what extent the fate of co-option and failure can be avoided. Examining the continuities *and* contrasts between past and present resistance movements advances such reflection. By questioning the direction, purpose and cohesion of resistance movements in this way, by reflecting on the potential of the ESFs to canalise resistance, it will be possible, finally, to distinguish between those movements that are engaged in historically organic transformations and those creating only individual movements grounded in extemporary polemics or ideologies that are arbitrary or willed. Highlighting in Gramsci's idiom 'real action on the one hand . . . and on the other hand the gladiatorial futility which is self-declared action but modifies only the word, not things, the external gesture' (Gramsci 1971: 307, 376–7). Four main sections bring the chapter into focus. The first develops our historical sociological approach to resistance by establishing a series of historical continuities and contrasts to present resistance movements embodied in the ESF. The second, third and fourth sections then reflect with the help of this approach on the Florence, Paris and London ESFs respectively, before developing in conclusion the difficulties to be faced in canalising resistance movements in the future.

Labour: left on the shelf?

In moving towards a historical sociological understanding of resistance, Hobsbawm has long noted that the real challenges to historical capitalism initially stemmed from extra-parliamentary movements, the 'labouring poor', who increasingly embarked on tactics of direct action leading up to the European revolutions of 1848. Yet the labour movement at this time was, neither in composition, nor ideology, a strictly 'proletarian' movement based on industrial and factory workers but a common front of all forces and tendencies representing mainly the urban poor. 'The public expression of their protest was, in the literal sense, a "movement" rather than an organisation', linked by little more than a handful of traditional and radical slogans and held together more by 'hunger, wretchedness, hatred and hope' than leadership or organisation (Hobsbawm 1962: 212–13, 215–16). It was only subsequently that the labour movement emerged in Europe, in the 1890s, channelled through industrial trade union struggle and political parties, the latter based on the model success of the German Sozialdemokratische Partei Deutschlands (SPD) in formulating core demands linked to the welfare state and labour market regulation (Sassoon 1996: 9, 24).

Similarly, the full array of social movement claim-making did not gain consolidation in France until around 1848 and even then workers' demonstrations did not become established until the final decades of the nineteenth century (Tilly 2004: 34, 41). At this time, structured mass movements in industrial economies threatened the stability of 'bourgeois civilisation' based on a combination of organisation and mass support. Yet they amounted to 'potential states': 'the major revolutions of . . . [the nineteenth century] were to replace old regimes, old states and old ruling classes by parties-cum-movements institutionalised as systems of state power' (Hobsbawm 1987: 95). The era of a flourishing and stable liberal capitalism during the mid-nineteenth century offered the nascent 'working class' the possibility of improving its lot through collective organisation within trade unions, offering the prospects of improvement but on bourgeois terms (Hobsbawm 1975: 224). Illustrative here is how the former anthem of the French Revolution, the *Marsellaise*, would be taken over by the State and, in Britain in the 1890s, how the phenomenon of organised national labour appeared within the framework of trade union struggle channelled through 'industrial unionism'. Here the inauguration of annual May Day demonstrations would become the effective framework of state-defined class consciousness whilst the British monarch also began annual appearances at that 'festival of the proletariat', the football Cup Final (Hobsbawm 1987: 107, 129). The lineal continuation of this tradition during the 'Golden Age' of the twentieth century, from post-World War II to the 1970s, was acceptance of a reformed capitalism within the fold of labour and social democratic aspirations. Labour movements were beset by a history of corporatist structures and institutionalism that amounted to an 'Enlightenment Left' based on values of progress applied through reason and science, education, and a future-oriented outlook (Hobsbawm 1994: 147, 272).

This sentiment is similarly highlighted in separate reflections on 'anti-systemic movements' that presents mobilisations of the nineteenth and twentieth centuries as 'children of the Enlightenment', which 'reflected in their formulation of long-term objectives, middle-range methods that reinforced the mechanisms of the capitalist world-economy' (Wallerstein 1982: 36). Historically, anti-systemic movements took the form of national(ist) and social(ist) movements clamouring for the occupancy of state power. No matter how egalitarian their objectives, they continued to function as part of the social division of labour altering state structures but not capitalist accumulation (Arrighi, Hopkins and Wallerstein 1995: 68, 71–2). In their generic forms anti-systemic movements thus represented a nexus that combined attempts to both challenge *and* reproduce the production of value underlying social productive relations so that transformations remained limited to the *politics* but not the *economics* of capitalism. 'A strong organisation became the primary weapon of revolution', argues Wallerstein (1984: 115), 'it simultaneously served as a constraint on revolutionary activity. This primary contradiction explains much of the subsequent history of workers' parties.' Anti-systemic movements therefore became the *interlocuteurs valables* of the defenders of privilege or the 'institutional products of the capitalist world-economy formed in the crucible of its contradictions, permeated by its metaphysical suppositions, constrained by the working of its other institutions' (Wallerstein 1991a: 27, 1999: 152).

From the 1960s onwards, though, social movements railed against these bureaucratic structures and realised once more the increased efficacy of direct forms of action embodied in emergent transnational methods of organising. '1968', Wallerstein (1991b:11) notes, 'reopened the ideological consensus that followed 1848' as the seeking of state power was no longer seen as the crucial strategy for transforming society. More controversially he also asserts that '1968 was the ideological tomb of the concept of the "leading role" of the industrial proletariat', after which labour was left on the shelf amidst those movements immediately challenging capitalist restructuring (Wallerstein 1991b: 72). This is also the theme of Herbert Marcuse's critical social theory in which labour itself is again predominantly regarded as a prop and affirmative force between the productive capabilities of society and their destructive and oppressive utilisation (Marcuse 1964: 35). In delineating the 'new sensibility' of non-violent direct action stemming from the context of 1960s radicalism, Marcuse noted a shift toward decentralised forms of organisation, which signalled a turning point in resistance. Whilst organised labour was seen to share the stabilising, counter-revolutionary interests of the middle-classes, a 'new historical subject of change' began to examine the contradictions of parliamentary democracy and raise the agenda of social transformation (Marcuse 1969: 43, 58). In Europe the evident manifestation of this 'new sensibility' was the 1968 French May movement based on a combination of student protests and the weapon of the general strike. Power here was seen to manifest in the streets, from *Le pavé* (the Parisian cobblestones that provided both a symbolic and tangible weapon against the established order) to the student demonstrations that passed peacefully by the National Assembly, whilst holding the Palais Bourbon in contempt because it was not even worth storming. 'Ten years as a Gaullist rubber stamp', Daniel Singer (2002: 27, 127, 129) reported soon after, 'had broken the remaining illusions about the importance of an already discredited institution.' With the widespread opposition to bureaucracy, the *comités d'action* attempted to mobilise through alternative instruments of spontaneous struggle whilst simultaneously giving dynamism to the general strike. Although the action committees suffered from incoherence and indecisiveness, 'their approach, even very existence, was a sign of the utter inadequacy of traditional parties for the tasks of [the] day' (Singer 2002: 274). Whilst the general strike was pivotal in supporting the response of the student rebellion, the institutionalisation of class struggle within the Confédération Générale du Travail (CGT) was a brake on the movement, whereas the Fédération de la Gauche Démocratie et Socialiste (FGDS) and the Parti Communiste Français (PCF) were dismissed by the radical contingent of students as part of the parliamentary opposition and thus the 'capitalist consensus'. 'The conduct of the PCF in May 1968 was no aberration, no slip by a revolutionary party that misjudged a situation. It was the natural behaviour of an organisation intrinsically incapable of evolving a revolutionary strategy' (Singer 2002: 289).

Miliband similarly indicates that the PCF 'was suddenly offered the opportunity to move in the direction of insurrectionary politics in May 1968 and rejected it with little if any hesitation' with Ernest Mandel tracing related problems in the reformist strategic position of labour taken at the time (Mandel 1968: 17–21; Miliband 1977: 174). Hence Marcuse's celebration of the rebellion that was taking place at the time, in all its 'weird and clownish forms', based on radical protest and an antinomian, anarchistic and, in his own words, 'anti-capitalist' ethos (Marcuse 1969: 64, 68). Yet all attempts to create a sustainable opposition to the traditional socialist and communist organisations prevalent at the time failed. 'No established party', argues Donald Sassoon (1996: 390, 399), 'suffered unduly, or prospered particularly, as a consequence of the movement', thus acting as 'no more than a cathartic hope for the future, an expression of a desire to escape from the constraints of electoral politics'.

Contemporary criticisms of established trade unions echo the above concerns about the constraining impact of institutionalised labour. An insight afforded by casting out a wider historical sociological net to understanding labour and social movement resistance. Co-opted into social partnership institutions, it is alleged that the European Trade Union Confederation (ETUC), especially, has participated in the implementation of neo-liberal restructuring across the European Union (EU), based on principles of monetary stability, market flexibility and a policy of 'employability' (Taylor and Mathers 2002: 48–50). This is particularly explicable in light of the comment that since its inception the ETUC can be regarded as 'firmly capitalist' (van der Pijl 1984: 249). It is as much a part of the post-World War II history of corporatist structures and reformist institutionalism, a 'politics of productivity' (Maier 1977: 607–33), which would bring into question its ability to lead the latest agenda of resistance. At the same time, the lessons of 1968 need to be kept in mind. The heavy focus on extra-parliamentary action did lead to clear defeats in the past, a risk that is always worth taking, but a result that has been partly reflected in an inability to break the structures of capitalism. The latter 'can be brought down only by those who still sustain the established work process, who constitute its human base, who reproduce its profits and its power' (Marcuse 1972: 132). Hence a blend of direct action and uncivil disobedience alongside a rejuvenation of the historical power of the general strike and the factory occupation can be seen as potential resources of hope. The possible radicalisation of labour through contact with other social movements should not therefore be discounted (O'Brien 2000: 533–55).

It is in this respect that we analyse the ESFs in Florence-Paris-London, regarded as a further expression and continuation of these historical continuities or, put differently, as 'new revolts against the system' that nevertheless carry over certain similar sentiments (Wallerstein: 2002: 29–38). It is asked whether the lessons from 1968 have been learned, in that trade unions as the institutionalised representatives of labour, on one hand, and social movements of extra-parliamentary opposition, on the other, have started to co-operate more extensively. Hopefully bringing the structural power of trade unions rooted in production and the weapon of the general strike together with the force of spontaneity, creativity and mobilisation characteristic of social movements.

The ESFs as new revolts against the system? The beginnings at Florence

The first ESF took place in Florence in November 2002. During 400 meetings ranging from small group workshops to large plenary sessions, around 32,000 to 40,000 participants from all over Europe plus 80 further countries debated issues related to the three main themes of the forum: (1) 'Globalisation and (neo-) liberalism'; (2) 'War and Peace'; and (3) 'Rights-Citizenship-Democracy' (Bieler and Morton 2004).

Trade unions and social movements were well presented in Florence. The former can be divided into established trade unions on the one hand, and new, more radical trade unions on the other. Overall, Northern European established trade unions were under represented. For example, the Union of Rail, Maritime and Transport Workers (RMT) was the only British union represented by a leading official whereas the two biggest German unions, IG Metall and the service sector union Ver.di, stayed away. In contrast, several Southern European peak trade union associations as well as the ETUC and some of its affiliated European Industry Federations (EIFs) participated actively in the proceedings through high-level delegates.[2] Though with significantly fewer members at the national level, radical, new unions were also strongly represented at the ESF, with most notable examples including the Italian Comitati di Base (COBAS); the main French education union Fédération Syndicale Unitaire (FSU); several of the French Solidaires, Unitaires et Démocratiques (SUD) unions; as well as their confederation L'Union Syndicale G10 Solidaires (or G-10) (also see ESF 2002).

There are clear differences between the established and new, radical trade unions as far as their history, their internal structure, as well as their strategies are concerned and these differences became all too apparent in Florence. The very emergence of the new, radical trade unions is a result of the perceived accommodationist position of established trade unions vis-à-vis neo-liberal restructuring in Europe. The French union SUD-PTT, for example, which organises workers in the postal services and telecommunications industry, was founded in 1988 after a split from the Confédération Française Démocratique du Travail (CFDT) over the latter's lack of support for strikes in these industries. In contrast with established trade unions, these new, radical unions regard themselves as rank and file unions, where strong emphasis is put on the opinions of members. COBAS unions, for example, emphasise the importance of members at the company level at the expense of hierarchical, centralised union structures. COBAS groups are independent, diverse and frequently have no regular link with their counterparts (Gall 1995: 13, 17–18). These different histories and structures have direct implications for strategy. Established trade unions continue to focus on 'social partnership' with employers and state representatives in order to assert the demands of their members. Representatives made clear at the Florence ESF that a Social Europe, where the market is embedded in a set of protective regulations, could be best achieved through bargaining with employers, backed up by the right to strike at the European level. In short, the focus is on institutionalised interaction with established trade unions as the most important representatives of the alternative forces (ESF-I, Sessions III, IV and VI).

Such positions were greeted with exasperation by new, radical trade unions and social movements alike. They in turn accused established trade unions of having participated in (and thus partly culpable for) neo-liberal restructuring projects such as Economic and Monetary Union (EMU) and the increasing flexibilisation of the labour market. Rather than concentrating on institutionalised interaction, it was argued that the emphasis should be on the formation of an extra-parliamentary opposition, based on rank and file organisation at the workplace, providing the basis for successful strikes if needed, combined with a strong focus on other social movements and their issues. COBAS advocated the formation of a new front that 'stems from the fundamental terrain of trade unions and is necessarily extended into the more general political terrain' to oppose 'the aggressive dynamics of capital, which invades all aspects of human activity' (COBAS 2002: 16). SUD unions and the G-10 also recognised that neo-liberal exploitation goes beyond issues at the workplace. 'It is, therefore, necessary to operate in relation to all these consequences in partnership with social movements, which also struggle on this terrain' (G-10 1998; SUD 2002a: 29–30). Hence, new radical trade unions not only raised demands related to the workplace, they also asked for the right to work, to accommodation and to health alongside raising ecological concerns. They demanded decent unemployment benefit as well as rights for 'illegal' immigrants, the so-called *sans-papiers*. For example, SUD éducation stated that 'it is our role as trade unionists to defend the basic rights of all – the right to work, to accommodation, to health care, to education, to culture . . . and, therefore, to co-operate with all those, who are excluded from them. This has been the reason for our engagement on the side of the *sans-papiers* since 1996' (SUD 2002b: 4).

Social movements are sceptical of established trade unions' motives. They question unions' hierarchical internal organisation and remain unconvinced about the willingness of unions to confront neo-liberal restructuring in Europe. Of course, social movements themselves differ drastically from each other. Some social movements such as ATTAC, who were co-initiators of the ESF and thus heavily represented at the meeting, concentrate on influencing policy-making via research and lobbying (ESF-I, Session I; http://attac.org/indexen/index.html). Others adopt the politics of more direct action, embodied at the ESF in the presence of groups like the disobediente, which is the wing of Italian autonomism that in previous incarnations has materialised as Ya Basta! and the tute bianche (also see Wright 2002). The latter social movements, akin to autonomous movements like Reclaim the Streets campaigners, Earth First!ers or People's Global Action (PGA), are pervaded by a different life-style ethos. A combination of more traditional and new currents of extra-parliamentary resistance can also be observed in groups such as the British Socialist Workers Party and Globalize Resistance, both well represented at the ESF in Florence. Another specific group of social movements are so-called single-issue alliances. For example, groups such as the Belgium Le Comité pour l'Annulation de la Dette du Tiers Monde (CADTM), which is closely linked to the international Jubilee South Campaign, founded in Johannesburg in 1999 for the cancellation of developing countries' debt (ESF-I, Session I; http://users.skynet. be/cadtm/pages/English); the Habitat International Coalition (HIC) and its commitment to secure housing for everybody; or the National Unions of Students in Europe and its emphasis on protecting the right of everybody to free education (ESF-I, Session IV; http://home.mweb.co.za/hi/hic/about.html and http://www. esib.org/). Associations such as the international peasant organisation La Via Campesina with its focus on the protection of the interests of small and medium-sized agricultural producers were also present (ESF-I, Session III; http://ns.rds. org.hn/via/). Finally, the pan-European social movement Euromarches, organising resistance against unemployment, job insecurity and social exclusion was active as both organiser and participant at the ESF (ESF-I, Session VI; http://www. euromarches.org).

All these different institutional structures and strategies clearly led to tensions within the labour movement itself as well as between trade unions and social movements. Nonetheless, this should not make us overlook the commonalities of these actors as well as the resulting joint actions. All sides stressed the importance of co-operation. This was easier for social movements and new, radical trade unions, but representatives of established trade unions were willing co-operators too. For instance, the representative of the Spanish CCOO argued that the union agenda had to be put forward at all levels in co-operation with social movements leading to the formation of a new international solidarity (ESF-I, Session III). It was acknowledged that in this process trade unions also have to defend the underemployed and the unemployed. Hence the main contribution of trade unions was their experience in mobilising people and organising strikes, which would caution against underestimating the weapon of the general strike. In a like manner, the representative of the CGTP emphasised the importance of trade union-social movement co-operation in the struggle for another Europe. While the former could concentrate on the daily defence of basic rights, the latter could focus on the formulation of 'utopian', yet inspiring, goals (ESF-I, Session IV). This relates directly back to the lessons of 1968. Extra-parliamentary opposition without the trade unions is likely to fail, whilst sole reliance on the activities of unions is liable to cement the system rather than changing it. A combination of both forces, however, may be the potential basis for a successful way forward. Florence, although just the beginning, was clearly a step in this direction.

Most importantly, despite all their differences, there was clear agreement between unions and social movements on the view that European integration has been constitutive of neo-liberal globalisation, which simultaneously has to be resisted in and beyond Europe. This is the fundamental common basis on which these groups meet and from which their co-operation starts (Ashman 2004: 150; Khalfa 2003: 6). Whereas the ETUC does not reject globalisation as such – based on the belief that workers too may benefit from global trade – it nevertheless agrees that a different globalisation is necessary. In this respect, additional regulation is demanded in order to further the development of a social dimension within Europe. 'The European social model must be defended and consolidated according to the needs of a different vision of economic and social relations on a global scale' (ETUC 2002). Unrestrained globalisation is therefore criticised for being unable to eradicate poverty, to combat social exclusion, and to provide decent work for all. New, radical trade unions are even more outspoken in their criticism of neo-liberal globalisation and the way it is implemented within the EU. FSU, for example, regards EMU and the neo-liberal convergence criteria as a reproduction of the Washington consensus, which enforces neo-liberal restructuring at the global level through structural adjustment programmes (Laval and Weber 2002: 109). Whilst SUD unions accept the EU as a fact, they also appreciate that its construction is not neutral but inscribed and proscribed within the remit of neo-liberalism. The European struggle, therefore, needs to be linked to the struggle against globalisation (SUD 2002a: 96, 102). Social movements make similar observations. Euromarches points out that 'since the ratification of the Treaty of Maastricht, the Stability Pact has imposed social regressions on every country, even those where the rights had been most secure' (Euromarches 2002: 6). HIC argues that 'regarding the challenges and damages provoked by [neo-] liberal globalisation, Europe continues to choose the market rather than rights' (HIC 2001).

On the basis of the above general agreements, a convergence of opinions emerged around several areas for joint activities. First, it was at the ESF that 'anti-war organisations in 11 European countries agreed to demonstrate against Bush and Blair's war on the same day: 15 February 2003' (Khalfa 2003: 5). The result was impressive. Estimates speak of 1 million people marching in London, 1 million in Madrid and Barcelona respectively, and even 2.5 million in Rome. Participants at the ESF recognised the new connection between the hegemony of neo-liberal restructuring and its ultimate extra-economic enforcement through military power (Rupert 2003: 197). Resistance to the war on Iraq is also resistance to neo-liberal restructuring itself. Second, neo-liberal restructuring of the public sector within the EU, pushed by the European Commission and the Lisbon European Council in 2000, and the GATS (General Agreement on Trade in Services) negotiations at the global level, were both perceived as the main threats to peoples' livelihoods and the focal point for joint struggle (ESF-I, Session IV). The consensus was that public services must not become a new realm for capital accumulation. As a result of the interaction at the ESF, demonstrations in Brussels were organised by Belgian unions and ATTAC, on 9 February 2003, to keep public services out of GATS followed by a day of national action, on 13 March 2003, linked to the same theme. Similar co-operation efforts were initiated and/or deepened in relation to the demand for a European minimum income, the combat of tax evasion, as well as the co-ordinated demands for the introduction of a Tobin Tax on currency speculations. Overall, Florence set the stage for intensified co-operation at the Paris ESF (Bieler and Morton 2004).

Paris: the ESF between moment of resistance and cultural happening

Although only a beginning, the ESF in Florence had raised hopes about possibly extensive future co-operation between trade unions and social movements. These hopes were not fulfilled in Paris. In contrast to the ESF in Florence, the ETUC organised its own forum prior to the ESF on 11 and 12 November 2003. No high-ranking ETUC official participated on panels of the ESF itself. Instead, three round tables were organised around the following themes: (1) Social Europe and Enlargement; (2) Europe and the Euro-Mediterranean space; and (3) Europe and Latin America (www.fse-esf.org/francais/article781.html). In other words, rather than participating in an open-ended process of discussion facing potentially critical questions, a format of debate was chosen, which could be controlled by the trade union hierarchy. Of course, some representatives of established trade unions still participated in panels of the ESF itself, but the separate trade union forum precluded, from the very beginning, the potential interaction with social movements. This is confirmed by the absence of panels specifically dedicated to the interaction between trade unions and social movements (ESF 2003). The concluding demonstration on 15 November 2003 further reflected the low profile of trade unions. The fact that the demonstration in Florence had been so large was mainly due to the mobilisation by the Italian CGIL. In Paris, the various unions were present, but they had not mobilised a large number of their members. This relates directly back to the experience of 1968 when established institutions of the labour movement were experienced as brakes on radical developments. The danger here, then, is that history comes to repeat itself. There was also stronger participation of political parties at ESF-II at the expense of direct discussions between trade unions and social movements. Several trade unionists participated in the sessions concentrating on the interaction between social movements and political parties, but the general emphasis here rested on parties, not unions (ESF-II, Sessions II, V). The contributions by these party representatives sounded more like electoral speeches full of empty slogans, greeted with enthusiastic chanting by the party faithfuls in the audience and, thus, expressions of the 'gladiatorial futility' of arbitrary ideologies rather than signifying any real potential movement for change. Again, there is a danger that institutions of organised labour, established trade unions and related political parties give the ESF an impetus towards stabilising the current order rather than challenging it. To be clear, the struggle against neo-liberal globalisation continued to be the common basis of participating organisations. Yet this frequently included mere repetition of positions already outlined at Florence (e.g. ESF-II, Session I).

Nevertheless, at times, new inflections, indicated by the growing presence of the Coordination Nationale des Sans-Papiers representing 'illegal' immigrants, were also evident. Indeed, the vocal and growing presence of the *sans-papiers* is significant given the way that social welfare structures, housing on short-stay estates, hospitals and benefits, are all brought to bear on the asylum world in a way that reinforces the European capitalist social division of labour inscribed within state frameworks. At issue here is the very reproduction of labour power through the normalisation of asylum seekers into state structures whilst simultaneously closing national space to foreign bodies within structures of isolation and 'parade-ground confinement'. As summarised in the words of Poulantzas such 'camps are the form of shutting up non-nationals (or, more precisely, "anti-nationals") within the national territory. They internalise the frontiers of the national space at the heart of that space itself, thus making possible the modern notion of "internal enemy"' (1978: 105).

The *sans-papiers* (especially in France against the background of the rise of new movements and the return of the social question) have close contacts to radical trade unions such as SUD with their interaction at the ESF in Paris, indicating an intensification of trade union/social movement co-operation (Waters 2003). This highlights the increasing importance attributed to resistance against the increasing exploitation of the sphere of social reproduction, which is one of the core features of capitalism at the beginning of the twenty-first century. Whilst this aspect was already present in Florence (exhibited by the joint initiatives against the increasing deregulation and marketisation of public services), it was extended at Paris. The fifth core theme of the Paris ESF substantiates this in terms of the stance against racism, xenophobia and exclusion to assert, instead, the equality of rights, dialogue between cultures, and greater openness across Europe to migrants, refugees and asylum seekers. Related to this continuing rejection of neo-liberal restructuring, the European Constitution, which can be regarded as an example of what Stephen Gill (1995: 47) labels 'new constitutionalism', where economic decisions are isolated from democratic influence and accountability, emerged as a new common focus for counter-projects. Speaker after speaker rejected the draft Constitution, criticising it for the lack of democratisation measures, its threat to the continuing general provision of public services and its general push towards the neo-liberal Anglo-American model of capitalism. For example, Angela Klein from *Euromarches* argued that the draft EU constitution would implement market competition as a constitutional principle (ESF-II, Session II).

Another encouraging development in comparison with Florence was the active participation by anarchist groups including the Italian *disobediente* within the ESF (ESF-II, Session III). Due to the general disillusion with political parties' endorsement of neo-liberal restructuring, disobedience in all aspects of daily life was presented as a way to regain political activism. This activism represents a critical base movement, expressing the wider crisis of parliamentarism, and thus echoes the extra-parliamentary resistance of 1968. Nevertheless, whilst contemporary social movements seem to resound with the symbols of 1968, such allusions are somewhat superficial, with the global presence of the Zapatistas and their struggle in Mexico being the more direct point of reference (on the latter see Morton 2002). As Luca Casarini, the main spokesperson of the *disobediente* has indicated elsewhere, the movement was informally born on 1 January 1994 alongside the Zapatistas, although the practical activities of resistance only unfolded in their wake (Hernández Navarro 2004: 3–4). The main themes by the speakers again here referred to issues such as the protection of 'illegal' immigrants and the countering of increasing state violence more generally through all possible forms of disobedience in daily life (ESF-II, Session III). Furthermore, European integration as expressed in EU enlargement does not only imply the extension and deepening of neo-liberal restructuring in Europe (see *inter alia* Bieler 2002: 588–9; Bohle 2000), but also provides the ground for new resistance movements. There were clear signs of an increased presence of representatives from Central and Eastern Europe in Paris in comparison with Florence. Jarosla Urbanski of Nowy Robotnik pointed out that the Polish delegation with 250 members alone had doubled its presence since Florence (ESF-II, Session I).

Several problems, however, can be deduced from the positive and negative characteristics of the Paris ESF. First, on many occasions, positions and arguments from the previous year were simply reiterated without substantive agreement or achievement. This potentially indicates that the ESF has been more arbitrary and willed in nature. Second, one can observe a sense of presentism, reflected in the issues that come to dominate the ESFs. For example, there was an emphasis on the looming negotiations of GATS and its negative implications for the public sector at Florence, while the draft EU Constitution dominated many discussions at Paris. While this is to some extent understandable, the danger is that a certain continuity of struggle is lost in this process. A further question mark also has to be attached to the danger of national characteristics dominating the various ESFs, thereby again threatening necessary continuity for a successful challenge against neo-liberal globalisation. In Florence, certain Italian parties and trade unions strongly influenced the proceedings, whereas the increased participation of *sans-papiers* organisations in Paris may simply be a result of the close link of these organisations with unions in France, and thus a temporary feature. Most importantly, however, Paris hardly offered a way forward in the crucial discussions about the future structure and strategy of the ESF. Thus, there were few sessions dealing with the question of whether the ESF should be organised along horizontal or vertical lines. When mentioned, it became clear that groups such as the Italian *disobediente* envisage a multitude of movements within the ESF, which would provide space for those wanting to practice another world (ESF-II, Session III). Representatives of the British Socialist Workers Party (SWP), on the other hand, prefer a more hierarchical structure, where the centre of the organisation can hand down clear instructions. Yet, even the public debate between Antonio Negri and Alex Callinicos on this issue concentrated less on political strategy and more on the definition of the working class (ESF-II, Session IV). In short, many issues were not only left open but did not even make it on the agenda at Paris. This is also due to the fact that the second ESF was much wider in coverage but less clearly focused than the first ESF. In contrast to the well-balanced and clearly linked themes of the programme in Florence, the Paris programme was structured around five themes, which were too complex and too detailed to provide a clear focus for debate (ESF 2003). They allowed for every potential topic to be included in the programme at the expense of providing some guidance for discussions and resulting actions. The pressure was thus on the third ESF in London held on 15–17 October 2004.

London calling: canalising resistance?

The ESF in London hosted about 25,000 participants from over 70 countries, less than in Florence and Paris but still considerable, especially as the novelty of the event had worn off.[3] The ESF in London was crucial in several respects. First, more discussion was needed about the future structure of the forum. Initially there were worrying signs that these debates might be stifled in the preparatory build up due to the dominance of the SWP within its organisation as well as at the root of the Stop the War Coalition.[4] The danger was that if this particular political current took over the ESF and imposed a hierarchical structure, many other groups in favour of a horizontal structure would be alienated, turned away and encouraged to set up their own parallel forum. Indeed, in many ways this possibility was confirmed when so-called 'horizontals', such as activists within the *disobediente*, effectively withdrew from the London ESF organising committee and developed alternative spaces in the manner of anarchist and autonomist groups instead.

Second, would the separation between trade unions and social movements evident in the Paris forum be repeated? London was reassuring in this respect. Instead of organising their own forum, trade unions participated fully in the programme as well as sponsoring the overall event. The ETUC was represented by its Deputy General Secretary Maria Helena André (ESF-III, Session I), other unions represented by leading officials included the established unions Fédération Générale du Travail de Belgique, the Austrian Railway Workers' Union as well as the German unions IG Metall and Ver.di. Radical unions present included the FSU, SUD, G-10 and COBAS. Noticeably, British unions were out in force for the first time. This may have partly been the result of presentism and thus the location but also the consequence of a more fundamental rethinking of strategy. Hence the inclusion, amongst others, of the peak association the TUC, the big general unions GMB and T&G and the large public sector union UNISON (ESF-III, Sessions I, II, III, V and VII). Importantly, the commitment to co-operation with social movements was revived by trade unions. Social movements were identified as adding a new dimension of struggle to that of trade unions, building substance on the anti-capitalist slogan 'Another World is Possible' (ESF-III, Session III). Piero Bernocchi from COBAS emphasised that the ESF needed to be based on the co-operation between unions and social movements (ESF-III, Session IV). Elsewhere, Frank Patta from IG Metall emphasised the importance of co-operation with social movements in addition to intensified international trade union co-operation, while Billy Hayes of the Communication Workers Union (CWU) argued for more effective tactics from trade unions that included recognising the changing nature of the workforce and the need to engage with anti-capitalist social movements to forge a new internationalism (ESF-III, Session V).

Third, would the ESF provide some continuity of themes and thus guarantee some kind of consistent strategy? At the London ESF the focus was still targeted against 'Project Neo-liberalism' (ESF 2004). The issue of precarity, or so-called flexible labour practices, was carried forward within the main ESF just as much as in the autonomous spaces. Attention was cast towards the realities of poverty and inequality created by the privatisation of services and the social exclusion of undocumented migrant workers in Europe and attendant problems of racism, discrimination and inequality. Piero Bernocchi (COBAS) highlighted the problems of concentration-camp style centres set up across Europe to control migrants, thus linking back to earlier sentiments concerning the *sans-papiers* raised at the Paris ESF (ESF-III, Sessions III and IV). Additionally, the fight against the privatisation of public services continued to be at the centre of the debate ensuring a clear continuity with the first ESF in Florence. Several sessions were specifically dedicated to the defence of public services (e.g. ESF-III, Sessions II and VII) and again and again trade union representatives and social movement activists pointed to the importance of preserving, but also developing further, public services. A representative of the Austrian Railway Workers' union pointed out that the corporate lobby pushes hard for the privatisation of areas such as education, health and transport because it is these areas, traditionally run by the state, where there is still money left and private industry can expect super profits (ESF-III, Session II).

To protect public services, Pierre Khalfa from ATTAC-France and SUD demanded that a joint struggle should be waged to change the ideology at the European level towards affirming that public services must not be subject to competition (ESF-III, Session IV). When discussing the sources of the pressures for privatisation, the market-oriented and neo-liberal character of the EU was singled out as the core culprit, with the Commission and its initiatives for liberalisation directives seen as the main force behind it (especially ESF-III, Session I). The draft EU Constitution, already under severe attack in Paris, was also criticised for enshrining neo-liberalism within Europe (ESF-III, Sessions I and IV).

Of course, old tensions from Florence also resurfaced. The presence of trade unions as such does not indicate a progressive strategy for change by itself. Often reformist tendencies and an exclusive focus on the workplace, political parties and government power were articulated in a limited and narrow sense, focusing on a promotion of democracy through the lowering of the voting age by Mary Senior, the Assistant General Secretary of the Scottish TUC, for example, or Maria Helena André from the ETUC arguing that collective bargaining and social dialogue would be the best way forward for trade unions (ESF-III, Session I). Thus, the predominant focus was often on constitutional rights and institutional building with specific demands based on establishing a workers' charter following the establishment of international labour standards (ESF-III, Sessions I and V). This reflected the worries of social movements and radical trade unions that established unions are accommodationist vis-à-vis neo-liberal restructuring, or facilitating it rather than forming a strong pillar of joint resistance. At times, moreover, unionists showed no interest in engaging with social movements. Bob Crow, General Secretary of the RMT, left the meeting immediately after his presentation without waiting for the discussion to unfold (ESF-III, Session II). In relation to concrete activities, Piero Bernocchi (COBAS, Italy) exposed the rhetorical nature of much of this posturing in haranguing the lack of public demonstrations on social issues. The ESF was accused of constant inactivity through its reliance on discussion, which would lead to the movement 'sinking into boredom' (ESF-III, Session IV). Questions therefore remain about the nature, aims, workings and future of resistance linked to the social forums with 'the constant risk of a collapse into enjoyable anarchy' (Houtart 2003: 15; Tormey 2004: 149–57). On the other hand, Olivier Besancennot from the French Trotskyist party LCR did argue that progress had been made within the ESF in that networks are continuously developed (ESF-III, Session IV). Clearly, in contrast to the first ESF's success in organising the large anti-war demonstrations across Europe and beyond in February 2003, the Paris ESF did not lead to a similar event. Perhaps, war is an easier issue to rally people around than neo-liberal restructuring. It was significant that the calls for demonstrations around European Council summit meetings were followed up.

Unsurprisingly, demands for drastic change beyond capitalism were not voiced at the official ESF. This took place in the alternative spaces for self-organised cultures of resistance called 'Beyond ESF'. This forum was held on 13–17 October 2004 and was posed as a gathering of those against hierarchically organised power (Beyond ESF 2004). The style was a mixture of workshops and strategy discussions for resistance, with the focus cast towards practically organising resistance, for example at the summit of the G8 leaders held at the Gleneagles Hotel, Perthshire in Scotland 6–8 July 2005.[5] The workshops, held at an alternative site to the official forum at Middlesex University in White Hart Lane, covered significant issues germane to the basis of co-operation between labour and social movements. Most significant here was the focus on autonomy and struggle directed towards anti-privatisation struggles and the focus on precarity, drawing attention to flexible labour conditions, casualisation and dole resistance (Beyond ESF, Sessions I and II). A transnational consciousness permeated these workshops notably in terms of identifying benefit discipline as a European-wide social and political practice.

Conclusion

The future of the ESF as a focal point for resistance to neo-liberalism in Europe is open-ended. Will it deteriorate into a cultural happening, an enjoyable event but empty in terms of political implications? If so, the ESF would then be unmasked as arbitrary and willed and the related resistance to neo-liberal globalisation would be in danger of petering out as did the previous resistances to capitalism linked to the upheavals of 1968. As Gramsci forewarned, political action has to take place on the terrain of 'effective reality' rather than an idle fancy, yearning or daydreaming. But at the same time, the endeavour to give shape and coherence to particular social forces within 'effective reality' necessarily involves concern about issues of 'concrete fantasy' within the extant equilibrium of forces. 'What "ought to be" is therefore concrete; indeed it is the only realistic and historicist interpretation of reality; it alone is history in the making and philosophy in the making, it alone is politics' (Gramsci 1971: 126, 171–2). The ESF may, then, still become consolidated as a meeting place for intensifying co-operation between trade unions and social movements leading to concrete joint activities of resistance. As Fausto Bertinotti, national secretary of Italy's Rifondazione Comunista, has declared in relation to the limitations of the alter-globalisation movement, there 'seems to be the lack of a connection between the great issues of globalisation, war and peace and the intermediate dimension of employment and production relations.'[6] Such demands go to the heart of the conflict within the ESF and need to be addressed, if the ESF wants to remain a place of progressive politics. Perhaps the ESF bears out the view that 'the late-twentieth-century crisis of labour movements is temporary and will likely be overcome with the consolidation of new working classes "in formation"' (Silver 2003: 171). This resonates comfortably with the ethos internal to the social forums in that the aim is not to prescribe how a future, post-capitalist order has to be organised. The ESF is akin to the WSF in this sense in that it, 'does not constitute a locus of power to be disputed by the participants in its meetings' (WSF 2002). It does not attempt to create a 'vanguard party' or a 'modern prince' based on conventional modernist practices of political association (Gill 2002: 211–21).

However, at the same time, there has to be an acknowledgement of the problems inherent in not effectively canalising resistance. As Ernest Mandel (1968: 27) said of the 1968 anti-capitalist resistance, 'the students, when in action, in their vast majority escaped all efforts to channel them in a reformist direction; the majority of the workers on the other hand once again allowed themselves to be so channelled.' There is a conundrum here that is still present. Namely whether to canalise resistance into focussed and mobilised organisational capacities at the risk of co-option and/or exclusionary practices, or to embrace autonomous self-organised sources of power. To reinvent the significance of political organisations and polities whilst shunning the leaderising tendencies of political parties, as advocated by Hilary Wainwright, or to change the world without taking power, as advocated by John Holloway thus remains a stark choice (ESF-III, Session VI; also see Holloway 2002; Wainwright 2004). The challenge, then, will be to appreciate a normative conception of radical subjectivity within existing struggles, movements and tendencies alongside a realism rooted in the potentialities of transformation and built on the lessons of history.

Sessions attended as participant observers

ESF-I in Florence, 2002
I   From the European Union shaped by neo-liberal globalisation to the Europe of alternatives (Thursday 7 November, 9.30am).
II   Recovery of European trade unions? 2002 strikes and conflicts (Thursday 7 November, 2:00pm).
III   Movements' and trade unions' struggle, (Thursday 7 November, 5.30pm).
IV   Europe is not for sale: new rights for a new social system (Friday 8 November, 9.30am).
V   Public services and privatisations (Friday 8 November, 2:00pm).
VI   Europe of workers between global production and social fragmentation (Saturday 9 November, 9.30am).

For details of the participants and topics discussed, see ESF (2002).

ESF-II in Paris, 2003
I   Report on social struggles in Europe and their ties with social movements (Thursday 13 November, 2:00pm).
II   Social and citizens' movements/political parties [1] (Thursday 13 November, 6:00pm).
III   Disobey! Disobedience and horizontality: strategies for our struggle? (Friday 14 November, 9:00am).
IV   Multitude or working class? (Friday 14 November, 2:00pm).
V   Social and citizens' movements/political parties [2] (Friday 14 November, 6:00pm).

For details of the participants and topics discussed, see ESF (2003).

ESF-III in London, 2004
I   For a democratic and social Europe (Friday 15 October, 9:00am).
II   Public ownership of the railways and domestic/international strategies for resisting rail privatisation (Friday 15 October, 1:00pm).

III Working together to fight inequalities and build social and economic alternatives (Friday 15 October, 4:00pm).
IV Privatisation, social movements and political parties (Friday 15 October, 7:00pm).
V International solidarity: trade union and workers' rights in the era of globalisation (Saturday 16 October, 9:00am).
VI Strategies for social transformation (Saturday 16 October, 11:30am).

For details of the participants and topics discussed, see ESF (2004).

Beyond ESF in London, 2004
I Plan Puebla Panama – Resistance in Mesoamerica (Thursday 14 October, 1:30pm).
II Dole resistance, unwaged activism and precarious work (Thursday 14 October, 5:00pm).

For details of the participants and topics discussed, see Beyond ESF (2004).

Notes

1 The research was based on an 'observer-as-participant' methodology, relying on direct observations and interviews with trade union and social movement representatives both during the forums and at follow-up meetings. The sessions observed are listed above and referred to in Roman numerals.
2 The unions present at the ESF included high level representatives from the French union Confédération Générale du Travail (CGT); the Italian, former communist union Confederazione Generale Italiana del Lavoro (CGIL) and its metal workers' federation Federazione Impiegati Operai Metallurgici (FIOM); the second most important Spanish confederation Confederación Sindical de Comisiones Obreras (CCOO); the main Portuguese confederation Confederação Geral dos Trabalhadores Portugueses (CGTP); and the Greek confederation Geniki Synomospondia Ergaton Ellados (GSEE). The EIFs present included the General Secretary of the European Transport Workers' Federation (ETF), participating actively in plenary discussions (ESF-I Session VI); the General Secretary of the European Metalworkers' Federation, although not in a speaking capacity; as well as the European Federation of Public Service Unions (EPSU).
3 *The Guardian*, 12 November 2003 and 18 October 2004.
4 *The Guardian*, 1 December 2003. See also the Communist Party of Great Britain (CPGB) on this issue, 'Control-freakery damps enthusiasm', www.cpgb.org/worker/547/esf.htm (accessed 18 October 2004).
5 This is organised by the Dissent! Network that works within the hallmarks of Peoples' Global Action, the radical social movement linked to Reclaim the Streets campaigners, the Landless Workers Movement (MST) in Brazil, and the Zapatistas in Mexico (EZLN). See www.dissent.org.uk.
6 *The Guardian*, 11 August 2003.

Bibliography

Arrighi, G., Hopkins, T. and Wallerstein, I. (1989) *Antisystemic movements*, London.

Ashman, S. (2004) 'Resistance to neo-liberal globalisation: a case of "militant particularism"?', *Politics*, 24:2.

Beyond ESF (2004) '5 days and nights of anti-authoritarian ideas and action', Alternative programme of the European Social Forum. London.

Bieler, A. (2002) 'The struggle over EU enlargement: a historical materialist analysis of European integration', *Journal of European Public Policy*, 9:4.

—— and Morton, A. D. (eds) (2001) *Social forces in the making of the new Europe: the restructuring of european social relations in the global political economy*, London.

—— and —— (2004) '"Another Europe is possible"? Labour and social movements at the European Social Forum', *Globalizations*, 1:2.

Bieling, H. J. und Steinhilber, J. (eds) (2000) *Die konfiguration europas: dimensionen einer kritischen integrationstheorie*, Münster.

Bohle, D. (2000) 'EU-integration und osterweiterung: die konturen einer neuen europäischen unordnung', in Bieling, H. J. and Steinhilber, J. (eds) *Die konfiguration europas: dimensionen einer kritishcen integrationstheorie*, Münster.

Cafruny, A. W. and Ryner, M. (eds) (2003) *A ruined fortress? Neoliberal hegemony and transformation in Europe*, Lanham, MD.

COBAS (2002) 'Confederazione Cobas: chi siamo e per cosa lottiamo', *COBAS – Giornale della Confederazione COBAS*, No. 12 supplement.

ESF (2002) *Un'altra Europa é possible*, Official Programme of the European Social Forum, Florence.

—— (2003) *Construire une autre Europe, un autre model*, Official Programme of the European Social Forum, Paris.

—— (2004) *For another Europe in another world*, Official Programme of the European Social Forum, London.

Euromarches (2002) 'Droits sociaux, convention, constitution européenne', *Marches Européennes/News*, No. 23.

ETUC (2002) 'European social forum: the European social model at the service of economic and political relations on a global scale' (6 September), www.etuc.org/en/ (accessed 29 January 2003).

G-10 (1998) 'Congrès constitutif: résolution générale', www.g10.ras.eu.org/ (accessed 20 May 2003).

Gall, G. (1995) 'The emergence of a rank and file movement: the Comitati di Base in the Italian workers' movement', *Capital & Class*, No. 55.

Gill, S. (1995) 'Globalisation, market civilisation and disciplinary neoliberalism', *Millennium: Journal of International Studies*, 24:3.

—— (2002) *Power and resistance in the new world order*, London.

Gramsci, A. (1971) *Selections from the prison notebooks*, ed. and trans. Q. Hoare and G. Nowell-Smith, London.

Hernández Navarro, L. (2004) 'The global Zapatista movement', America Program. Silver City, NM: Interhemispheric Resource Centre, 16 January.

HIC (2001) 'In Nice the debut of a new, yet very ancient, movement', 20 February, www.habitants.org/index.php3?file=newsfull.php3&id=67 (accessed 26 May 2003).

Hobsbawm, E. (1962) *The age of revolution, 1789–1848*, London.

—— (1975) *The age of capital, 1848–1875*, London.

—— (1987) *The age of empire, 1875–1914*, London.

—— (1988) 'Working-class internationalism', in van Holthoon, F. and van der Linden, M. (eds) *Internationalism in the labour movement, 1830–1940*, vol.1, Leiden.

—— (1994) *Age of extremes: the short twentieth century, 1914–1991*, London.

Holloway, J. (2002) *Change the world without taking power*, London.

Houtart, F. (2003) 'Another world is possible', *Le Monde Diplomatique*, 15 November.

Khalfa, P. (2003) 'War on Iraq, what's next?', *Sand in the Wheels – ATTAC Newletter*, 154: 6.

Laval, C. and Weber, L. (2002) *Le nouvel ordre éducatif mondial: OMC, Banque mondiale, OCDE, Commission européenne*, Institut de Recherches de la FSU, Paris.

Maier, C. (1977) 'The politics of productivity: foundations of American international economic policy after World War II', *International Organisation*, 31.

Mandel, E. (1968) 'The lessons of May 1968', *New Left Review* 52.

Marcuse, H. (1964) *One-dimensional man*, London.

—— (1969) *An essay on liberation*, London.

—— (1972) *Counterrevolution and revolt*, London.

Miliband, R. (1977) *Marxism and politics*, Oxford.

Morton, A. D. (2002) '"La resurrección del maiz": globalisation, resistance and the Zapatistas', *Millennium: Journal of International Studies*, 31.

O'Brien, R. (2000) 'Workers and world order: the tentative transformation of the international union movement', *Review of International Studies*, 26.

Poulantzas, N. (1978) *State, power, socialism*, London.

Rupert, M. (2003) 'Globalising common sense: a marxian-gramscian (re-)vision of the politics of governance/resistance', *Review of International Studies*, 29 (Special Issue).

Sassoon, D. (1996) *One hundred years of socialism: the west European left in the twentieth century*, London.

Silver, B. J. (2003) *Forces of labour: workers' movements and globalisation since 1870*, Cambridge.

Singer, D. (2002) *Prelude to revolution: France in May 1968*, 2nd edition. Cambridge.

SUD (2002a) *Qu'est-ce que sud solidaires*, Paris.

—— (2002b) 'Sans-papiers', *Le journal*, 148.

Taylor, G. and Mathers, A. (2002) 'The politics of European integration: a European labour movement in the making?', *Capital & Class*, 78.

Tilly, C. (2004) *Social movements, 1768–2004*, Boulder CO.

Tormey, S. (2004) 'The 2003 European Social Forum: where next for the anti-capitalist movement?', *Capital & Class*, 84.

van der Pijl, K. (1984) *The making of an atlantic ruling class*, London.

Wainwright, H. (2004) 'Change the world by transforming power – including state power!', Transnational Institute, 26 October, www.tni.org (accessed 28 October 2004).

Wallerstein, I. (1982) 'Crisis as transition', in S. Amin *et al.*, *Dynamics of global crisis*, New York.

—— (1984) *The politics of the world economy: the states, the movements, and the civilisations*, Cambridge.

—— (1991a) *Unthinking social science: the limits of nineteenth-century paradigms*, Cambridge.

—— (1991b) *Geopolitics and geoculture: essays on the changing world-system*, Cambridge.

—— (1995) *Historical capitalism with capitalist civilisation*, London.

—— (1999) *The end of the world as we know it: social science for the twenty-first century*, Minneapolis.

—— (2002) 'New revolts against the system', *New Left Review*, 18.

Waters, S. (2003) *Social movements in France: towards a new citizenship*, London.

Wright, S. (2002) *Storming heaven: class composition and struggle in Italian autonomist marxism*, London.

WSF (2002) 'Charter of principles', www.fse-esf.org (accessed 14 November 2002).

Index